The View from the Bench and Chambers

Constitutionalism and Democracy

GREGG IVERS AND
KEVIN T. MCGUIRE,
EDITORS

The View from the Bench and Chambers

EXAMINING JUDICIAL PROCESS AND DECISION MAKING ON THE U.S. COURTS OF APPEALS

Jennifer Barnes Bowie,
Donald R. Songer,
and John Szmer

UNIVERSITY OF VIRGINIA PRESS CHARLOTTESVILLE AND LONDON

University of Virginia Press

Printed in the United States of America on acid-free paper

First published 2014

9 8 7 6 5 4 3 2 1

LIBRARY OF CONGRESS CATALOGING-IN-PUBLICATION DATA

Bowie, Jennifer Barnes, author.

The view from the bench and chambers : examining judicial process and decision making on the U.S. Courts of Appeals / Jennifer Barnes Bowie, Donald R. Songer, and John Szmer.

pages cm. — (Constitutionalism and democracy)

Includes bibliographical references and index.

ISBN 978-0-8139-3599-7 (cloth : alk. paper) — ISBN 978-0-8139-3600-0 (e-book)

1. Appellate courts—United States. 2. Judicial process—United States. I. Songer, Donald R., author. II. Szmer, John J., 1970– author. III. Title.

KF8750.B69 2014

347.73'24—dc23

2014007111

For Gavin Bowie and my family.—JBB

For Michael. Now you have a hammer.—DSS

For Martha Kropf and Gwen and Zach Szmer.—JSS

CONTENTS

ACKNOWLEDGMENTS

We began this book in the hope of shedding new light on the U.S. courts of appeals. To do so required help of both a personal and a professional sort from many individuals. First and foremost, we owe a large debt of gratitude to all the judges who gave their time to speak candidly with us about the nature of decision making by courts of appeals judges; without their willingness and openness this book would not been possible.

University of Virginia Press editors Kevin McGuire, Gregg Ivers, and Dick Holway lent enthusiastic support to the project, each providing enormous assistance at various stages of the publication process. In addition, we are grateful for the recommendations of the anonymous reviewers of the manuscript, whose thoughtful suggestions improved the book.

Some of the ideas for the manuscript stemmed from earlier work. Chapter 6, for example, includes a version of "Assessing the Applicability of Strategic Theory to Explain Decision Making on the Courts of Appeals" (Bowie and Songer 2009), which was published in *Political Research Quarterly*, and part of a conference paper, "Decision Making on the Courts of Appeals: Can Judges Predict the Likelihood of En Banc Review?," by Bowie, which was presented at the 2009 Annual Meeting of the Midwest Political Science Association.

Several individuals read different parts of the manuscript. For such critical readings we thank Susan Haire, Kirk Randazzo, Wendy Martinek, and Christopher Zorn. We also thank Michael Giles, Thomas Walker, and Christopher Zorn for their Fifth Circuit en banc data set, which they made available to us to use in the analysis in chapter 6, and

Stephen Wasby for the Ninth and First Circuits en banc case data, also used in the analysis in chapter 6.

We would like to specially recognize Rob Christensen, who almost achieves the status of a fourth author. Rob played a major role in putting together much of the quantitative data we analyzed. He also worked on several prior conference papers (particularly those analyzing dissent and opinion assignment) and a published article (in the *International Review of Law and Economics*) that heavily influenced several empirical analyses. While Rob may not have written the book, his ideas and understanding permeate the work.

Jennifer Barnes Bowie is immensely grateful to her husband, Gavin Bowie, for his consistent support over the course of her career, and particularly during the writing of the manuscript. She also thanks her family, who have supported her in many ways, in particular Maureen and Paul Williams and The Honorable Peter W. and Sarah Bowie. Additionally she would like to thank Wendy Martinek, Christopher Zorn, and Bob Dudley, for their unwavering guidance and encouragement, and the University of Richmond, which provided financial research support for this project. She is especially grateful to the judges who took time to speak with her. Finally, thanks are owed to S. J. Hightower, Emily Vanover, Liz Dedman, and Sara Krauss for their invaluable research assistance.

Donald R. Songer thanks the many judges of the U.S. Courts of Appeals who took time from their busy schedules to talk to him, and especially Judge Robert Katzman, who facilitated an invitation to Songer to attend the annual retreat of the Second Circuit Court of Appeals and the gracious hospitality accorded him there by the judges on the Second Circuit. Songer is grateful to his family for their patience and support during his extensive travels to visit judges, and especially his son, Michael, and Michael's wife, Erica, who shared their perspective as clerks to judges on the courts of appeals.

John Szmer is thankful for the continuing support of his family, especially his children—constant sources of amusement—and his wife and colleague, Martha Kropf. Without her encouragement and support this project could not have been completed. He also thanks Mason DeCammillis, a former student, for research assistance; Reese Manceaux, the University of North Carolina at Charlotte Data Services Librarian, for extremely helpful assistance in merging the yearly Federal Judicial Center databases into one data set; and the University of North Carolina at Charlotte, for granting the research leave that helped make this project possible.

The View from the Bench and Chambers

INTRODUCTION
The Courts of Appeals in the U.S. Legal System

For much of their history, the U.S. courts of appeals have toiled in obscurity, well out of the limelight of political controversy. But as the number of appeals has increased dramatically in recent decades, while the number of cases heard by the Supreme Court has remained the same, the courts of appeals have increasingly become in practice the courts of last resort for the vast majority of litigants. This enhanced status has been recognized by important political actors, and as a result, appointments to the courts of appeals have become increasingly controversial since the 1990s (Binder and Maltzman 2009). This combination of increasing political salience accompanied by increasing political controversy finally led scholars, particularly in the past two decades, to undertake serious empirical studies of the role of the courts of appeals in the U.S. legal and political system. In particular, a number of studies have sought to test theories developed to explain the politics of the Supreme Court in the context of the courts of appeals (see Cross 2007; Hettinger, Lindquist, and Martinek 2006; Klein 2002; Sunstein et al. 2006). As a result, scholars now debate the applicability of both attitudinal and strategic models to describe decision making on the courts of appeals. With that said, the courts of appeals still remain understudied compared to the more extensive body of scholarship on the Supreme Court, but both the volume and quality of empirical work on the intermediate courts have risen sharply in the past two decades.

Despite the increased scholarly attention, one relevant line of inquiry remains largely ignored: the perspective of the judges themselves. This book seeks to fill that lacuna in the literature with a comprehensive examination of processes and politics on the courts of appeals as seen from the dual perspectives of the judges and their clerks, on the one hand, and empirical research grounded in statistical analysis on the other.

The Evolution of the Courts of Appeals

A decade ago, commentators wrote that "the average American is barely aware (if at all) of the courts of appeals, in spite of their importance" to the legal system in the U.S. (Songer, Haire, and Lindquist 2000, 3). In the words of other scholars, they are the "least noticed of the regular constitutional courts" (Carp and Stidham 1991, 13). The national media largely confine their attention to the decisions of the Supreme Court, because that is where the most dramatic and controversial issues appear to be resolved. The local media often cover the decisions of the federal district courts in their state when local celebrities and politicians take center stage in the hottest local political controversies. But the courts in the middle, the U.S. courts of appeals, appear to have no natural constituency and thus receive very little systematic attention from the media. This limited visibility to the American public notwithstanding, the courts of appeals occupy a pivotal position, the "vital center of the federal judicial system" (Howard 1981, 8). The courts of appeals have long played a central role in maintaining the uniformity of national law and in maintaining judicial oversight of the federal regulatory agencies whose rulemaking authority in an increasingly national and international market is vital to the economic well-being of the country. Moreover, with the Supreme Court able to review only one in every five thousand decisions of the district courts, the courts of appeals have become the primary creators and enforcers of federal legal policy. With the courts of appeals deciding roughly 60,000 cases per year, and with fewer than three-tenths of 1 percent of those decisions undergoing Supreme Court review, the U.S. courts of appeals have become the de facto courts of last resort for most litigants in the federal judicial system. Thus, the appeals courts have become important policymakers, announcing the final word on most questions of statutory interpretation of federal laws, the meaning of federal rules of civil and criminal procedure, and the limits of the powers of the administrative state.

The structure of the federal court system is not spelled out in the Constitution. Instead, that document confines itself to the general proposition that there will be a single Supreme Court and "such inferior courts as Congress may from time to time establish."[1] The basic current structure of the lower federal court was not established until the passage of the Evarts Act in 1891. With modifications in the law adopted in 1911, 1925, and 1988, the current system consists of three main layers. At the bottom of the structure, the U.S. district courts serve as the basic trial courts for virtually the entire range of federal jurisdiction. These courts are divided into ninety-one geographically defined units (called districts), with each state having one to four judicial districts that are completely encompassed by the state boundaries. The courts typically are presided over by a single judge, frequently sitting with a jury, though the total number of district judges serving within a district varies substantially across districts.

Almost all litigants losing a decision in the federal district courts are entitled to one appeal.[2] Those appeals compose the mandatory jurisdiction of the U.S. Courts of Appeals, which form the middle layer of the federal judicial system. The appeals courts are divided into eleven numbered, geographically defined circuits that comprise all the federal districts within a contiguous group of from three to nine states, plus the districts in various U.S. territories, such as Guam and Puerto Rico. A twelfth circuit is limited to hearing appeals from the district court of the District of Columbia and from a number of federal administrative agencies. A final (thirteenth) circuit, the Federal Circuit, sits in the District of Columbia and has a specialized jurisdiction, including customs and patent appeals. Each circuit is presided over by between six and twenty-nine full-time appeals court judges, who typically sit in panels of three judges to decide their appeals. On occasion, a retired judge or an active judge from another court sits "by designation" with two regular appeals court judges to make up the three-judge panel of the court of appeals. Losing litigants may petition for a review of the panel's decision by the entire membership of the circuit sitting en banc, or may petition for review by the Supreme Court.

At the top of the federal judicial hierarchy, a single Supreme Court, currently composed of nine justices, is empowered to review any of the decisions of the federal courts of appeals, and may also review decisions of the highest court in each state if a federal question is involved (e.g., in state cases raising an issue related to the interpretation of a federal statute or the Constitution of the United States). The Supreme Court has nearly complete discretionary control of its docket and typically grants full review to fewer than one hundred of the nearly 10,000 petitions for review (e.g., petitions for certiorari, or requests for the Supreme Court to use its discretionary jurisdiction to call up the records of the lower court so that the Supreme Court can review the decision below) it receives each year.[3]

The Data

The study reported here utilized two major sources of data—the most comprehensive sets of both qualitative interviews and quantitative case data ever assembled. First, we conducted a set of in-depth interviews with current and former judges sitting on the U.S. courts of appeals and with their law clerks (the general text of the interview questions is provided in the technical appendix following chapter 7). In all, formal interviews were conducted with sixty active and senior judges of the courts of appeals. We also held more informal discussions with several groups of additional judges at the circuit retreats of the Second and Ninth Circuits. Most interviews were conducted in the offices of the appellate court judges and typically lasted about an hour. While we tried to ask all the judges a similar set of questions, the interviews were conversational in nature. Our goal, first and foremost, was to allow the judges to speak freely about the various topics we covered in response to our asking open-ended questions. The interviews were conducted over seven years and included judges from every circuit. Judges were promised as a condition of their participation in interviews that none of their comments would be attributed to them by name or through a combination of characteristics that could reveal the identity of the judge (e.g., "a female appointee of Clinton in the Third Circuit"). Consequently, in the discussions cited in this book, judges are typically referred to by an alphabetic code (e.g., Judge W, Judge BB). Male pronouns are occasionally used to refer to judges regardless of their actual gender to further maintain anonymity.

While we sought a richer understanding of the courts of appeals by hearing from the judges themselves, we also understood that interview data have limitations. First, the interview sample is not random. Because of this, we are cautious in making generalizations about judge behavior. On the other hand, we can and do draw several inferences from the interviews about how the courts of appeals and judges operate. Second, because of the conversational format of the interviews, the questions posed to the judges were not identical in every case. We made every attempt to ask the judges similar questions and tried to follow a general format, but at times the interview veered in a different direction, or we simply ran out of interview time. Finally, the judges may have been guarded in their responses, which is not unusual with interview data. However, even with these limitations in mind, we believe the information gleaned from the judge interviews far outweighs the possible limitations presented.

The perspectives gained from the interviews are supplemented by quantitative analyses of an empirical database of decisions spanning more than three-quarters of a century and aggregated from every region of the country. Specifically, we utilized the United States Courts of Appeals Database (Songer 2002) and its update.[4] These databases consist of a stratified random sample of more than 20,000 cases decided by the U.S. Courts of Appeals from 1925 through 2002. The databases report information on more than two hundred variables for each case, including the votes of the judges and a detailed coding of the issues and the litigants. We extended the coding of the existing database through the year 2005.

The analyses we present in this book are among the first, if not the first, to combine the insights gained from in-depth interviews with appellate court judges with quantitative analyses of judicial decisions. The addition of interviews with law clerks, whose daily close working relationships with their judges provided a unique insider perspective, lent a richness to the analysis not available in any previous work on courts of appeals in the United States.

The interviews with the judges were used to derive a thick description of the actual practices of courts of appeals judges as they select panels to review each case, prepare for the judicial hearing, interact with attorneys during oral arguments, reach a tentative decision in conference, and then negotiate over the substance and style of the final opinion. The interviews also explored the perceptions of the judges as to possible patterns of decisions, the extent of collegiality and conflict, and the substantive nature of the decisions.

To supplement the perspectives of the judges gained from the interviews, each chapter presents a set of descriptive statistics to provide an empirical overview of the work of the courts. In addition, several statistical models are estimated to illustrate the perspective of the court developed in recent scholarly work. In particular, we empirically model the likelihood that an oral argument will be granted, the nature of the opinion assignment process, the likelihood that the decision will be published, factors affecting both the time to decision and the length of the majority opinion, the grounds of dissent, and attitudinal and strategic accounts of judicial decision making.

Theoretical Perspective

While one might argue that there is a single dominant model of Supreme Court behavior (Segal and Spaeth 1993, 2002), no one appears to have posited a single dominant model of U.S. appellate court behavior.

Based on the qualitative and quantitative analyses presented in this book, in every aspect of court of appeals decision making, we found that the judges are influenced by a variety of factors. In other words, following the language of other scholars who have examined a variety of courts, we posit an integrated model of decision making (Brace and Hall 1993; George and Epstein 1992; Songer and Haire 1992). While this theoretical perspective is not novel, it is the truest reflection of the behavior of the U.S. intermediate appellate courts. Moreover, the combination of the comprehensive examination of different types of decisions with the mixed methods research design is novel. Before sketching the contents of the book, we briefly describe some of these theoretical approaches that, we believe, together contribute to the integrated model.

A variety of models of judicial behavior have been theorized, with three alternatives having the most traction in the community of judicial scholars: the attitudinal, strategic, and legal models. Attitudinal explanations of judicial decision making typically contend that a judge will take the position that is closest to his or her policy preferences. Specifically, judges "decide disputes in light of the facts of the case vis-à-vis" their ideology and values (Segal and Spaeth 2002, 86).

Like the attitudinal model, strategic accounts assume that judges are motivated by policy goals (see Epstein and Knight 1998). Moreover, while many statements of the theory suggest that judges can have a variety of goals (e.g., Baum 1997), empirical studies usually focus on policy preferences (e.g., Cross 2007; Hettinger, Lindquist, and Martinek 2006). The real distinction between attitudinal and strategic accounts is the context in which the actor is situated. The former assumes that the judge does not factor in institutional constraints, while the latter theory assumes that judges consider the context, including institutional rules and the behavior of external actors, when taking a position. Given these constraints, according to the strategic account, a judge will behave in the manner that he or she believes will result in the outcome closest to his or her goals. The key distinction may thus be phrased in the following way: the attitudinal account suggests that judges will always take the position closest to their ideal position (sincere behavior), while the strategic account posits that judges will sometimes behave insincerely, depending on the contextual setting.

The other major model of judicial decision making, the legal model, comes in two basic flavors. The first conception of the legal model assumes that legal factors such as the text of the law, original intent or meaning, precedent, and other elements determine judicial behavior

(Segal and Spaeth 2002, 48). Often labeled "mechanical jurisprudence," this approach has largely been discredited. Instead, most scholars posit that the law functions to constrain the number of potential choices available to a judge but does not determine any one choice (e.g., Bailey and Maltzman 2011; Songer and Lindquist 1996). This modern approach is not inconsistent with the attitudinal model: within the constraints of the law, judges are free to take positions that are consistent with their policy preferences. This version of the legal model also shares a similarity with the strategic approach: judges take into account the constraints of institutions. However, the strategic model tends to focus on extralegal institutions, while the legal model does not assume judges will behave insincerely.

These are only the most dominant approaches to describing judicial decision making, and scholars have also posited alternative explanations. Of those, new institutionalism is perhaps the most prominent. New institutionalism designates a broad approach with many flavors, including both strategic and legal approaches. New institutionalism holds that institutions, both formal and informal, affect the behavior of political actors. Whether judges are strategic or sincere depends on the flavor. Moreover, some new institutionalist approaches hold that institutions can affect how preferences form, or may even take on a life of their own (Gillman and Clayton 1999). Another variant contends that we must look not just at the effects of institutions but also at the broader social context, which includes a variety of social constructions such as race and gender (Gillman and Clayton 1999, 7).

In light of the breadth of the theory, a variety of influences and causal mechanisms fall under the purview of new institutionalism. For example, a judge might feel constrained by nonlegal formal or informal institutions without choosing the goal-maximizing alternative. Alternatively, nonlegal institutional factors could determine the judge's behavior, regardless of goals or preferences. Finally, characteristics such as race or gender could influence judges' decisions.

In our analyses of various aspects of judicial behavior on the U.S. courts of appeals, we found evidence that each of these models could explain some of the judges' choices in a variety of different contexts. Hence, we prefer what we call the integrated model (i.e., a perspective that combines or integrates the insights gained from the legal, attitudinal, and strategic approaches to understanding judicial behavior). We found evidence that appellate court judges are sometimes guided by policy preferences, but judges are also often constrained by the law or other institutional factors. Sometimes judges react strategically when considering these constraints, but in other instances they appear to consider these institutions without attempting to maximize goals. Finally, characteristics such as race and gender sometimes influence judicial decisions.

An Overview of the Analysis

Most scholarship that exists on the courts of appeals is limited to attempts to explain the ultimate decisions of the courts. Much less is known about the processes used by the courts to reach those decisions. In the first two chapters we seek to fill that gap in the understanding of the appellate courts, drawing heavily on our interviews with the judges and their clerks.

Before turning to the details of the way the courts operate, the first chapter describes the institution, from the basic structure to the selection and characteristics of judges, followed by the workload of the court. The chapter presents a portrait of who the judges are, focusing on characteristics such as partisanship, gender, and race. It also provides a broad statistical overview of the business of the courts of appeals, highlighting the dramatic changes that have occurred in the workload and agenda of the courts of appeals over the past half century.

Because the workload crisis described in chapter 1 has led judges to modify their procedures for handling the cases appealed to them, chapter 2 examines the screening procedures used by the courts of appeals, utilizing both the detailed explanations of the judges themselves about how such procedures work and why they are needed and statistical accounts. The procedures discussed include the process used to decide which cases are favored with oral argument. The chapter then moves on to other preliminary procedures, starting with the selection of panels and a discussion of another method for dealing with the caseload crisis, the use of designated judges. After reviewing how cases are assigned to panels, we examine the role of oral arguments. Finally, we address the panel conference, focusing primarily on the assignment of the opinion of the court. In general, institutional factors, both formal and informal, appear to influence most of these preliminary processes.

Chapter 3 describes the process of decision making, particularly the important process of arriving at the opinion of the court, from the perspective of the judges. In contrast to the extensive literature on the patterns of *votes* of judges in appellate courts (particularly in the United States), much less is known about how the final decision of the court is reached. Here we describe, from the judges' viewpoint, what happens after a tentative decision has been reached in the private conference proceedings. We include a description of the role of clerks in writing the initial draft opinion, as well as the bargaining and negotiations that sometimes occur. Overall, opinion writing is a collaborative process, though the named author of the opinion does primarily control the direction and content of the majority opinion.

Chapter 3 then examines two different indirect measures of the length of the panel's deliberations: the amount of time it takes to produce an opinion of the court and the length of that opinion. Once again, the workload crisis plays a role in whether the opinion is published. We end the chapter with a discussion of the likelihood that a three-judge panel decision will be reviewed, either en banc or by the U.S. Supreme Court. For the most part, consistent with the integrated model we pursue in this book, a combination of legal, attitudinal, strategic, and institutional influences plays a role in these aspects of the appellate process.

In the following chapters we turn to factors that affect the judges' disposition of a case. Chapter 4 looks at the decision to cast a dissenting vote. Again combining judge interviews with quantitative analyses, we identify a variety of factors—attitudinal, legal, and institutional—that affect the decision to dissent. In the end, it appears that collegial norms exert the most influence—most disagreements are worked out during the postconference stage discussed in chapter 3.

Chapters 5 and 6 attend to the three most prominent models of judicial decision making noted earlier in this introduction. In chapter 5, relying primarily on the perspectives of the judges, with some supplemental quantitative analyses, we explore the degree to which legal and attitudinal factors affect the decisions of judges as to the merits of cases. It appears that both legal and attitudinal factors play a role, though the law clearly constrains judges in most cases. Conversely, in chapter 6 we look at strategic behavior. While earlier chapters found some support for this model, particularly in the bargaining and negotiations that often occur during the opinion-writing phase, our interviews and analyses in chapter 6 suggest one type of strategic behavior likely does not occur. Specifically, we examine the frequently posited view that the possibility of review, either en banc or by the Supreme Court, encourages the three-judge panelists to decide cases strategically. If this were so, these types of review should be frequent and predictable. However, they are not. These empirical findings appear to confirm the results of our judicial interviews.

The concluding chapter begins by pulling together the results presented in the previous chapters. Two key themes are examined. First, we examine the extent to which the perspectives of the judges and their clerks are consistent with the picture painted in mainstream analyses of the courts by empirical social scientists, as well as by our own analyses. Second, we discuss how well our integrated model of judicial behavior is supported by the qualitative and quantitative evidence.

ONE

The Judges and Cases

Most scholarship pertaining to the courts of appeals is limited to attempts to explain the ultimate decisions of the courts. Much less is known about the processes used by the courts to reach those decisions. This book fills in many of the gaps concerning how the courts of appeals operate on a-day-to day basis, drawing heavily on an extensive set of interviews we conducted with judges from every circuit. Before taking up the details of the way the courts operate, this chapter first turns a spotlight on the central actors on the courts of appeals, the judges. Appellate court judges' decisions often represent the last word on many of the important legal questions of our time—but no one knows who they are. This chapter, then, constructs a portrait of appellate court judges, noting how the changing partisan balance on the courts has reflected trends in partisan control of the presidency, and the increasing gender and racial diversification of the appellate judiciary.

The Judges

Judges on the U.S. courts of appeals are among the most powerful people in American politics. As authors of the final decisions on important social and legal questions affecting large constituencies, they occupy a position quite different from that of many other key players in American politics, including governors, senators, and big-city mayors, all of whom are public personages living in the public spotlight.

However, this is not the fate of even the most influential or powerful of the judges on the courts of appeals. One of the most well-respected judges in the country, one who in addition to taking a leadership role on one of the busiest circuits in the country has written more than a dozen influential books on law, after noting this treatment of many of the celebrities in American politics had this to say about the reception of judges:

> I can be holding a hearing in the morning on the interpretation of some new federal law, knowing that our decision is going to make new law that will affect millions of people, and it is easy to start thinking, hey, the three of us—we are pretty important people. Then after the hearing we walk out of the courthouse together and walk two or three blocks down a busy street to a popular restaurant for lunch, passing several hundred people on the sidewalks along the way, and not a single person—not even the waitress who takes our three credit cards to pay our lunch bill—recognizes us or pays any attention to us. It reminds me that regardless of how important I think my job is, the fact is that probably no one but a dozen or so lawyers in this town have any idea about who I am.

As this anecdote suggests, courts of appeals judges often go unnoticed even though their decisions affect millions of people.

Our goal in this chapter is twofold. First, we seek to describe who these mysterious key figures in American politics are. Second, we explain and analyze the structure and procedures of the courts of appeals. Both goals incorporate the perspectives of the judges along with empirical data. We begin our discussion with the process of selecting courts of appeals judges.

THE SELECTION OF JUDGES

The formal process for selecting judges on the courts of appeals is straightforward. Nominees are selected at the discretion of the president and take office if confirmed by a majority vote in the U.S. Senate. Once appointed, judges serve during "good behavior," which effectively means they remain in office until they voluntarily retire or die.[1]

This seemingly straightforward practice is complicated by the political geography of the courts of appeals. As can be seen in the map of the circuits in figure 1, each circuit encompasses multiple states, but each state lies wholly within a single circuit. Consequently, each seat on the circuit is filled by a nominee from a particular state located within that circuit, and as a result, each U.S. senator is typically more concerned with nominees from her state than with those from other states (Steigerwalt 2010). In practice, the selection of an appeals court judge is a political process that involves negotiations between the White House and home

FIGURE 1. Circuit boundaries of the U.S. Courts of Appeals

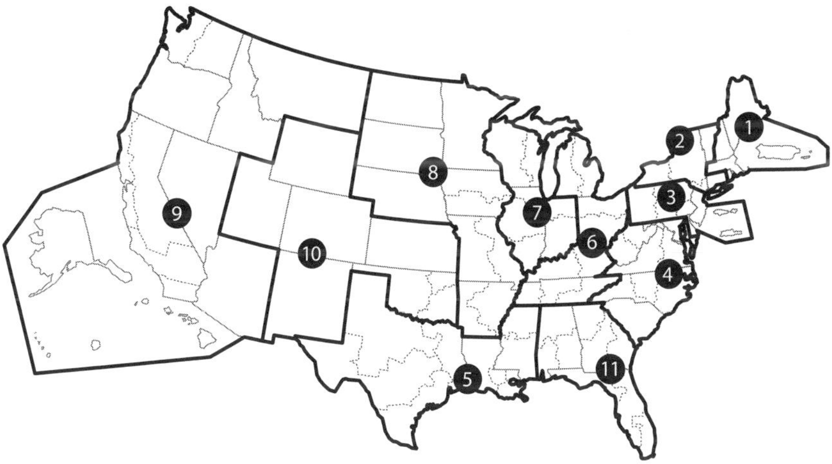

Note: Numbers indicate circuits. *Source:* www.uscourts.gov.

state senators. Under the informal but strong norm of "senatorial courtesy," a president is expected to confer with any senators of his party who are in the home state of the prospective nominee before the nomination is formally announced.[2] Such home state senators can effectively veto the president's choice if they are sufficiently opposed to the nominee, and on occasion the home state senator may convince the president to abandon his preferred nominee in favor of the senator's choice. However, most nominations for the courts of appeals result from informal negotiations and bargaining between the president and the home state senators. Presidents usually have the upper hand in such negotiations, but the relative influence of the president and home state senators varies considerably from case to case, depending on the priorities, power, and policies of the relevant policymakers, including the president, the home state senators, the Senate majority leader, and the chair of the Senate Judiciary Committee (see Binder and Maltzman 2009; Goldman 1997; Howard 1981; Songer, Sheehan, and Haire 2000; Steigerwalt 2010).

The politicization of the confirmation process has resulted in significant delays, as well as an increase in the number of rejected nominations, leading to a vacancy problem on the courts of appeals (Binder and Maltzman 2009). As an illustration of the vacancy problem, while there are 167 authorized courts of appeals judgeships, every year for the past twenty years between eleven and twenty-three of the positions have gone unfilled.

Of course, the vacancy problem is offset in part by the increased number of judges (from fifty-six in 1990 to 103 by 2007) who have taken "senior status" but are still participating in cases (we discuss the implications of this, as well as the use of designated judges, in chapter 2).[3] Judge P explained that judges can remain on active status as long as they want (or until they die). Alternatively, a judge may voluntarily elect to take senior status at age sixty-five if he or she has at least fifteen years of service—but moving into senior status is not automatic. More precisely, Judge Q explained that eligibility for senior status is governed by the "rule of 80." If a judge is at least sixty-five years old, has served for at least ten years, and his age plus years of service as an appeals court judge equals eighty, he is eligible to take senior status (see also Block 2007). As Judge E pointed out, judges on senior status may be as active or as inactive as they like; they may continue to hear a regular load of cases or they may sit for a reduced caseload. But, as Judge P pointed out, the general rule of thumb is that judges on senior status work half-time—that is, they hear half the number of cases heard by a judge on active status—and they are assisted by two law clerks and one secretary, rather than by the full-time judge's allotment of four clerks, a secretary, and an administrative assistant. Judges on senior status receive full salary but generally may not participate when the circuit sits en banc to resolve a conflict in circuit law.[4] According to our interviews, judges on senior status are also somewhat isolated from the administrative proceedings of the circuit and are usually not involved in the screening of cases.

PARTISANSHIP

Having described the appointment process, we now turn to a quick portrait of the types of people currently serving on the courts of appeals.[5] The selection of appeals court judges is a partisan process, with more than 90 percent of the judges representing the party of the president who appointed them. Thus, the partisan balance on the court has largely followed the electoral successes of each president. The proportion of appeals court judges appointed by a Democratic president has ranged from slightly over 20 percent in the early 1930s to over 80 percent at the end of the Truman administration (Songer, Sheehan, and Haire 2000, 30). Party control of the courts of appeals has split nearly evenly in the twenty-first century.

Turning our attention to the specific presidents who appointed the judges serving between 2000 and 2011, we see from figure 2 that four presidents, Reagan, Clinton, and the two presidents Bush, accounted

FIGURE 2. Judges sitting on U.S. Courts of Appeals in 2000–2011 (N = 229) by appointing president (percent)

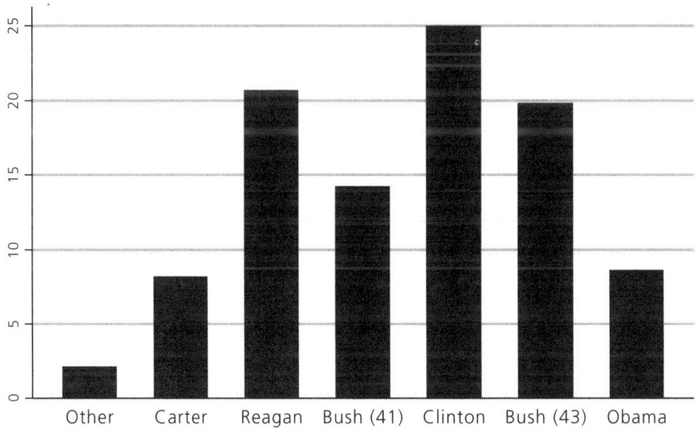

for most of those who have served recently. However, president Obama had appointed twenty judges by the end of September 2011,[6] and during his second term it is likely that the total number of judges appointed by Obama will eventually pass the appointment numbers of some of the other presidents reported in figure 2. Fewer than 10 percent of those serving in this century were appointed by President Carter, and almost no one remains who was appointed by a president before Carter.

The relative influence of the most recent former presidents on the U.S. courts of appeals primarily reflects the lengths of presidential terms (the three presidents with the most appointees served two terms) and recency. However, the numbers also reflect a decreasing trend in the rate at which presidents appoint judges to the intermediate federal appellate courts. In a four-year term, Carter appointed fifty-six judges. By comparison, Reagan and George H. W. Bush appointed judges at relatively similarly rates to one another, but much lower than Carter's (Reagan appointed eighty-three judges in two terms, an average of forty-one and one-half per term, and Bush appointed forty-two judges in his single four-year term). After that we see a precipitous drop, as Clinton and George W. Bush each appointed thirty-three judges, while Obama appointed thirty in his first term.

Part of this steep drop surely is due to the increasing delays in the confirmation process (see Binder and Maltzman 2009). However, part of the delay reflects the static number of judgeships on the courts of appeals since Clinton took office. During Carter's administration, Congress added thirty-five new seats to the appellate courts. Under the next two presidents, twenty-four (under Reagan) and eleven (under George H. W. Bush) new judgeships were created. However, since 1990, the total number of court of appeals judgeships has remained stable at 167.

GENDER, RACE, AND ETHNICITY

Historically, the federal appellate bench was almost entirely composed of white men. Before the election of Jimmy Carter, only two women had ever served on a court of appeals. Franklin Roosevelt appointed the first female federal appeals court judge, Florence Allen, to the Sixth Circuit in 1934. It took another thirty-four years before the second woman, Shirley Hufstedler, a Lyndon Johnson appointee, was appointed to serve on the Ninth Circuit (Ginsburg and Brill 1995).

Beyond the two token women judges, the process of gender diversification on the court really began under President Carter. Figure 3 shows the proportion of court of appeals appointees who were women for each appointing president since 1977. Overall, just over 20 percent of judges appointed in the past thirty-four years were women. Two additional trends stand out in the graph. First, Democratic presidents have tended to appoint more women than their recent Republican counterparts. As the graph reflects, Carter appointed a larger proportion of women appeals court judges than did the two subsequent Republican presidents,

FIGURE 3. Percentage of U.S. Courts of Appeals judges who are women, by appointing president

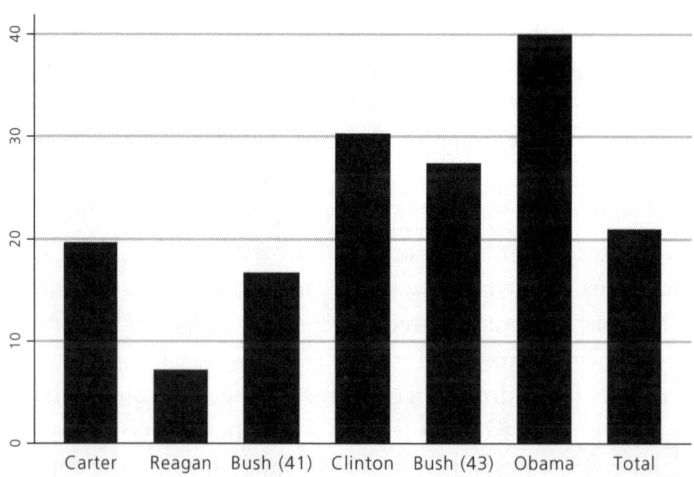

and Clinton and Obama each appointed a larger percentage of women than did any Republican president. Indeed, during this time period, 27.5 percent of the Democratic appointees were women, compared to 16 percent of the judges appointed by a Republican. In other words, the last three Democratic presidents were 1.7 times more likely to appoint a woman than the last three Republican commanders in chief.

Second, after accounting for partisanship, the general trend is toward appointing an increasing share of women judges to the appellate courts. Among Democrats, Clinton appointed about 10 percent more than Carter, and Obama appointed about 10 percent more than Clinton. A similar temporal pattern holds for the Republicans.

What accounts for these trends? The partisan difference may result at least in part from the gender gap—the tendency, since the 1970s, for women to affiliate with the Democratic Party more frequently than men (Norrander 1999). In other words, because there are more women Democrats and because presidents almost always select members of their own party, Democratic presidents are more likely to select women than are Republican chief executives. This preference is potentially compounded by the related presidential desire (though constrained by senatorial courtesy) to pick ideologically proximate nominees (Epstein and Segal 2005), combined with the tendency to perceive women as more liberal (Koch 2000). Finally, Democratic presidents appear to have had informal, if not formal, affirmative action plans (Slotnick 1984; Tobias 2010). The most obvious explanation for the tendency toward appointing more women (after accounting for partisanship) is an increasing proportion of women in the pipeline, which is roughly a reflection of the lagged proportion of women graduating from law schools. However, this does not appear to be the case. We can estimate the relevant lag by starting with the median age of judges when they are appointed, which, from the Carter administration through the first term of George W. Bush, has been fifty-one years. Assuming that the typical judge graduated from law school around age twenty-five or twenty-six years, the relevant lag is just under twenty-five years. In other words, the demographic breakdown of the total pool of potential federal appeals court appointees should be roughly reflected in the demographic breakdown of law schools thirty years prior to the appointment. Interestingly, twenty-five years before this writing, in 1976, approximately 10 percent of law school graduates nationwide were women (Sarver, Kaheny, and Szmer 2008). Five years before that, approximately two in one hundred law graduates were women. In other words, when the new judges added to the bench over the last thirty-four years were in law school, the pool of potential women judges was very shallow, and for most of this time it was miniscule.

In all likelihood, the trend toward more women appointees to the federal appellate bench resulted from several factors. First, the virtual quantum leap in the Carter administration—from one woman intermediate appellate court judge appointed in the previous five administrations to eleven appointed during Carter's single term—likely owes at least in part to his innovations in the judicial selection process. Carter created a White House nominating commission for judicial appointees, and he encouraged senators to do the same (Ginsburg and Brill 1995). This could have increased the effects of merit and decreased the effects of the "good old boy" network (Ginsburg and Brill 1995; but see Hurwitz and Lanier 2008, who found that state merit systems are no more likely to select diverse appellate judges). Also, Carter implemented an affirmative action plan when selecting judicial nominees (Slotnick 1984). Once Carter opened the door, other presidents may have felt compelled to pick female nominees, perhaps for political gain. Finally, the trend may also reflect the influence of the women's movement, which hit full stride in the 1970s.

The racial diversification of the appellate bench also started with President Carter. Prior to his administration, only five minority judges—four African Americans and one Asian American—had been appointed to the U.S. courts of appeals. Truman appointed the first African American judge, William Hastie, to the Third Circuit in 1949. It took another twelve years before Thurgood Marshall, Hastie's former law student and protégé, was appointed to the Second Circuit by President Kennedy. Kennedy's successor, Lyndon Baines Johnson, appointed two African American judges, Wade McCree (Sixth Circuit) and Spottswood Robinson (District of Columbia Circuit), to the U.S. Courts of Appeals in 1966. Finally, President Nixon appointed Herbert Choy, the son of Korean immigrants, to the Ninth Circuit in 1971. Prior to 1977 no president had appointed Latino or minority women judges to the courts of appeals.

As indicated by figure 4, just under 17 percent of U.S. appellate court appointees since 1977 have been racial minorities (either African American, Latino, or Asian American; no Native Americans have ever been appointed to a U.S. Appeals Court). Also, the same patterns identified with respect to gender exist for race, only they are starker: Democratic presidents are significantly more likely to appoint racial minorities and, after accounting for partisanship, the percentage of minority appointees has increased over time.

FIGURE 4. Percentage of U.S. Courts of Appeals judges who are minorities, by appointing president

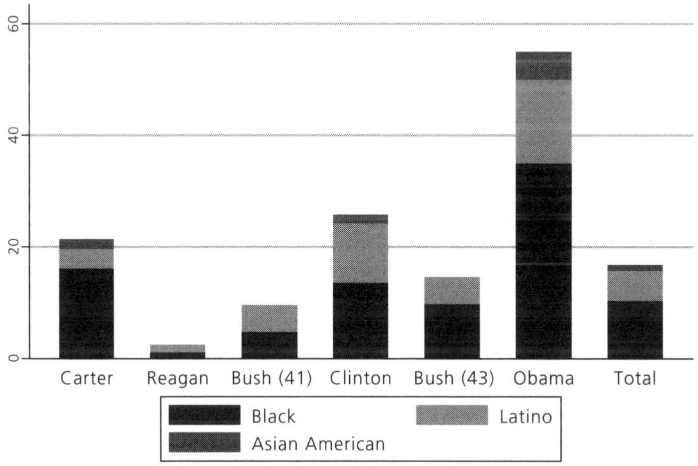

With respect to partisanship, 28.2 percent of Democratic presidents' appointees to the intermediate appeals courts have been racial or ethnic minorities, compared to 8 percent of Republican appointees. Put another way, Democratic presidents are three and one-half times more likely to appoint a racial minority. Of course, much of this disparity is driven by President Obama, who in his first thirty-three months in office appointed more nonwhites than whites to the U.S. Courts of Appeals. As of this writing, 35 percent of his appointees have been African American, 15 percent Latino, and 5 percent Asian American.

Why is the disparity so dramatic? The answer probably lies in some of the same explanations for the gender differences. First, partisanship and ideology are primary factors in the judicial selection process, and racial minorities, particularly African Americans (where the gap is most prominent), are much more likely to affiliate with the Democratic Party and espouse liberal views. Second, Democratic presidents, such as Carter (Slotnick 1984) and Clinton (Tobias 2010), have often employed affirmative action plans.

The change in time (after accounting for partisanship) is also striking. Overall, each president appointed a larger percentage of minority appellate judges than the prior president from his party. The most striking difference is among African American judges. Except for Clinton, each president appointed more than twice as many African American appellate court judges than any prior president from his party.

Once again, the changes over time are not entirely a reflection of increases in the size of the potential pool of minority judges. While the percentage of appointees overall during this time period generally does not reflect the racial breakdown in the entire population (approximately 13 percent of the U.S. population is African American, while only 10 percent of the appointees between 1977 and 2011 were African American), the entire population is not a macrocosm of the potential pool. Instead, we must look at the percentage of minority law school enrollees twenty-five to thirty years prior to the year of appointment to estimate the pool. As with gender, for most of the period (pre-1970s), the percentage of minority law students was relatively small, in large part owing to prior discrimination in law school admissions and financial barriers to accessing higher education. For the period 1971–1976, between 4 and 5 percent of all law students were African American, between 1 and 2 percent were Latino, and between 0.5 and 1 percent were Asian American. This reflects the pool for some of the George W. Bush and Barack Obama appointees. Both presidents appointed relatively higher percentages of African Americans (9.7 percent and 35 percent, respectively) and Latinos (4.8 percent and 15 percent). Additionally, Obama appointed a much higher proportion of Asian Americans (5 percent) than is represented in the pool.

Recent research on the intersectionality of judge race and gender suggests that both characteristics are too intertwined to examine separately (e.g., Collins and Moyer 2008). One thing stands out: most of the racial and ethnic minority judges are men. No Asian American women have ever sat on a U.S. court of appeals. Additionally, since 1977, African American and Latino men are more than three and a half times as likely to serve as U.S. Courts of Appeals judges than are African American women and Latinas. In the context of intersectionality, this is important, because minority women are more likely to be "tokens," which can affect behavior (Hawkesworth 2003).

PRIOR EXPERIENCE

While the U.S. Constitution sets no formal qualifications for appeals court judges, in practice, it would now be unthinkable for the president to nominate anyone without a law degree and a distinguished law career. However, no judicial experience is required, and most judges appointed in the last century did not have any formal judicial experience before taking their place on the courts of appeals (see Songer, Sheehan, and Haire 2000, 39, for details on the trend over time). Those with any judicial experience most frequently obtained it as a trial judge on the U.S. district courts. The data show that this is still the case, with more than one-third of the judges serving on the courts of appeals between 2000 and 2011 coming to the appellate bench after service on the main federal trial court.

In summary, while the backgrounds of appeals court judges are not representative of a cross section of the American public, there is substantial diversity within the judicial ranks, and the court has become more diverse over time. While women and racial minorities remain underrepresented compared to the population as a whole, the representation of women and minorities is substantially greater than it was even twenty years ago. Moreover, the representation of both groups appears to be greater than one would expect given that judges typically have more than twenty-five years of experience in the profession prior to appointment, and the pool of women and minorities with that level of experience is quite shallow as a result of historical discrimination and social pressures. At present, there is substantial parity in terms of the representation of political parties, but that could change depending on the outcome of future elections.

Managing Appeals on the Courts of Appeals

The U.S. courts of appeals exercise only appellate jurisdiction. They are responsible for hearing all appeals raised by litigants who lost in the U.S. district courts within their circuit and those raised by losing litigants from a broad array of federal administrative entities (Howard 1981).[7] They conduct no trials—no cases originate in the courts of appeals. Instead, the courts of appeals review the decisions of the courts and administrative agencies below in proceedings that typically are limited to the judges and the lawyers for the litigants. Although hearings conducted by the courts of appeals are open to the public, neither the actual litigants nor any witnesses typically appear before the courts.

One basic premise of the common law is that everyone has the right of one review of an adverse decision reached at trial. This led to the early creation of the U.S. courts of appeals as an intermediate court between the nation's trial courts and its Supreme Court to handle these mandatory appeals.[8] As a result of this absence of docket control, the number of appeals that must be terminated by the courts of appeals depends not on their own decisions but on the decisions of the losing litigants in the lower court (see Songer, Sheehan, and Haire 2000).

The courts of appeals hear appeals from both the civil and criminal decisions of the district courts and from the administrative rulings of many federal administrative entities within their geographic jurisdiction. Thus, the courts of appeals are empowered to hear appeals raising questions relating to the interpretation, application, or validity of federal laws, federal administrative regulations, treaties of the United States, or the Constitution of the United States. Moreover, when hearing appeals from cases brought under diversity of citizenship jurisdiction of the federal district courts or cases in which the U.S. government is a party, the courts of appeals are also involved in the interpretation of state law.[9]

There are now thirteen U.S. courts of appeals. One of the courts, that for the Federal Circuit, has broader geographic jurisdiction but more limited subject matter jurisdiction. The Federal Circuit hears cases in a hodgepodge of subject areas, including intellectual property and international trade.[10]

Because of the idiosyncratic nature of the Federal Circuit, we focus on the other twelve courts of appeals, which have broader subject matter jurisdiction but limited geographic jurisdiction. These courts are divided into twelve geographic circuits, one for the District of Columbia and eleven numbered circuits that each have jurisdiction over all cases arising in a multistate region. Circuit boundaries follow state boundaries, with the result that no state is in more than one circuit. Circuits and their borders are created by acts of Congress and presumably reflect political considerations, but do not necessarily reflect easily identified objective criteria. As can be seen from figure 1, each circuit covers a geographically contiguous set of states, but the groupings of states do not follow conventionally understood regional boundaries. For example, the Eighth Circuit extends from Arkansas to the Canadian border. Moreover, as shown in table 1, the circuits vary dramatically in terms of the proportion of the nation's population within each circuit. Additionally, the circuits vary widely in the number of cases filed per year and in the average workload of the judges in each circuit. The Ninth Circuit, which includes California, represents almost one-fifth of the nation's population and decides almost 13,000 cases per year. At the other extreme, both the District of Columbia Circuit and the First Circuit process fewer than 2,000 cases per year and represent a combined total of less than 5 percent of the nation's population.

Within this organizational structure, the procedures in each of the courts are governed by the Federal Rules of Appellate Procedure (FRAPs), a body of law promulgated by the Supreme Court of the United States and subject to amendment by Congress.[11] The FRAP rules apply uniformly to

TABLE 1 Number of judges and cases per circuit, 2009

CIRCUIT	CASES COMMENCED	AUTHORIZED JUDGESHIPS	PERCENTAGE OF U.S. POPULATION IN THE CIRCUIT	WORKLOAD (CASES COMMENCED PER JUDGE)
District of Columbia	1,272	11	0.19	116
First	1,646	6	4.58	273
Second	6,175	13	7.66	475
Third	3,879	14	7.17	277
Fourth	5,629	15	9.38	375
Fifth	7,507	17	10.27	442
Sixth	4,805	16	10.37	300
Seventh	3,463	11	8.08	315
Eighth	3,067	11	6.56	279
Ninth	12,912	29	19.75	445
Tenth	2,224	12	5.40	185
Eleventh	7,785	12	10.60	649

Source: Administrative Office of the United States Courts Director's Annual Report.

all the circuits. They cover a variety of topics, from the process for initiating an appeal, to the length and format of briefs and oral arguments, to guidelines for granting en banc rehearings. Additionally, under FRAP 47, each circuit authors a set of local rules that expound on the overarching FRAP rules. Each circuit also typically drafts internal operating procedures (IOPs), which, unlike the FRAP and local rules, are nonbinding. The IOPs often expand or clarify rules enunciated in the formal rules, as well as describe internal processes, which often are not covered formally. For example, some IOPs discuss the process for assigning judges to panels. Since the local rules and IOPs may not conflict with FRAP rules, the circuits each operate in a similar institutional setting. However, within these constraints there are some variations, which we address throughout the book.

The first step in the appellate process is for the losing party in the district court (or administrative entity) to file with the clerk of the court of appeals a notice of intent to appeal. That party (now designated the "appellant") proceeds to assemble a record of the trial court proceeding for the appeal (including a verbatim transcript of the proceeding), specify a list of errors alleged to have been made during the trial, and write a legal argument, designated the appellant's "brief" (Songer, Sheehan, and Haire 2000, 8–9). Copies of the record, the alleged errors, and the appellant's brief are sent to each of the three judges on the panel and to the opposing party, designated the "appellee."[12] The counsel for the appellee then files a brief detailing the reasons why the trial court decision should be affirmed. After the appellant receives a copy of the respondent's brief, the appellant has the opportunity to file a "reply brief" in which it attempts to refute or answer the allegations in the respondent's brief.

Once all these motions and briefs have been assembled, the case is typically assigned to a three-judge panel. The process generally involves two levels of at least quasi-random assignment. First, the chief judge or the clerk of court randomly assigns judges to panels, which typically meet for one week at a time.[13] (The chief judge is generally the active judge on the circuit with the greatest seniority among those who have not yet turned sixty-five and have not previously served as chief judge. Chief judges may not serve past seventy unless no one else is eligible.) Then the clerk randomly assigns the case to the panel. In some circuits this process is truly random. In other circuits, such as the Ninth, the clerk first (typically based on assessments from staff attorneys) weights the cases according to complexity to ensure a relatively equal workload across panels (Cohen 2002).

Typically, once a case has been assigned to a panel, the three judges must decide whether to hear oral arguments.[14] According to FRAP 34, oral argument must be granted unless a panel of three judges has examined the brief and record and unanimously agrees that oral argument is not warranted. However, as discussed further in chapter 2, the actual practice for deciding whether or not to set a case for oral argument varies substantially across the circuits.

When the panel decides to hear oral arguments, the length of the hearings is at the discretion of the judges (sometimes based on recommendations from the clerk or staff attorneys), but in recent years the majority of hearings have limited attorneys to an argument of no more than twenty minutes per side. Similar to Supreme Court oral argument practices, judges may, and frequently do, interrupt the presentations of the attorneys with questions, and the time taken up asking and answering those questions counts toward the twenty minutes allotted to each side.

Shortly after each hearing, the three judges hold a meeting, called a "conference," at which they discuss the case just heard and take a preliminary vote on the outcome. These meetings are held in strict confidence; even the law clerks of the judges are excluded. However, the decision of the court is not formally announced until after an opinion of the court has been written and is ready for formal distribution to the parties. While the hearing itself is open to the public and the final opinion of the court is by law a part of the public record, the deliberations of the three-judge panel at the conference and during the opinion-writing process remain secret even after the final decision is announced.

The Caseload Explosion

With the rapid expansion of caseloads, the intermediate appellate courts have come in practice to provide the final as well as the first review of alleged errors in the federal trial courts. A major problem faced by the courts of appeals has been the dramatic increase in the number of cases appealed to the courts in the past half century. As indicated in table 2, for much of the twentieth century the courts of appeals were required to decide only a modest number of cases. As late as 1960, fewer than 4,000 appeals were filed in the courts per year. But that changed rapidly beginning in the 1960s. Between 1960 and 1970, the number of appeals tripled. In the following decade, the number of cases filed in the courts of appeals more than doubled again, and between 1980 and the end of

TABLE 2 Increase in caseload of the U.S. Courts of Appeals, 1925–2009

YEAR	CASES FILED
1925	2,525
1930	2,874
1940	3,446
1950	2,678
1960	3,765
1970	11,440
1980	23,155
1990	40,893
1995	50,072
2000	55,626
2001	56,067
2002	56,534
2003	60,661
2004	60,505
2005	70,003
2006	70,375
2007	60,668
2008	61,492
2009	57,138

Source: Administrative Office of the United States Courts Director's Annual Reports.

the century the number of appeals more than doubled again, exceeding 55,000 cases in the year 2000. In the twenty-first century the rate of increase has slowed, and the total number of cases filed has even declined recently from the high of more than 70,000 filings reached in 2006, but the total number of appeals filed has remained above 60,000 cases per year for most of the past decade.

This rapid rise in the number of cases appealed to the circuit courts has had a number of consequences. A major consequence has been the emergence of the courts of appeals as the de facto courts of last resort. Successful appeal to the Supreme Court has been relatively rare for at least the past century. For example, in the late 1920s, after the Supreme Court gained largely discretionary control of its docket, it decided an average of roughly 150 cases per year at a time when the courts of appeals were deciding more than 2,500 cases per year. Thus, no more than 6 percent of the appeals court decisions were typically reviewed in a given year. In contrast, for most of the past decade the courts of appeals have been deciding more than 60,000 cases per year, while Supreme Court review of U.S. Courts of Appeals decisions has dropped to less than 150 cases per year (counting the summary decisions of the Supreme Court), making the probability of review less than three-tenths of 1 percent. Put differently, the proportion of appeals court decisions reviewed by the Supreme Court in the late 1920s was roughly twenty-five times as great as the proportion currently being reviewed.

For the courts of appeals, the biggest problem caused by the explosion in the caseload is that the number of judges has not kept up with the rising demand represented by the number of appellate filings, and these workload issues were addressed by many of the judges interviewed. While Congress has, over time, approved a substantial increase in the number of federal appeals court judges, the increase pales in comparison to the increase in the number of appeals filed in the courts of appeals in the same period. For example, while the number of authorized judgeships for the twelve geographic circuits of the courts of appeals has more than tripled since 1930—rising from forty-five judgeships in 1930 to the current number of 167—the increase has not come close to matching the caseload increase. The result is that the average workload for appellate court judges has exploded.

Figure 5 traces the increase in the average workload of courts of appeals judges, calculated as the number of cases filed per year divided by the number of appeals court judgeships authorized by Congress. The increase is dramatic. For the first three decades after 1925, the workload of

FIGURE 5. Average workload of U.S. Courts of Appeals judges, 1925–2010

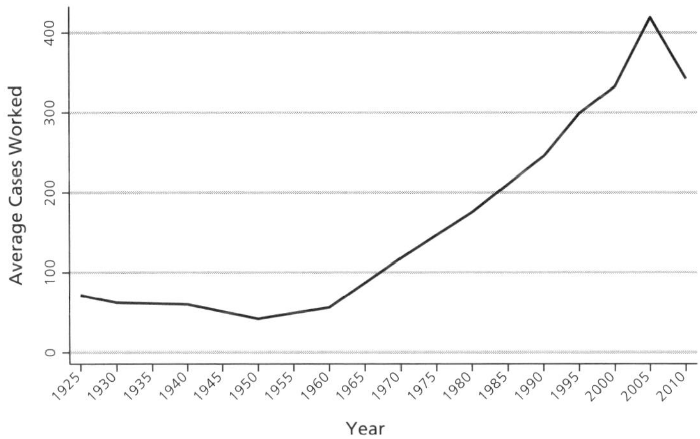

the judges remained relatively flat, even declining in some years. But after 1960 the number of appeals filed increased rapidly, while the number of judges available to decide the appeals did not. In the late 1950s and early 1960s, there was an average of fewer than sixty cases per judge on the docket of the courts of appeals. But in the most recent decade, the average workload has ballooned to more than 360 cases per judge in many years (reaching a high of more than 400 per judge in 2005)—a sixfold increase in the workload of the court. To make matters worse, the increasing political controversy surrounding appointments to the courts of appeals since the Clinton administration has meant increasing delays in the confirmation of appeals court nominees, with the result that there are often several vacancies on the courts. For example, in November 2010, twenty authorized judgeships were unfilled, increasing the workload for the remaining judges.

Issue Agenda

While we know much about the judges and the caseload, we know little about the extent to which the nature of the cases filed with each circuit are similar, because there is currently no available database of all cases filed that includes a categorization of the issues raised in the appeals. We do, however, have a database containing the issue areas discussed in a broad sample of reported cases. As such, we can discuss the output of the courts in the cases they deem important (i.e., those with reported opinions), including the variations across circuits and over time.[15]

Using data from the United States Courts of Appeals Database

(Songer 2002), we calculated the proportion of the courts of appeals decisions devoted to each of the major categories of issues heard by the circuit courts. The data represent only those cases that resulted in published opinions during the first eight years of the twenty-first century. Thus, while this is not a comprehensive look at the business of the circuit courts, it represents those cases that the judges themselves considered to be most important and therefore worthy of publication.

The most dramatic aspect of the agenda of the courts of appeals is that nearly half of all appeals that result in published opinions deal with issues raised by defendants in either federal or state criminal prosecutions.[16] Because of the constitutional prohibition against double jeopardy, virtually all of these appeals are brought by defendants who are challenging either their conviction or the sentence imposed at their trial. (A small number of these cases involve appeals brought by the government to pre-trial rulings in criminal cases [e.g., a decision by the trial court to deny the admissibility of the fruits of an alleged illegal search].) A much smaller proportion of cases (fewer than 7 percent) also involve defendants who were previously convicted in a criminal trial and sentenced to prison and who now challenge not the original conviction but some other aspect of their confinement, such as a claim that the extent of the crowding in the prison violates the prohibition of cruel and unusual punishment.

The second largest category of cases, accounting for more than one-fifth of all cases resulting in published opinions, are those raising claims under federal civil rights statutes. Most of these raise a claim of discrimination on the basis of race, gender, age, religion, or disability. A large majority of the cases in this category raise statutory rather than constitutional claims. Appeals raising other civil liberties claims, especially constitutional claims of the denial of due process or the right to privacy, make up a much smaller portion of the appeals court docket. Even when the categories of privacy and due process are combined with all other civil liberties claims (e.g., those raising First Amendment claims relating to freedom of speech, press, or religion; claims of the denial of equal protection; or Second Amendment gun rights claims) into a general civil liberties category, they constitute fewer than 8 percent of the cases receiving published opinions from the courts.

In some ways, the current agenda of the courts of appeals represents a major change from the business of the courts in previous years. In particular, economic disputes between private litigants, either individuals or corporations (combining torts, commercial cases, and the category of "other economic cases"), now make up slightly more than 10 percent of the published opinion cases. But an earlier study discovered that such private economic disputes accounted for more than 35 percent of the circuit courts' docket in the 1960s, and that in the 1920s and 1930s nearly half the docket was devoted to these private disputes (Songer, Sheehan, and Haire 2000, 54). Similarly, the proportion of the courts' published opinion docket involving action by the U.S. government in economic affairs (i.e., the categories of taxes, government regulation of business, the provision of government benefits such as Social Security and Medicare, and government involvement in labor management relations) is also much smaller than it was in the twentieth century. Government economic cases account for fewer than 6 percent of all cases with published opinions. But in the 1960s the courts decided four times as many of these cases (24.3 percent), and during the New Deal era close to two-fifths of all published opinions dealt with the role of the national government in the economy.

The big winners in gaining the attention of the courts of appeals in the twenty-first century are criminal and civil rights cases. To highlight, criminal cases, which now account for almost half of all published opinions, made up fewer than 20 percent of all cases with published opinions before 1960. And civil rights appeals, which now account for 21 percent of all cases with published opinions, made up fewer than 4 percent of published opinions in the 1960s and miniscule proportions of the docket before then (Songer, Sheehan, and Haire 2000, 54).

Conclusion

Having described the judges and the size and nature of the appellate court docket, in the rest of the book we examine how the courts treat the cases once the cases appear on the docket. In the next chapter we examine the process from the moment the appeal is filed, including case screening, oral arguments, and case conferences. Our interviews with sixty appeals court judges provide an insider's look at the processes followed by the courts. We then empirically test the implications of some of these judicial insights using statistical analyses of the actual outcomes of judicial decisions.

TWO

The Preliminaries: Setting the Agenda, Oral Argument, and Assigning the Opinion of the Court

Much happens before the announcement of a U.S. Court of Appeals decision. The existing scholarship, however, virtually ignores these procedures. Although significant research attention has been devoted to the U.S. courts of appeals (e.g., Cohen 2002; Cross 2007; Hettinger, Lindquist, and Martinek 2006; Howard 1981; Klein 2002; Songer, Sheehan, and Haire 2000), by and large, most of that attention has focused primarily on either judicial selection (e.g., Binder and Maltzman 2009; Goldman 1997; Steigerwalt 2010) or case outcomes in decisions (e.g., Hettinger, Lindquist, and Martinek 2004, 2006; Songer and Sheehan 1992). The process leading up to the outcomes, however, has been largely unstudied (but see Atkins 1974; Cohen 2002). For example, how do courts of appeals judges screen cases, prepare for oral argument, and make opinion assignments? We know little about any of these matters. The last lacuna is particularly troubling in light of the importance of the assignment of the opinion, which affects the content of the policy promulgated by the panel.

In this chapter, we fill this gap in our understanding of the literature through a combination of judge interviews and empirical analyses. For example, we explore the factors that influence panel screening decisions (e.g., whether to hear oral arguments) and opinion assignments. These analyses not only enhance our understanding of largely ignored yet important court processes, they also test a variety of theories incorporated into our integrated view of judicial behavior, including new institutionalism and the strategic model of decision making, which describes judges' consideration of contextual factors in reaching an opinion.

Screening Appeals

How do courts of appeals judges decide whether a case deserves oral argument, and what are their screening mechanisms? Although many judges spoke about the importance of understanding the processes prior to making a final panel decision in a court of appeals case, one judge's comment captured the complexity and significance of understanding these procedures: "The real question or determination in whether a case is given oral argument is whether there is something to be obtained for oral argument—meaning the case is not a 'slam dunk.' Something in the case puzzles you, and you want to explore it more. Ordinarily, if there will be a published opinion in the case, or [if] I think there will be, I will favor oral argument." Although this explanation does not provide specifics as to what makes a case worthy of an oral argument hearing, it demonstrates to some extent that the cases that make up the appeals courts' oral argument agendas should contribute to the state of the law and not be merely routine matters. This description also implies the importance of understanding how and why appeals court judges screen cases for oral argument.

As we discussed in chapter 1, the dramatic increase in the workload of the courts of appeals has created a major problem for the courts. The U.S. Supreme Court and many state supreme courts have handled the problem of an increasing number of appeals by limiting access to their courts (e.g., by denying an increasing number of petitions for certiorari, thus limiting the number of appeals scheduled for full consideration). But because recipients of an adverse decision in a lower court or administrative agency have the right to appeal, the courts of appeals lack such a direct means of controlling their docket. We asked the judges we interviewed how the courts have handled this problem.

All the judges we interviewed recognized this problem of rapidly increasing appeals at a time of only modest increases in the number of judges added to the courts of appeals. Several of the judges labeled the caseload increase an "explosion" or "the biggest crisis" confronting the courts during their lifetime. Three of the judges suggested that if Congress did not stop its partisan bickering and address the problem, the resulting deterioration in the working conditions of judges on the courts of appeals would make it increasingly difficult to attract quality judges to the appellate bench or to keep them from taking early retirement.

While the judges appeared to be unanimous in their recognition of the problems caused by the explosion in the number of appeals filed in their court, there was no consensus on the specific changes that should be taken to avert a crisis. Nevertheless, if one steps back from the details of the corrective measures taken by the circuits to deal with the problem, several general patterns emerge. Over the past several decades, every circuit has adopted means to deal with the problem of increasing workloads, and by and large most of the judges are satisfied with the way their circuit handles the problem. In fact, when discussing procedural changes adopted to deal with the caseload explosion, we noticed a pattern emerging in the descriptions of circuit practices. Most of the judges appeared to identify strongly with their own circuit and to approve of the way things were done in their circuit. Almost without exception the judges used "we" when discussing their own circuit and implied that all the judges in their circuit were of one mind about their particular procedures or approaches to judging. For example, judges would frequently say something like "On Circuit X, they do x, y, and z, but *we believe*"—"we" meaning the judges on the interviewee's circuit—"that is not the appropriate way to deal with the problem." So the circuits have adopted a variety of different ways to deal with the caseload explosion, and while the judges appeared to be fairly familiar with the way other circuits do things, they tended to think their own solution worked best (at least for their circuit).

Though the specifics of the procedural changes adopted vary, in general, all the circuits have implemented some variation of four practices. First, circuits make increasing use of staff attorneys (usually hired by the chief judge of the circuit) to examine appeals for technical defects that will allow for procedural termination of the appeal without full consideration by a panel of three judges. For example, appeals may be dismissed on the grounds of jurisdictional problems, mootness, lack of standing of the appellant, or failure to meet circuit requirements relating to the time allotted for appeal. In addition, all the circuits have adopted some sort of screening, even of those appeals meeting the technical requirements, which results in expedited decisional processes for appeals judged not to raise any important or significant legal issue. Most often, the result is that the less important appeals are not granted a hearing for the presentation of oral argument and instead are decided solely on the basis of the written materials submitted to the court, the lower court record and the litigant's briefs. In addition, many of the appeals granted oral argument are decided with an "unpublished" opinion or an opinion designated as not for citation as precedent. (We examine this method in substantial detail in chapter 3.) Finally, all circuits now make use of "outside" judges on some of their three-judge panels.

Analysis of data available through the Administrative Office of the United States Courts provides an indication of how frequently some of the screening techniques have been used during the past two decades. First, it is clear that a large number of appeals are now disposed of by procedural termination without a panel of judges making a decision as to the merits of the case. Since 2005, the number of procedural terminations has typically approached 30,000 cases per year. In an average recent year, only about half of the appeals filed with the courts of appeals are decided on their merits by a panel of three judges. In addition, even those cases slated for a decision on the merits often are not granted a full hearing with oral argument. Since 2005, on average fewer than 30 percent of terminations on merits have been decided after a hearing before a three-judge panel with oral argument. Combining these two figures, it appears that only about 15 percent of all appeals filed with the courts of appeals receive the "full treatment" of oral argument before a three-judge panel prior to the final decision. Since the full treatment of oral argument is by far the most time-consuming way to resolve appeals, the sharp limitation in the use of oral argument makes a major contribution to the ability of the courts to handle their increasing caseloads.

Consistent with the comments of the judges, the use of procedural terminations and denial of oral argument appear in all circuits, but there is considerable variation across the circuits. As can be seen from table 3, the frequency with which cases are resolved on their merits rather than receiving a procedural termination varies substantially across the circuits. At one extreme, almost two-thirds of all appeals filed in the Tenth Circuit are resolved on the merits. The rate in the First Circuit is nearly as high (62.0 percent). But at the other end of the continuum, fewer than two out of five cases receive a merits resolution in the Seventh and Eleventh Circuits.

Decisions to hear cases without oral argument are governed by Federal Rules of Appellate Procedure (FRAPs) rule 34. The rule requires the courts to allow oral arguments unless a panel of three judges unanimously decides that oral arguments are unnecessary for one or more of the following reasons: "the appeal is frivolous," "the dispositive . . . issues have been authoritatively decided," or "the facts and legal arguments are adequately presented in the briefs and the record" such that "the decisional process would not be significantly aided" by oral arguments. (The

TABLE 3 Procedural and merits terminations by circuit, 2008

CIRCUIT	CASES COMMENCED	CONSOLIDATED AND PROCEDURAL TERMINATIONS	MERITS TERMINATIONS (% OF TOTAL TERMINATIONS)	MERITS TERMINATIONS AFTER ORAL HEARING (% OF TOTAL MERITS TERMINATIONS)
District of Columbia	1,272	715	557 (43.7)	270 (48.5)
First	1,646	626	1,020 (62.0)	337 (33.0)
Second	6,175	3,316	2,859 (46.3)	1,111 (38.9)
Third	3,879	1,579	2,300 (59.3)	389 (16.9)
Fourth	5,629	3,048	2,581 (45.9)	395 (15.3)
Fifth	7,507	3,386	4,121 (54.9)	1,066 (25.9)
Sixth	4,805	2,236	2,569 (53.5)	909 (35.4)
Seventh	3,463	2,125	1,338 (38.6)	787 (58.8)
Eighth	3,067	1,145	1,922 (62.7)	576 (30.0)
Ninth	12,912	7,112	5,800 (44.9)	2,036 (35.1)
Tenth	2,224	751	1,473 (66.2)	468 (31.8)
Eleventh	7,785	4,717	3,068 (39.4)	639 (20.8)

Source: Administrative Office of the United States Courts.

three-judge panel deciding whether to hear argument need not be the same three-judge panel that decides the case.)[1] The rule also gives the circuits discretion to establish local rules requiring parties to file written statements "explaining why oral argument should, or need not, be permitted."

While FRAP 34 sets certain requirements for granting oral arguments, the circuit local rules and internal operating procedures (IOPs) still suggest there is significant variation across circuits. For example, while most circuit rules are silent on the issue, the Fourth Circuit mandates that all non-orally argued cases must be decided unanimously, while the Fifth Circuit allows dissents unless the court denied a party's request for an oral argument. Similarly, local rules outline a variety of provisions regarding litigant requests for or against oral arguments. Some circuits, like the Second and Sixth, require written statements within a certain time period or the party is presumed to have waived oral argument. Although the other circuits do not have explicit presumptions regarding the effects of the absence of a statement requesting or waiving oral argument, some, including the First, Third, Fourth, and Fifth Circuits, have promulgated rules governing the process for submitting such statements.

In light of the variation in local rules and procedures governing the process for granting oral argument, it is not surprising to find significant variation across the circuits in the proportion of the merits cases that are granted a hearing with oral argument. The 2008 data in table 3 show that the Seventh Circuit appears to be an outlier in its willingness to grant oral argument. Almost three in five (58.8 percent) cases decided on the merits received oral argument in the Seventh Circuit. In contrast, only one in six merits cases received oral argument in the Third Circuit (16.9 percent) and in the Fourth Circuit (15.3 percent). To explain these circuit differences and to understand the nature of the screening process more generally, we turn to the interviews with our appeals court judges.

The data in table 3 suggest that oral argument is most common in the Seventh Circuit, and the comments of the judges suggest that is not accidental. One judge[2] insisted quite forcefully, "We have a strong preference for oral argument," and then accurately noted, with considerable pride, "I believe we have the highest rate of oral argument of any circuit." Another Seventh Circuit judge reaffirmed this sentiment, asserting, "We generally grant oral argument in all cases that are not pro se"—pro se cases are cases in which litigants, usually prisoners, represent themselves, without an attorney—and then indicated that all of the judges were proud of this fact and saw it as part of the circuit's culture. Indeed, this is reflected in the Seventh Circuit's local rules. Unlike any of the other circuits' rules, the Seventh Circuit's local rules do not include any provisions that would make it easier for the court to deny oral arguments. For example, in the Second and Sixth Circuits, failure to affirmatively request an oral argument is deemed a waiver. Moreover, the Seventh Circuit is unique in that it has a rule (Local Rule 22(d)(1)) requiring oral arguments in certain cases (e.g., direct appeals of death penalty decisions).

The Seventh Circuit judges indicated that when the briefs first arrive at the clerk's office, they are screened by one of the circuit's twenty staff attorneys before they go to the judges. These attorneys first screen the appeals for technical defects and make recommendations for procedural termination of those that have such defects. Those that survive that initial screening are further evaluated by the staff attorneys, who then make a recommendation about whether to grant a request for oral argument. For the less complicated cases, the staff will recommend that a case be set for just ten minutes of oral argument per side, and that twelve such cases be scheduled for a single day's sitting by a panel of three judges. Appeals raising more important issues in the minds of the staff attorneys are recommended for twenty minutes of oral argument per side. All of these recommendations go to a panel of three judges. While the panels have the power to accept or reject the recommendations of the staff attorneys, most are routinely accepted. However, one Seventh Circuit judge said that just because most staff recommendations on oral argument are accepted by the panel of judges does not mean that the high actual rate of oral argument in the Seventh Circuit is the result of the preferences of the staff rather than the judges. Instead, he suggested that because of the close working relationship between judges and the circuit staff, the staff attorneys understand the preference of the judges for oral argument and make their recommendations accordingly. He also noted that the staff attorneys have a special responsibility to examine all pro se briefs carefully (because the judges themselves usually do not give much initial attention to pro se briefs since so many are frivolous) and to make recommendations if they think the pro se position has merit, and usually if they make such a recommendation, the court will appoint an attorney for the indigent defendant.

Judges on the Second Circuit also asserted strong preferences for oral argument. For example, one of the Second Circuit judges told us, "We don't really screen—we will grant oral argument to anyone who asks for it except in the case of prisoner petitions." Two other judges agreed with this assessment regarding oral argument. Another judge maintained that "We don't have a screening process like some circuits—we will let anyone have an oral argument." However, unlike in the Seventh Circuit, this informal preference is not reflected in the Second Circuit's local rules, which are among the least permissive of oral argument. For example, as previously noted, failure to file a request for oral argument within two weeks of the filing date of the last brief submitted for the appeal signifies a waiver of oral arguments (Local Rule 34.1(a)). In addition, the Second Circuit appears to have the only rule (34.2(a)(1)) actually requiring that certain cases (a subset of immigration appeals) must be decided without oral argument. Nevertheless, the data available from the Administrative Office of the United States Courts (see table 3) indicate that their rate of oral arguments is the third highest of all the circuits', though litigants are only two-thirds as likely to actually receive oral argument on the Second Circuit compared to the Seventh Circuit.

Table 3 suggests that in the First Circuit, a relatively high percentage of cases survive the threat of procedural termination and are decided on their merits, with a moderate proportion of those receiving oral argument. When asked about the screening process in the circuit, one judge initially responded, "There is minimal screening in our circuit." But as he and other judges in the circuit talked further, it evolved that there was actually a fairly elaborate process. This same judge indicated that when the cases come in, they go to a senior staff attorney, who takes a quick look at the case. Any case he thinks has an arguable issue is forwarded to a three-judge panel for further action. Other cases are sent to staff attorneys. The staff identifies the "open-and-shut" cases or issues that are not fully developed, and these are recommended for summary disposition. Another judge elaborated that the staff prepares a list of such cases to dismiss—with a memo explaining why—and these memos are circulated to all the judges in the circuit (only six, in the First Circuit). A single judge can put the case back in for assignment to a panel. But if no judge objects to summary treatment, a staff attorney then prepares a draft of a proposed opinion disposing of the case without argument. According to these judges, this draft memo is then sent to the circuit's "duty panel" of three judges for final approval.[3] Formal approval is routinely given, resulting in the issuance of a formal disposition in a short unpublished opinion.

Next, the staff attorneys prepare a list of cases that appear to warrant consideration by a panel of judges but the staff attorneys believe do not warrant oral argument. This is done about two months before the panels are to meet. In preparing this list, staff attorneys pay particular attention to pro se and habeas cases, where it is necessary to examine the extensive records of the trial. They also pay particular attention to Social Security claims and immigration appeals. These cases are also circulated to all judges with a memo recommending the disposition of the case (usually a dismissal or an affirmance). Again, a single judge can put the case back on the calendar for oral argument.

The rest of the cases are assigned to a three-judge panel, which may still decide not to grant an oral hearing after examining the full case file. Usually a hearing is denied only if all three judges agree that it is an obvious affirm or reverse, and this happens in only about 5 percent of the cases sent to the panels. The presumption is that all orally argued cases will result in a published opinion, but the panel on occasion may decide not to publish after an oral hearing.

In the Fourth Circuit, which has both a relatively high rate of procedural terminations and the lowest rate of granting oral argument, the judges take pride in the efficiency of their screening procedures. All the judges interviewed agreed that ultimately the judges decide which cases will receive oral argument. Nevertheless, thirty staff attorneys (i.e., two staff attorneys for each authorized judge in the circuit) working in the clerk's office are active in screening.

One Fourth Circuit judge explained that all cases go first to the head staff attorney, who decides whether they should be "screened." If he decides that the case is of such clear importance that it does not require the normal screening but needs to be scheduled for oral argument, it is immediately forwarded to a panel of three judges, randomly selected in the clerk's office. This usually results in an oral argument hearing and full consideration by a panel of judges. Nonetheless, even if the clerk has scheduled a case for oral argument, if all three judges agree that it should not be heard, it is removed from the oral argument docket.

In a large majority of cases, however, the importance of the case is not immediately obvious to the head staff attorney. Then the head staff attorney assigns the case to one of his staff for their normal screening of cases. If the staff attorney thinks the case is worthy of oral argument, it is sent to the senior clerk for assignment to an oral argument panel. There are no formal rules about which cases should be decided without oral argument, but many are jury cases in which there are only factual issues on appeal, or else they are cases that are frivolous or do not have the potential for any precedential significance.

Alternatively, the staff attorney will examine the appeal for procedural defects (e.g., appeal "out of time," a problem of mootness or standing, or a jurisdictional defect). If such a defect does exist, another judge explained that no memorandum will be written by the staff attorney; instead, the attorney will propose procedural termination in the form of a summary disposition. After receiving such a recommendation, the judges on the panel who would have decided the case on its merits have a conference call with the staff attorney and agree on the phone to summary dismissal. The decision for such a procedural termination must be unanimous: a single judge can send the case to the argument calendar for full consideration on its merits.

If the staff attorney decides that there are no procedural defects but that a full hearing is not warranted, staff will write a draft of an opinion and send it to the "top" judge of a panel (this is the judge whose name is listed at the top of the three judges' names, not necessarily the most senior judge). That judge then writes a letter to the other two judges on the panel to ask whether they agree with the proposed disposition. If they write back and agree, then the opinion is filed as the disposition of the court. Such opinions are virtually never published. If, however, a single judge disagrees with such a summary disposition, the case is scheduled for a full hearing. It was noted in our judge discussions that this process allows the "vast majority" of cases to be decided without oral argument (a conclusion supported by the data presented in table 3).

Once the panel of judges receives a case on the argument calendar, the presumption is that the case will be scheduled for oral argument. Nevertheless, the judges can remove it and designate it for summary judgment if all agree. After oral argument, the panel decides whether the opinion announcing its judgment should be published; usually this decision is made at the initiative of the judge assigned to write the opinion.

The Tenth Circuit makes much less extensive use of staff attorneys in its screening. As one judge recounted, "All of our screening is done by the judges. We have a three-judge screening panel whose composition changes every year. The bottom line is that if any one of the three judges wants to schedule oral argument, the case gets oral argument." Other cases are disposed of summarily.

The remaining circuits appear to use some variant of the procedures used on the First and Fourth Circuits. A judge of the Third Circuit explained that they always grant an oral argument "if we think there is a chance for reversal or if the appellant really needs to be heard" (e.g., in civil rights cases). "We want to make sure that the loser feels that he has had a fair shake." Nevertheless, as our judges from other circuits also mentioned, they wouldn't hear any appeals that appear to be frivolous.

A judge on the Sixth Circuit spelled out some of the rules of thumb that appear to be used to varying degrees in most circuits. He said that "paid" criminal appeals—those in which the defendant is represented by a lawyer, whether privately retained or appointed from the Public Defender's office—were treated as having a right to oral argument in that circuit (though they do not always request it). Similarly, civil cases with counsel are given the presumption of oral argument if the claim is reasonable, but it is up to the panel assigned the case whether to grant oral argument. In contrast, pro se cases generally are not argued orally, but if the Sixth Circuit decides to hear oral argument, then counsel will be assigned. Staff attorneys have the primary responsibility to screen the pro se applications, but any judge on the panel assigned to hear a case can insist on an oral argument. Similarly, a judge from the Ninth Circuit indicated that usually if there is no oral argument, it means there is a very clear decision. Elaborating on this theme, one of the Ninth Circuit judges explained that the real question or determination in whether a case is given oral argument is whether there is something to be obtained for oral argument. For example, "oral argument is granted when the case is not a 'slam dunk.' Something in the case puzzles you, and you want to explore it more. Ordinarily, if there will be a published opinion in the case, or [if] I think there will be, I will favor oral argument."

In general, then, all circuits make use of staff attorneys to reduce their workload by identifying cases with clear legal defects or cases not broaching an important legal issue. Such cases are disposed of with some form of summary disposition that requires minimum involvement by the judges. While all judges indicated that they agreed with the proposed dispositions offered by staff attorneys in a large majority of the cases, the judges are careful to reserve the final disposition to themselves, and the rules of most circuits provide there will ultimately be a full hearing with oral argument if even one of the three judges assigned to the panel to hear the case thinks that such full treatment is warranted.

Modeling Decisions to Hear Oral Arguments

While some aspects of the screening process are difficult to test empirically owing to data restrictions, we can examine the decision to hear oral arguments. Those who have scrutinized appellate decision making have directly studied the content of oral arguments (e.g., Johnson 2004) and the effects of oral arguments on Supreme Court outcomes (e.g., Johnson, Wahlbeck, and Spriggs 2006). They have also indirectly examined the effects of oral arguments on U.S. courts of appeals decisions in studies examining the impact of the characteristics of the orally arguing attorneys (e.g., Szmer et al. 2013). However, no one has previously modeled decisions by the U.S. Courts of Appeals to offer oral arguments. In light of evidence that oral arguments affect judicial behavior, the decision to hear oral arguments can have profound effects on judicial outcomes. To better understand this process, we synthesized the comments of the judges, along with the formal circuit rules, to develop a set of hypotheses explaining oral argument decision making, which we then tested.

HYPOTHESES

Obviously, oral arguments have temporal costs. They delay the advancement of a specific case, as well as the disposition of other cases. As such, the judges noted in their interviews that decisions without oral arguments are more efficient. Given this, we would expect oral argument to be less likely to occur when the circuit overall, and panelists specifically, are faced with greater workload pressures. So factors like circuit docket size, judicial vacancies on the court, and the workload of the panelists (e.g., the relative number of opinions of the court the judge is responsible for writing at that point in time) should all affect the decision to hear oral arguments.[4] This situation leads to the following set of hypotheses:

H1: The likelihood that a case is orally argued decreases as the docket size of the circuit increases.
H2: The likelihood that a case is orally argued decreases as the number of judicial vacancies on the circuit increases.
H3: The likelihood that a case is orally argued decreases as the workload of the panelists deciding the case increases.

It is also possible that rules matter. Whether a court will hear an oral argument provides a nice venue to test the new institutionalism theory (Smith 1988) that behavior is constrained by the formal and informal rules that govern the institution. The decision to hear oral arguments provides an appropriate context for examining this theory because we have two levels of formal rules. While FRAP 34 governs all circuits, within the constraints of the broad rule, each circuit has the power to craft its own procedures. This leads to two sets of hypotheses to test the effects of these rules.

According to FRAP 34, circuits must hear oral arguments unless three judges agree the case is frivolous, or the issues have already been authoritatively decided, or the legal arguments have been adequately presented in the briefs. The first two criteria are essentially aspects of legal complexity. As such, we hypothesize the following:

H4: The likelihood that a case is orally argued increases as the complexity of the issues presented in the case increases.

Several of the judges we interviewed also discussed the tendency not to allow oral arguments in pro se cases. In part, pro se cases are heuristics that reflect the legal salience of the issues raised by the appellant.[5] Additionally, judges likely have low expectations for the utility of oral arguments presented by pro se litigants. Therefore, we hypothesize the following:

H5: The likelihood that a case is orally argued decreases when the appellant is a pro se litigant.

While FRAP 34 governs all the circuits, it expressly and implicitly leaves plenty of room for the individual circuits to construct different local rules and IOPs governing the decision to hear oral arguments. For example, FRAP 34(a)(1) explicitly gives the circuit the discretion to craft a rule requiring litigants to file "a statement explaining why oral argument should, or need not, be permitted." While none of the circuits requires such a statement, many of the circuits have created rules regarding the manner, timing, and effects of the failure to file such statements. For example, the Second and Sixth Circuits treat failure to file a statement requesting oral argument by a certain time as a waiver of oral argument, or at least a signal that the litigant does not want the opportunity to present an oral argument. Other circuits, including the First, Third, Fourth, and Fifth, set time limits for the litigants to file requests for oral argument. Additionally, some circuit rules require that some cases be automatically placed on the nonargument calendar (e.g., the Second Circuit), while the Seventh Circuit expressly requires oral arguments in direct death penalty appeals. These rules vary in their likely influence over the decision to grant oral arguments. For example, treating failure to file a statement requesting oral argument as a waiver decreases the likelihood the court will hear oral arguments. Based on this discussion, we posit the following general hypothesis:

H6: The likelihood that a case is orally argued is lower in circuits with local rules or procedures that make it easy for the court to decide the case without oral arguments.

Data and Methods

What follows is a nontechnical description of the data sources, the variables used in the statistical models, and justifications of the precise statistical model employed in each analysis. Similar nontechnical discussions are provided for each of the statistical models throughout the book. For some variables, these nontechnical descriptions are sufficiently precise and do not require additional explanation. For variable names followed by an asterisk (e.g., Orally Argued Case*), these descriptions are supplemented with a more detailed discussion found in the technical appendix.

Ideally, we would have liked to examine the entire population of U.S. courts of appeals cases, including both reported and unreported cases. However, the only available data set of that magnitude, maintained by the Federal Judicial Center, does not include the requisite information to test all of our hypotheses and adequately control for additional factors, particularly those at the panel level. As such, we analyzed those cases decided by three-judge panels in the United States Courts of Appeals Database from 1971 to 2002 (Songer 2002).[6] There is, of course, one major limitation: the Songer (2002) data set includes only cases that were eventually published in the *Federal Reporter.* These cases as a whole are systematically distinct from the nonreported cases. In general, they are more salient and more complex. Of course, if anything, this should make it more difficult to support our hypotheses, as we will have less variance. Still, all of our conclusions need to be interpreted in light of this limitation.

The dependent variable, Orally Argued Case*, is dichotomous, coded one if the case was orally argued, zero if it was not orally argued. Given the level of measurement, we estimated the model coefficients using logistic regression. Additionally, to account for potential correlated error structures within circuits, we estimated a circuit-level fixed effects model.

INDEPENDENT VARIABLES

We included three independent variables to operationalize the effects of workload pressures: Circuit Docket Size, Circuit Judge Vacancies, and Panel Opinion Caseload. Since higher values for each construct indicate increased workload pressures, we expect to find negative coefficients for each of the three variables.

Circuit Docket Size:* Variable measured as the number of terminations per three-judge panel during the corresponding fiscal year by that circuit.

Circuit Judge Vacancies:* A measure of the number of judicial positions vacant in a given circuit in a given year.

Panel Opinion Caseload:* A measure of the workload facing each judge at the time of the decision on whether to grant oral argument.

Hypothesis 4 states that oral arguments are less likely to occur as case complexity increases. Unfortunately, no one definitive measure of complexity has been operationalized. The typical measurement strategy relies on one or more proxy measures. Some of the proxies, such as length of the opinion of the court (e.g., Hettinger, Lindquist, and Martinek 2006), could be a function of the decision to hear oral argument, so we could not include them in the model. In the end, we chose three different measures, Number of Issues, Cross Appeal, and Criminal, to assess complexity.

Number of Issues: A variable indicating the number of substantive issues addressed by the court in the published opinion.[7] Higher values indicate increased complexity; therefore, we would expect to find a positive coefficient.

Cross Appeal: A dummy variable, coded one if the case included a cross appeal. Since cases with cross appeals are presumably more complex, we would expect to find a positive coefficient.

Criminal: A dummy variable, coded one if the case was a criminal case. Based on our interview material, appeals court judges tend to perceive criminal cases as less complex. Therefore, the coefficient should be negative.

Pro Se: A dummy variable, coded one if the appellant was a pro se litigant and zero if she was not. Given Hypothesis 5, we would expect to find a negative coefficient.

Circuit Rules:* A dummy variable, coded one if the circuit had rules discouraging oral argument and zero if it did not.

We also included a variety of control variables. For example, we posited that courts are more likely to hear oral arguments in more salient cases. As with complexity, no one salience measure has been devised for courts of appeals cases. As such, we included several proxy measures: Civil Rights, Amicus Curiae, Constitutional, and Prior Publication.[8] Since higher values of each construct indicate higher levels of case salience, the coefficients for each variable should be positive.

Civil Rights: A dummy variable, coded one if the case involved a statutory or constitutional civil rights issue, zero if it did not.

Amicus Curiae:* Measured as the natural log of the number of amicus briefs filed in the case.

Constitutional: A variable, coded one if the case involved the application of the U.S. Constitution, zero if it did not.

We also included two additional circuit-level measures that controlled for logistical difficulties in arranging to hold oral arguments: Circuit Active Judges and Circuit Area (per judge). Presumably, circuits with more judges, as well as circuits that cover more area, incur greater temporal and possibly financial costs when they hear oral arguments. As such, both coefficients should be positive.

Circuit Active Judges: The total number of active judges on the given circuit during the year the case was decided.

Circuit Area: The number of square miles of land in the circuit.

Finally, the model includes seven panel-level controls:

Panel Ideological Range:* The ideological distance between the most liberal and the most conservative member of the panel.

Panel Law School Prestige:* A proxy measure of judicial expertise, like the ABA rating measure (below). At least one recent study suggests that expert judges are less likely to utilize information from oral arguments (Szmer and Ginn forthcoming). As such, we posited that experts are less likely to grant them. The variable is a count of the number of graduates of prestigious law schools sitting on the panel.

Panel ABA Extremely Well Qualified: A proxy measure of judicial expertise. The American Bar Association (ABA) rates the federal judicial nominees based on their qualifications (Songer, Sheehan, and Haire 2000). The rating is ordinal, with judges receiving extremely well qualified, well qualified, qualified, and not qualified ratings. The variable is a count of the number of extremely well qualified judges serving on the three-judge panel that decides the case.[9]

Panel Senior Judge/Visiting Active Appeals Judge/District Court Judge: Three dummy variables, each coded one if that particular type of designated judge sat on the panel.

Panel Tenure: The average number of prior years on the U.S. courts of appeals served by each of the three panelists.

Analysis of Decisions to Hear Oral Arguments

The results of the analysis, presented in table 4, support three of our five hypotheses. One of the three workload measures, Panel Opinion Caseload, appears to affect the decision to hear oral arguments. The coefficient is negative, as posited, and statistically significant at the 0.001 level. However, the direct measure of circuit level workload, Circuit Docket Size, is not statistically significant. Neither is Circuit Judge Vacancies. This suggests that the judges are influenced by more personally tangible workload pressures.

All three of our measures of complexity—Number of Issues, Cross Appeal, and Criminal—are statistically significant in the posited directions. Panels are more likely to hear oral arguments in cases with cross appeals and more substantive issues and are less likely to hear appeals in criminal cases.

The coefficient for the Pro Se and Circuit Rules variables, as anticipated, are negative and statistically significant. In other words, oral arguments are less likely to be held in pro se appeals and by circuits with formal rules discouraging oral arguments.

With respect to the controls, three of the four salience variable coefficients are statistically significant (Civil Rights is neither significant nor in the expected direction). Among the circuit- and panel-level control

TABLE 4 Logistic regression of decisions to grant oral arguments, U.S. Court of Appeals published opinions, 1971–2002

VARIABLE	B	DISCRETE CHANGES IN PREDICTED PROBABILITIES: CONTINUOUS INDEPENDENT VARIABLES	DISCRETE CHANGES IN PREDICTED PROBABILITIES: DUMMY INDEPENDENT VARIABLES
Circuit Docket Size	0.000 (0.000)	—	—
Circuit Judge Vacancies	0.000 (0.002)	—	—
Panel Opinion Caseload	−0.041*** (0.014)	−0.04	—
Number of Issues	0.264*** (0.030)	0.08	—
Cross Appeal	0.586*** (0.160)	—	0.07
Criminal	−0.336*** (0.071)	−0.05	—
Circuit Rules	−0.627*** (0.206)	—	−0.11
Pro Se	−2.503*** (0.121)	—	−0.54
Civil Rights	−0.149 (0.083)	—	—
Amicus Curiae	0.924*** (0.249)	0.03	—
Constitutional	0.332*** (0.098)	—	0.04
Prior Publication	0.201*** (0.075)	—	0.03
Circuit Active Judges	0.014 (0.014)	—	—
Circuit Area	−0.000*** (0.000)	−0.30	—
Panel Ideological Range	0.020 (0.093)	—	—
Panel Tenure	0.020** (0.007)	0.03	—
Panel Law School Prestige	0.006 (0.040)	—	—
Panel ABA Extremely Well Qualified	−0.054 (0.056)	—	—

(continued)

TABLE 4 (*continued*)

VARIABLE	B	DISCRETE CHANGES IN PREDICTED PROBABILITIES: CONTINUOUS INDEPENDENT VARIABLES	DISCRETE CHANGES IN PREDICTED PROBABILITIES: DUMMY INDEPENDENT VARIABLES
Panel Senior Judge	0.499*** (0.074)	—	0.06
Panel Visiting Active Appeals Judge	0.701*** (0.171)	—	0.08
Panel District Court Judge	0.763*** (0.088)	—	0.08
Constant	1.978		
N	9,940		
Nagelkerke R^2	0.242		

Notes: B (column 2) = maximum likelihood coefficient; robust standard errors in parentheses; circuit fixed effects not reported.
$^*P < 0.05$, $^{**}P < 0.01$, $^{***}P < 0.001$.

variables, only Circuit Area (per judge), Panel Tenure, and the three judge type variables are statistically significant. Interestingly, cases with designated judges are more likely to hold arguments. Perhaps this is a function of a selection effect: these judges choose to take on extra work, and therefore, perhaps, feel less workload pressure. In particular, senior judges should have diminished workloads.

Of course, tests of statistical significance tell us very little about substantive significance. To get a fuller understanding of the magnitude of the effects of the statistically significant independent variables, we generated discrete changes in the predicted probabilities (see Long and Freese 2006, and the discussion in the technical appendix).

Among the main independent variables, the Pro Se variable exerts the most influence on the likelihood the panel will hear oral arguments in a case. The discrete change suggests that the probability of an oral hearing is 0.54 less in pro se cases than in cases in which the appellant is represented by counsel. Of the other main independent variables, Circuit Rules appears to have the strongest effect. Specifically, the probability of an oral argument occurring is 0.11 less in circuits with formal rules discouraging oral arguments. Of the other main causal variables, Number of Issues has the third highest discrete change (0.08). Among the control variables, Circuit Area has the strongest effect. The probability of an oral argument occurring in a circuit with a value one standard deviation above the mean is 0.30 less than in a circuit with a value one standard deviation below the mean.

Overall, the model provides strong support for the institutionalism hypotheses. We found evidence that both the FRAPs and the local rules and IOPs influence decisions to hear oral arguments. FRAP 34 creates a widely applicable rule calling for oral arguments in all but the simplest cases. We found that oral arguments are more likely to occur as the case complexity (measured using the number of substantive issues, the presence of a cross appeal, and whether it was a criminal case) increases. Additionally, we found evidence that circuits' local rules and IOPs influence decisions to hear arguments. While we found some evidence that workload matters, it appears that it is the workload of the judges on the panel, not that of the circuit as a whole, that affects whether oral arguments are heard. Finally, we reiterate that our data include only those cases in which the decision of the court was eventually published in the *Federal Reporter.* While this should make our hypothesis tests more conservative, the results should be interpreted in light of this limitation.

Who Sits on the Panel?

In addition to screening, the panel assignment process is another behind-the-scenes procedure with important implications. Indeed, as the analysis below demonstrates (see chapters 5 and 6), who sits on the three-judge panels that decide appeals sometimes makes a major difference in who wins and who loses an appeal. The judges we interviewed also suggested that panel composition may affect the content of the legal rules fashioned in the majority opinion. Not surprisingly, in the 1960s, there was considerable controversy on at least one circuit about the selection of judges for panels that heard appeals in school desegregation cases. The Fifth Circuit was split 5–4, with the more conservative judges in the majority, about the extent to which the circuit should vigorously demand compliance with the landmark Supreme Court case of *Brown v. Board of Education.*[10] Some suggested that the liberal chief judge of the circuit used his control of panel assignment to ensure that a liberal majority existed on all panels hearing appeals of school desegregation decisions (Atkins and Zavoina 1974). In light of the potential importance of which judges heard the appeals in politically important cases and the past controversy over the selection of panels, we felt it was critical to explore both the formal rules and the informal practices that determine which judges are selected to sit on each appeals court panel.

The consensus in the answers that the judges we interviewed gave to our questions about panel selection was striking. Almost all the judges appeared to be familiar with the controversy in the 1960s, yet all the judges whom we interviewed were adamant in asserting that nothing similar had happened in recent years.[11] Many went on to volunteer the observation that given current practices in their circuit, it would be unthinkable for any chief judge to try to stack a panel in an attempt to influence the outcome of an appeal.

Judge C expressed a sentiment that appeared to be shared by the judges in all circuits, saying, "There has never been any controversy in our circuit over an allegation that the panels have been 'rigged' or 'stacked.' The panels are assigned by the administrative staff; opinions are assigned by the senior judge on the panel." Judge J agreed, asserting emphatically, "Panel selection is essentially random; we have never had any complaints." Judge D agreed with his colleagues and elaborated on the specifics of the process used in their circuit. He indicated that the judges and cases were independently assigned by different clerks (i.e., one assigned cases to panels and the other assigned judges without knowing the cases). According to Judge D, "The judges are assigned to panels in a basically random process about a year in advance; about two months before the panel is to meet, the clerks assign the cases to panels. This assignment of cases is not strictly random—there is an attempt to assign a mix of heavy and light cases to balance the workload of the panels, but none of us has ever seen any evidence that the panel assignments were being used for political purposes."

While the specific procedures used to assign judges and cases to panels vary across the circuits, all the judges we interviewed indicated they were confident that the process was essentially random and contained no political bias. For example, Judge R asserted, "It is completely random now. Even if a judge has to recuse, the replacement is picked randomly." Judge P agreed, adding that the calendar clerk oversees the process. For many years, the three judges' names were literally drawn out of a hat, producing a completely random assignment. Now the names for the panel are computer generated by a program designed to ensure that every judge sits with every other judge the same number of times per year. Litigants do not learn the names of the judges to hear their argument until they show up on the day of the hearing. This approach is designed to prevent forum shopping by litigants and their attorneys.

Like Judge R, several other judges noted that there was now little concern over the possibility of stacking panels to achieve political goals, and instead randomized procedures were often seen as a necessary device to prevent forum shopping. As Judge G commented, "No, there has never been any attempt to 'stack' a panel that I know of. Assignments are usually generated by the computer—completely random. We don't even use expertise or seniority in making panel assignments. There is no way that the litigants will know who will hear their case if they decide to appeal—the assignments are not announced until about two weeks before oral argument." Judge N concurred, noting that while it might sometimes make sense to take account of expertise or experience, the greater concern with forum shopping meant that even such "benign" reasons for departing from random selection were not used.

Judge S indicated that the only departures from random assignment were those designed to eliminate schedule conflicts among the judges and conflicts of interest. He indicated that on his circuit, the cases are assigned by date before the judges are assigned, and the judges are sent lists of the days on which they are tentatively scheduled to hear oral argument without identifying which cases they will hear. Judges are asked to indicate whether they have any conflicts that would prevent them from sitting on those dates, and only after they have indicated their availability are they sent the list of cases they are scheduled to hear. Judges are then asked to indicate whether they need to recuse themselves from any case because of a conflict of interest. Vacancies created by such recusals are then filled randomly from among the judges who previously indicated they were available on the given date.

Of course, with the case explosion noted in chapter 1, the circuits have also had to look beyond their own active judges to fill some panel seats. And, as with many other internal processes, there are considerable differences in practice across the circuits in the extent to which the courts attempt to deal with the case explosion by supplementing the work of the judges on active service in the circuit with additional judges. To some degree, all circuits use these additional judges to sit with two active circuit court judges in order to make up the three-judge panel. This process was implemented to help the circuit courts manage the large caseloads that come before their respective circuits. Most of these additional "designated" judges come from one of two categories: (1) senior circuit court judges from the same circuit who have expressed their willingness to continue to hear cases in the circuit (usually hearing the equivalent of half the load of judges remaining in active service) and (2) district court judges from the same circuit who are in active service.

However, other federal judges are eligible for appointment on an ad hoc basis to serve on appeals court panels as "judges sitting by designation." Consequently, on occasion appeals court panels sit with one judge who is an appeals court judge or a district court judge from another circuit (either in active service or on senior status), or with a variety of other judges, including circuit judges from the Federal Circuit, judges from specialized courts or, more rarely, a retired Supreme Court justice. This latter method is a relatively recent phenomenon. In a Lexis judge field search of names of justices who retired after 1945, Justice Tom C. Clark (who retired in 1967) appears to have been the first former justice to have sat on a U.S. court of appeals by designation after retirement. He is also the most prolific, by almost threefold. The Lexis search for Justice Clark returned 390 separate decisions over an eight-year period. Since then, approximately half (seven) of the subsequent High Court retirees have sat by designation on the lower appellate court. Of those seven, two—Justices Marshall and Brennan (both of whom died shortly after retirement)—sat in a handful of cases (five and two, respectively). After Clark, the three most prolific former justices are recent retirees. Following his departure from the Supreme Court in 1993, Justice Byron White appeared in seventy-four cases. As of September 2011, former Justices Sandra Day O'Connor and David Souter have both appeared in more than one hundred U.S. courts of appeals cases as designated judges. Interestingly, while most of the retired justices sat on multiple circuits, Souter, known as a homebody who retired relatively young to return to his home in New Hampshire, sits only on First Circuit panels.

Our interviews noted that in all circuits, the use of designated judges is seen as one of the devices that the circuit has been able to implement to handle increasing caseload pressures. Designated judges are assigned at the discretion of the chief judge of the circuit or the chief justice of the United States, but their appointment appears to be noncontroversial.[12] All the judges we interviewed appeared to be comfortable with the idea of using judges to reduce workload pressures, and no one complained about the criteria used to select these additions to their panels.

Despite the lack of controversy surrounding their use, there are substantial variations across circuits in both the frequency of use of designated judges and the balance achieved by doing so. The data in table 5 indicate that at one extreme, designated judges were used in slightly

TABLE 5 Use of designated judges in cases terminated on the merits, by circuit, 2008

CIRCUIT	TOTAL JUDGE PARTICIPATIONS	RESIDENT ACTIVE CIRCUIT JUDGES (%)	RESIDENT SENIOR CIRCUIT JUDGES (%)	VISITING JUDGES (%)
District of Columbia	1,680	1,522 (90.6)	143 (8.5)	15 (0.9)
First	3,060	2,260 (73.9)	536 (17.5)	264 (8.6)
Second	8,571	6,102 (71.2)	1,757 (20.5)	712 (8.3)
Third	6,931	5,020 (72.4)	1,468 (21.2)	443 (6.4)
Fourth	7,747	6,555 (84.6)	901 (11.6)	291 (3.8)
Fifth	12,377	10,651 (86.1)	1,673 (13.5)	53 (0.4)
Sixth	7,771	5,305 (68.3)	1,235 (15.9)	1,231 (15.8)
Seventh	4,032	3,270 (81.1)	762 (18.9)	— (0.0)
Eighth	5,828	5,049 (86.6)	691 (11.9)	88 (1.5)
Ninth	17,762	11,424 (64.3)	5,198 (29.3)	1,140 (6.4)
Tenth	4,428	3,196 (72.2)	1,174 (26.5)	58 (1.3)
Eleventh	9,249	8,215 (88.8)	603 (6.5)	431 (4.7)
Total	89,436	65,569 (76.7)	16,141 (18.0)	4,726 (5.3)

fewer than 10 percent of the cases decided by panels in the District of Columbia Circuit in 2008. At the other end of the spectrum, such judges sat on more than a third of the panels of the Ninth Circuit. The balance between the use of senior appeals judges from their own circuit and bringing up district judges for temporary service or drawing judges from other courts also varied substantially across circuits. The Fifth, Seventh, and District of Columbia Circuits almost exclusively used senior appeals court judges from their own circuit. In contrast, the Sixth Circuit was almost equally likely to use judges from other courts as to use its own circuit judges on senior status. Most circuits relied primarily on their own senior circuit judges but also included a nontrivial number of district judges or judges from other courts. Interestingly, while the judges we interviewed were overwhelmingly positive about the use of judges sitting by designation, no one mentioned a circuit policy that would explain the variation among the circuits (no one said something like, "we only use designated judges when we have to" or "we prefer to use our own senior judges than to go outside our circuits").

In the course of discussing the use of designated judges, six of the judges we interviewed spontaneously mentioned their own service as a visiting judge either sitting on panels of another circuit or sitting on an appeals court panel while still serving as a district court judge. All six reported being positive about the experience as a designated judge, and none felt that either of the regular judges on the panel treated them any differently than they treated their other colleague. The only negative comments came from two judges from other circuits who had sat on panels of the Ninth Circuit. Both spontaneously mentioned their dislike of that circuit's practice of having one clerk write a memorandum of law that was distributed to all three judges on the panel and indicated they went along only because they thought it was not their place as outsiders to challenge what appeared to be an established practice of their "host" circuit.

All the judges we interviewed who had already achieved senior status described their job as a judge on senior status in terms that were substantially similar to the descriptions of judges on active service.[13] Notably, all the judges on senior status retained a strong identity with their home circuit and its practices, and no one commented on any differences they had noticed between either their own role or the way other judges treated them when they were active circuit court judges compared to how they were treated after they had taken senior status. One judge specifically commented that the only difference in his job, now that he was a senior judge, was that he played more golf (because he sat on only half as many cases).

While the judges generally stressed that designated judges behave and are treated similarly to active court of appeals judges, the empirical research contradicts this view from the bench and chambers. For example, the scholarly literature shows that district court judges sitting by designation often are influenced by the policy preferences of their appellate court co-panelists (Collins and Martinek 2011) and are less likely to dissent (Hettinger, Lindquist, and Martinek 2006).

Preparation for Oral Argument

Once the composition of the three-judge panel has been set and the cases are assigned to that panel, the real work of the judges begins. Supreme Court justice Sandra Day O'Connor was once asked what Supreme Court justices actually did—what was their day-to-day life on the Court like? She answered succinctly, "We read."[14] Our interviews with appeals court judges indicate that Justice O'Connor's answer would be a pretty good summary of the normal day of an appeals court judge as well. A normal appeal arrives at the court with a tremendous amount of dense, often complicated legal material that must be examined and digested before the case can be decided. A case file in a case scheduled for oral argument typically contains transcripts of the lower court proceedings, as well as principal "briefs" (not so brief legal arguments of up to 14,000 words, not counting appendices and other "supplementary material") filed by the appellant and appellee, and a somewhat shorter "reply brief" from the appellant (typically capped at fifteen pages, according to FRAP 32). FRAPs 28 and 32 painstakingly detail the format of the litigants' briefs, down to the color of the cover (e.g., the appellant and appellee principal briefs must have red and blue covers, respectively). Failure to follow the rules can pack a punch: as Bast and Harrell (2004) noted, the U.S. Courts of Appeals have sanctioned litigants for failing to follow the formatting guidelines in the FRAP; sanctions have included dismissing appeals and refusing to award attorney's fees to successful appellants. Additionally, the case file may include information from the parties, including motions and briefs supporting and challenging the motion. Finally, amici curiae may submit briefs.

Judge E put the total amount of reading in perspective by noting that "we each have eight sittings a year; each sitting is for four days of oral argument, in which time we hear thirty-five to forty cases," or 250 to 300 cases a year. In contrast, Supreme Court justices typically decide fewer than 150 cases per year. After confirming the annual total, Judge E was quick to add, "I'm talking about just merits cases" (i.e., this doesn't include the time needed to decide which cases will receive a decision on the merits or the time required to review the recommendations of the staff attorneys for summary dispositions). Summing up, Judge S said, "We read about a thousand pages a day."

What do judges read? The answer varies somewhat from judge to judge, but one of the striking things about appeals court judges—to one who is familiar with the work of other elites who have similar important roles in national policymaking, such as members of Congress, cabinet members and their deputy secretaries, and top White House staff—is how small the staffs of appeals court judges are. A typical staff is limited to four law clerks (recent top graduates of elite law schools) and one or two secretaries. One consequence of such a small staff is that the judges do most of their own work, and this includes reading most of what is contained in each case file.

Judge E described the typical process he uses to prepare in the following way:

> When I get the case I first skim the briefs and then the opinion, to see if there is any reason for oral argument. At this stage there is little involve-

ment by the clerks. Some judges may think you should have an oral argument only when you think there is a chance of reversal, but for me there are a number of other reasons to have an oral argument—if the circuits are split, if this circuit has not written on the question before, if the "intensity" of the issue is particularly high or if it is a high-profile case (so the public will know it has been fully vetted), or simply if the attorney has done a bang-up job and deserves a chance to argue the case orally. And occasionally you wish to develop an area of law further, even if the outcome for the litigant is clear-cut. If any judge in our court wants oral argument, it is granted. Then, after the cases are set for oral argument, I assign each case to one of my clerks and ask for a bench memorandum (normally fifteen to twenty-five pages). The memorandum from the clerk should analyze the issues and lay out the facts and attach other precedents [opinions in cases relevant to the legal issues raised in the appeal] that I should read before oral argument. After reading the bench memorandum and the attached precedents, I go back to the briefs filed by each party and look at them in light of the additional research brought to me by my clerk. Then, right before oral argument I meet with my four clerks in the library for a "tribal council," and each clerk presents his or her conclusion on cases they did a memo on, and the five of us bat the issues around. These sessions might last anywhere from a few minutes to five or six hours. Generally we come up with a tentative outline of how to decide the cases and questions to ask during oral argument.

While the details of their preparation vary for other judges, most indicated using a process roughly similar to that described by Judge E. All judges indicated that they paid close attention to the arguments in the briefs, all relied on their clerks to do additional, independent research on the key legal issues in the case, and all judges gave at least a quick reading of the opinion of the court below. Judges seldom read the complete transcript of the trial, instead relying on their clerks and the briefs of the litigants to highlight the portions of the record below that was most relevant to the resolution of the issues raised on appeal.

For example, Judge O said, "I'll read all of the briefs and skim the opinion of the district judge, and the clerk assigned to the case will also read the briefs" (Judge O assigns each case to one of his four clerks). Then, he said, "The clerk and I will sit and discuss the case before anything is written. I always ask them to tell me what they think before I say anything because I want to get their ideas without bias. Only after we both talk through the case—trying to get as close as possible to agreeing—will I ask the clerk to write a bench memo for me." Judge O indicated that after reading the clerk's bench memorandum summarizing the additional legal research done by the clerk, he would often go back and read—or at least skim—the actual texts of the precedents that the clerk's memo identified as the most important for the case and take notes on those precedents to use in the questions he asked during oral argument.

Judge W ends up doing most of the same reading as the other appeals court judges we talked to, but proceeds in a different order. According to Judge W, "When the cases come in I divide them among my clerks and ask them to write a bench memo. I don't start my preparation until I get that memo, which I read first. Then I read the briefs and any supplementary materials the clerks have highlighted for me; I look directly only at those portions of the record that either the briefs or the bench memo have highlighted as important for the appeal. I usually will make extensive (handwritten) notes directly on the briefs which I use for oral argument."

The biggest difference in the way judges prepare for oral argument pits the judges in the Ninth Circuit against everyone else. In the Ninth Circuit, after the cases are assigned to a given panel of judges, the cases are divided equally among the judges, with one judge being given specific responsibility to pick one of his clerks to write a bench memo, which will then be distributed to all three judges on the panel. In all other circuits, bench memos are not shared with other judges on the panel. Rather, each clerk writing a memo communicates only with his own judge.

All the judges we interviewed indicated that each judge prepares for oral argument in virtual isolation; his only interaction is with the clerks in his office. As Judge H explained, "Generally there is no discussion with other judges on the panel before conference, so I am often surprised what my colleagues think." Judges A, F, N, and R specifically confirmed this observation of Judge H, and in discussions about the way they prepared, no judge mentioned any interactions with anyone outside his or her own office. There is absolutely no lobbying of the judges on the panel. Litigants, lawyers, interest groups, and others are specifically forbidden by federal ethics standards from attempting to influence the outcome of any case through any means besides the submission of briefs and other written motions. Moreover, Judges F, H, and N specifically confirmed what appears to be a widespread norm on the courts of appeals: there is never any discussion with any judges not on the panel either before oral argument or during the writing of the opinion of the court.

This absence of interaction with anyone outside the panel (e.g., the litigants, lobbyists who favor one side or another, government officials) dramatically contrasts with our understanding of the legitimate decision-making processes employed by other branches of government, including both Congress and the executive branch. Members of Congress frequently discuss, bargain, and negotiate with other members before they enter formal sessions of their committee or floor sessions of the full chamber where the formal decisions are made. Members often actively seek input from their constituents, and it is considered normal and legitimate for them to listen to the pitches made on behalf of one or both sides of an issue from lobbyists, party officials, government spokespersons, or key campaign supporters. But none of this happens before the judges meet to hear oral argument or retire to their conference to discuss and vote on the outcome. The judges readily admitted to reading the newspapers and watching television presentations of the news, and thus of having some awareness of the general political context in which their decisions would be made, but they all explicitly shunned any direct contact with anyone who had a view about how a specific case should be decided (except, of course, for their reading of the formal briefs and motions submitted by the official litigants, and their discussions with their law clerks concerning the case). The judges shared a strong consensus that any other contact with any outside individuals or groups (including government officials) who wanted to influence the outcome of the case would be a severe violation of judicial ethics. In informal conversations at the Second Circuit retreat, all the judges around the dinner table one night agreed that discussions or contacts with any other persons outside the formal parties to the case simply never happened. They agreed that none of them could think of a single scandal (because they also agreed that such contact would constitute a scandal) that had ever come to light in the history of the courts of appeals. And they all agreed that the recognition of this prohibition against attempting to influence judicial decisions is so pervasive that none of them had ever been faced personally with an attempt by a lobbyist, political activist, or government official to influence their vote in a pending case.

Discussion before oral argument with the other two judges on the panel assigned to hear a given appeal is not considered unethical, but the judges indicated that it rarely happens. Ten of the judges we interviewed specifically commented on whether they discuss the case with their colleagues on the panel before oral argument, and all indicated that it rarely or never happened. The comments of Judge O were typical:

"The general rule is that the judges do not discuss the case at all before oral argument—but occasionally you might exchange a few comments in passing in the hall." Judge H agreed, noting, "Generally there is no discussion with other judges before conference, so I am often surprised [when I hear what they say at the hearing] what my colleagues think." Judge DD had a different take: "The panel judges usually do not talk about the case before oral argument, and we don't do this because it is dangerous to do so. You don't want to get locked into a decision because you just may change your mind after oral argument—although that does not occur often" (i.e., changing one's mind). Judge W added that not only is there rarely any discussion among the judges before the hearing, but clerks almost never communicate with clerks in other chambers either.

To these disclaimers about any pre-conference discussion with colleagues, one caveat should be added. This absence of specific discussion before the hearing does not necessarily mean that the judges go into the hearing with no idea at all about how the other judges on the panel are likely to react to the various arguments. Life tenure of the judges and the constant rotation of panel memberships mean that after a few years, judges, especially those in relatively small circuits, will have sat with all the other judges in their circuit on many previous occasions and thus may have a fairly good idea of the approaches their colleagues take to a variety of issues. As one judge on a small circuit said, "As soon as I start reading the materials in a new case, the first thing that comes to my mind is how the other two judges on the panel are likely to respond to these issues."

When panels of judges are created, they are typically assigned twenty to thirty cases to hear. After preparations are completed the judges travel from their individual offices in their home state to the site of the hearing. Most hearings are held at the circuit headquarters, though some circuits designate several cities scattered across the circuit as locations for hearings of the circuit.[15] Typically the judges sit together for four to five days, hearing four to six cases per day. Once the hearings and the conferences at which the cases are discussed are completed, the judges return to their individual home offices to begin work on the drafting of opinions. The main exception to this process occurs in the Seventh Circuit. There, panels are assigned for sessions of a single day.

Oral Argument

The actual procedure used in the oral argument hearings appears to be substantially the same in all circuits and is quite similar to the procedures used by the U.S. Supreme Court (though Supreme Court hearings are longer). As a judge on the Third Circuit explained, the presiding judge for the hearing is the most senior active appeals court judge from the respective circuit court. In other words, designated judges can never be the presiding judge, regardless of experience. Typically, the only people in the room are the judges, their law clerks, and attorneys representing each side (and other essential courtroom staff such as the court reporter). Witnesses do not testify, and although the actual litigants have a right to attend the hearing, they seldom do. As with virtually all court proceedings in the United States, hearings are open to the public, but few people attend, and most hearings are not covered by members of the press.

Once the hearing is called to order, each side is typically given fifteen to twenty minutes for its presentation. A lectern is in the center of the courtroom with green, yellow, and red lights. When the attorney begins speaking, the light is green. The light turns yellow when five minutes remain in the attorney's allotted time, and in some circuits it blinks during the last minute. When the light turns red, counsel is expected to finish her sentence and then sit down, though the amount of flexibility given attorneys with their time limits varies according to who the presiding judge is at the hearing. There is a counsel table on each side, and there is an elevated bench with nameplates for each of the judges in the center facing the lectern. Attorneys are expected to come prepared to make a fifteen- to twenty-minute argument, but all three judges will ask questions and generally feel free to interrupt counsel. According to Judge H, the questioning is generally gentle in tone; voices are not raised, and the questions rarely devolve into extended arguments. The judges' questions and counsel's answers count against the allotted minutes. Counsel for the appellant is allowed to reserve three minutes for rebuttal, and usually the appellant avails him- or herself of that chance to speak both first and last.

As Judge O noted, "Oral argument is always interesting—it is your chance to see what the attorneys will be arguing and what the perspectives of the other judges are, because usually this is your first chance to get an idea of what your colleagues are thinking about the case." Judge UU voiced a similar perspective. He said that oral argument is useful because it is a dialogue among the judges and lawyers. "You bounce ideas off the lawyers and listen to the other judges. It is the most public part of the process—where the lawyers get to be the participants."

The amount of time allowed for oral argument does vary somewhat across circuits. A Fourth Circuit judged noted that their general rule is twenty minutes per side, but judges can request more time. Even with a twenty-minute time limit, it depends on who the presiding judge is—some are much more lenient about letting counsel run over time than others. In the Seventh Circuit the judges we interviewed agreed that while twenty minutes per side is the norm, cases that appear to be less complex are often allotted only ten minutes per side.

Does Oral Argument Make a Difference?

We were struck by the extent to which all the judges we interviewed seemed to believe in the utility of the limited form of oral argument practiced in their circuit and appeared to be satisfied with the ways in which the hearings were conducted in their circuit.[16] So we asked them whether oral arguments ever changed their minds or served any other important purposes. Virtually every judge interviewed felt that the hearings served some purpose, but their specific responses were quite different.

The most impassioned defense of the utility of oral argument came from Judge YY. He was emphatic that oral argument is critical. For one, he said, "it is an opportunity to meet people from outside the court. Two, it is a way the public can see what we do. Three, it aids in the decision-making process. You may think you know how a case will come out, but if the lawyers are well prepared, one of two things will happen: (1) the lawyers will validate your view by filling the nooks and crannies, or (2) the lawyers will point to the record or to the law you had not thought about. Either way, the hearing is crucial."

Most of the judges made general remarks about oral argument being helpful, and then went on to provide their own estimates of how frequently the arguments changed outcomes. Judge E estimated that "30 percent of the time oral argument is significantly helpful in addressing issues and developing my understanding of the issues. However, probably in only 5 to 10 percent of the cases do I change sides as the result of oral argument. But I find oral argument to be fun—it is intellectually challenging!"

Only one judge claimed to have thought about the effect of oral argument systematically. Judge S asserted, "I kept track for a couple of years and found that I changed my opinion on what the outcome of the case should be in only 5 to 10 percent of the cases after (and as a result of) oral argument."

Different judges gave different estimates of how frequently oral argument changed anyone's mind, but all of those commenting on oral argument then went on to suggest that it was valuable even when minds were not changed. For example, Judge S stressed that oral argument was especially useful in complex cases because it often helped judges clarify their understanding of the key issues. He added, "Only 5 to 10 percent of the time has my mind has been changed because of oral argument. . . . It may not have changed the outcome in the end but it changed the way I thought about the issues in the case." Similarly, Judge VV said, "Since I first joined the court, less than 5 percent of the time [has] it made a difference and changed my mind. But even if it doesn't change settled expectations, I go into the oral argument more unsure of the final decision than I am when I come out. Oral argument is an opportunity to continue the discussion of the case even if I don't end up changing my mind. I suppose in close cases it matters, but I do often make my mind up early on in cases that come before me." In contrast, Judge UU asserted that oral argument could make a difference "very frequently." He then clarified that statement: "Sometimes you change your mind, and sometimes the argument refines your mind in how to approach the case" even if the judge does not end up voting differently. He added, "I am of the school of thought that you don't have to make up your mind about the case until oral argument ends, and I try to follow that. I want to have an open mind."

In contrast to the conclusion that oral argument changed minds "very frequently," Judge XX maintained that oral argument made a difference in the outcome of the case in only one or two cases per year. Yet even he thought that oral argument was frequently useful. "You see more about where the parties are going, and that isn't always apparent from the briefs. . . . In two or three cases I will have a question mark, and oral argument is very important in those cases even if it doesn't change the outcome." These thoughts were echoed by Judge F, who said that oral argument infrequently changed the tentative decision already arrived at, "but sometimes the argument makes you stop and think or something comes out that seems significant that was not in the briefs."

Other judges indicated that oral argument did not often change their vote on the actual outcome but refrained from giving a quantitative assessment of how often their votes were changed. Nonetheless, these judges felt oral argument served important functions. Judge T said that oral argument was always useful: "It doesn't change minds very often, but it often clarifies what the implications of ruling each way are." He added that oral argument was also important because it was psychologically important for litigants to "have their day in court," to feel they had a chance to make their case before the judges. Thus, even though he contended that "it is the written submissions and the comments of our colleagues that have the greatest impact on our thinking," he was still a strong proponent of continuing to have oral argument in all cases that were not "slam dunks." Judge T agreed on the utility of oral arguments for enhancing the legitimacy of the courts, saying, "Oral arguments are useful because we can ask questions—this is the most useful part. Also, it is important for the litigants to have an advocate out there. It gives litigants the feeling they had their opportunity in court. It helps to make litigants feel better about the process."

Judge TT agreed with those who maintained that even when it did not change votes, oral argument often helped clarify key issues. He said, "Oral argument is helpful because it forces the attorneys to really break down complex issues. Attorneys have a very limited time period, and they don't want to get hung up on complex issues, so they do their best to get to the point." And Judge WW added, "If I have questions, I will ask them, and the attorneys can convince me, and often even if my mind doesn't change on how I think the case should be decided, the oral argument matters because it often confirms my initial impressions of the case and issues."

In summary, the judges we interviewed were largely in agreement that oral argument changes the outcome (i.e., who wins and who loses) in only a relatively small portion of cases. Yet there was widespread agreement that oral arguments are useful in many cases in which outcomes are not changed, since they often help the judges clarify their thinking about the ways in which an opinion should be written. And finally, several judges noted that in addition to the utility of the arguments to the judges on the panel, oral arguments enhance the legitimacy of the court by giving litigants "their day in court."

The Judges' Conference

Before the judges return to their home offices, they meet in what is called the judges' conference to make tentative decisions on the cases argued during the week. Our interviews indicated that in some circuits, the judges hold a separate conference for each case immediately after the conclusion of oral argument. In other circuits the judges hold a conference at the end of each day to discuss all the cases heard that day. Much as is done on the Supreme Court, only the judges attend these meetings, and the proceedings are considered confidential and private. Even though most judges will later give their clerks an overview of what happened, none of the judges we interviewed could recall a single time that the security of the conference was breached with the result that either the litigants in the case or the media learned of the conference decision before the official opinion of the court was released a month or more later.

Judges expect that three things will occur at these conferences. First, a tentative decision will be made about the outcome of the case (either by a formal vote with a majority determining the outcome or more informally by consensus). Second, there will be enough discussion of the case to reach informal agreement on at least an outline of the reasons that will be given for the majority decision. And finally, one judge will be selected to write the "opinion of the court."

The first theme that we heard in some form or another by almost every judge was voiced in a straightforward manner by Judge N, who began his comments about conferences by volunteering that "most conferences don't last very long." In fact, he suggested that even if the conference was considering five or six cases, it would be unusual for the meeting to last more than an hour. Judge UU agreed, explaining that the conference tends to be short because "many cases are simple and most of the judges will agree on the outcome of the case." Similarly, when asked about bargaining, Judge VV responded, "Is there a lot of give-and-take? I would say not much because [in] a large percentage of the cases we are already in agreement so there isn't much to discuss and there is not much to give and take with." As a result, he agreed that most of the conferences are short. The nearly identical point was made by Judge O, who responded to the same question by saying, "On the majority of cases after oral argument the initial vote is unanimous, so there is no need to negotiate or try to influence another." Judge Q joined the chorus, saying that usually discussion is pretty brief because the judges quickly see to what extent they all agree and then can easily decide the main bases for the opinion. To this agreement that the high degree of initial consensus on how many cases should be decided results in a short conference, Judges G, UU, and WW added that the heavy workload faced by the judges also acts as an incentive to keep the meetings short.

The procedure used in all circuits tends to be quite informal even though the precise details vary across circuits. For years, scholars who studied the Supreme Court debated whether the order of speaking in the Court's conference was most senior to most junior or the reverse. In the courts of appeals, our interviews indicated no ambiguity on this question. The answer is simply that the order of speaking is determined by informal circuit rules, and in practice, the order varies across circuits.

Regardless of the order of speaking, the process in all circuits appears to follow the procedure laid out by Judge E: "We first go around the table, junior to senior—everyone indicates how they see the first case, then there may be a good bit of back-and-forth to see if there is a way we can reach consensus—it is all very collegial. I can't think of a single conference in which any hostility was expressed even when we disagreed." Then Judge E indicated that the judges went on to the next case, following the same process. Eventually, he said, "By the end of the conference we will have decided who is in the majority in each case and whether we will publish a decision, who will write the opinion, and the general direction of the opinion." He noted that the judges took their own notes on the discussion: "There is NO memo from the chief judge setting out points of agreement." If Judge E is assigned the opinion, he will first talk to his clerk who wrote the original bench memo regarding the outline of the case he had already developed with the clerk before conference, and add any changes as a result of the conference discussion. Judge E then usually assigns that same clerk to write the first draft of the opinion.

Judge G agreed that there is a great degree of civility in the conferences, saying, "If you disagree, you feel obligated to explain the reasons for your disagreement and to consider counter arguments. . . . Where possible, we try to tone down our disagreements and to reach compromises when possible." But while no judge disagreed with the observation that discussions in conference are marked by a high degree of civility, there was no consensus about how much give-and-take there was in dealing with cases in which there was not an initial agreement as to how the appeal should be resolved. At one end of the spectrum, Judge WW observed there was usually a lot of give-and-take in the conferences. And Judge MM noted that "once all three judges air their points of view, many times I have been persuaded by another judge's point of view. But sometimes we agree to disagree."

Judge C was similarly adamant, saying, "There is a strong attempt to reach agreement in our circuit, and it begins at conference. All the positions taken when we start discussing a case are taken by everyone to be tentative. It is not viewed as unseemly to change your mind. A judge who is writing our opinion may even switch sides from what was agreed to at conference, though that is certainly not routine." Likewise, Judge Q asserted that if substantial differences emerge after the initial expression of positions by the judges, there is usually an attempt to work out those differences to see if there is some basis—perhaps a narrower opinion—on which all can agree. Judge GG elaborated that when there isn't consensus, the judges will usually "try our best to hash it out, but it doesn't always work out, and then one of the judges dissents." Judge K continued in a somewhat similar vein, noting that discussion in conference on the easy cases was usually quick—"we just compare notes and see that everyone is in agreement." He went on to say that in cases of medium difficulty, "we generally have a good discussion."

In contrast, Judge K noted that in hard cases, "we may not completely resolve the case at conference—that occurs mainly after conference through the exchange of memos; in fact, the exchange of memos may begin even before anyone starts writing an opinion."

Other judges expressed a less sanguine view of the effects of conference discussion in the hard cases. Judge N noted that most of the judges go into the conference with their minds made up, and as a result, there usually wasn't much negotiating or bargaining. Judge VV went further, arguing that for cases in which there is controversy or disagreement, "it can be futile during conference to try to change someone's mind." Substantive discussion, he said, comes out in the written memos they send during the opinion-writing phase. Judge AA agreed with Judge VV that arguing over substantive differences was futile: "If a judge has a strong feeling, there isn't much point in trying to hash it out in conference." Moreover, Judge AA suggested that the pressure of heavy caseloads made many judges "anxious to get through conference as quickly as possible." As a result, he concluded that conferences were generally inadequate for resolving important disputes.

Bargaining during conference depends on who is in the conference. As Judge YY noted, "If you have sat with judges many times, there isn't much need for discussion. There maybe a little discussion. I understand my fellow colleagues, so we don't have to sit there and hash it out. More accommodation occurs during the draft opinion-writing process, when judges may write something like, 'if you make these changes I can sign on.'"

The Assignment of the Opinion of the Court

Once agreement has been reached in conference or the judges have concluded that no agreement is possible, the final task for the conference is to decide who will write the opinion of the court (the majority if the panel is split). Court opinions matter. In fact, the opinion of the court is the core of the policymaking power of the courts. The majority opinion lays down the broad principles that govern the decision in the case before the court, and these principles are binding on the lower courts (Rohde and Spaeth 1976, 172; see also Richards and Kritzer 2002). It is the opinion that "guides the lower courts in deciding future cases, and it establishes precedents for the Court's own subsequent rulings" (Segal and Spaeth 1993, 261; but see Lax and Rader 2010). In addition to shaping policy and guiding lower courts, the majority opinion serves an important role in justifying and legitimizing the decision of the court. An important function of the opinion is to "persuade us that the law ought to mean what the judge has decided" (Carter and Burke, 2010, 10). Or, in the words of one long-serving judge on a U.S. Court of Appeals, the opinion serves three functions: "it decides the case . . . it continues the story by making some law . . . and it projects the story into the future by giving intimations of future directions" (Coffin 1994, 171).

Because opinions are important, the assignment to write the court's opinion is also important. While there is a fairly extensive body of scholarship on opinion writing and the assignment of the majority opinion on the Supreme Court, less is known about these important processes on the U.S. Courts of Appeals.

Because of the importance of the majority opinion and the view that who writes the opinion may have a substantial impact on the precise policy supported by the court, it is important to understand how the opinion writer is selected and what criteria guide that selection. While the formal opinion assigner may not be completely free in practice, the assigner is important as an agenda setter. As one classic study of judicial politics notes, "the power of agenda setting should not be underestimated" (Maltzman, Spriggs, and Wahlbeck 2000, 33; see also Hausegger and Haynie 2003, discussing opinion assignment as a function of individual policy preferences).

Our interviews indicated that the opinion is usually formally assigned by the most senior active judge in the majority on the panel.[17] This norm provides an opportunity for opinion assigners to attempt to affect the court's decisions (Baum 1977; Epstein and Knight 1998). For example, the influence might be achieved by assigning a case to a judge who will represent the assigner's own preferences (Maltzman, Spriggs, and Wahlbeck 2000, 15). But the extent to which the senior judge on panels of the courts of appeals uses the power to assign the majority opinion to advance his own policy interests rather than to achieve other goals, such as satisfying norms of equality or promoting the efficiency of the court, is largely unknown. Despite a steadily expanding body of empirical scholarship on many aspects of decision making and policymaking on the courts of appeals, little is known about who writes for the court or what criteria are used in practice to make the assignment. Thus, we asked our judges to describe the process of opinion assignment.

Opinion Assignment—The Judges' Views

The judges we interviewed all said that in practice, the presiding judge on the panel is responsible for the assignment of the opinion of the court. Even in circuits like the Sixth Circuit where the formal assignment is made by the chief judge of the circuit, the presiding judge on the panel typically makes a recommendation to the chief judge about who should write the majority opinion, and that recommendation is almost always followed. Since the presiding judge is the most senior active appeals court judge from the given circuit (i.e., a judge who has not taken senior status and is not sitting by designation) with the most seniority, in a given year a substantial number of different judges in the circuit will end up being the presiding judge on some panel, with the result that decisions about opinion assignment are made by a large number of judges.

Assignment in practice by the presiding judge appears to be the rule in all circuits. There is some variation in actual assignment practices, but they appear to be related to the preferences of individual judges rather than circuit-wide rules or norms (except for the Ninth Circuit, whose special practices are described below). For example, some judges rely on volunteers to write the opinion, but that is not a common practice. However, Judge S noted that when it is not a case that he wants to self-assign and it is not one he feels strongly about, he will ask if someone has a particular interest in a case before announcing the opinion assignment. The comments of the judges indicated that most judges don't feel strongly about most opinion assignments, and thus if one of the other judges expresses a strong interest in being the author of a particular opinion, the assigning judge will usually honor that request. Similarly, a few judges indicated that when they assigned opinions, they considered whether any judge on the panel had a particular expertise related to the issues in the case, but no one indicated that expertise was regularly taken into account. While no judge claimed that it was a norm on their circuit to favor those with expertise, a couple of the judges in the Ninth Circuit argued that they (meaning Ninth Circuit judges) took a more generalist approach in their circuit and usually did not assign opinions based on expertise, but they "knew" that other circuits did rely on expertise as a criterion.

Whether opinion assignments are made on the basis of expertise would be hard to test empirically because existing data sources do not include many of the specific sources of particular expertise possessed by judges. And it is not always obvious what type of expertise is relevant for every case on the courts of appeals dockets. But, as noted above, criminal cases are the biggest category of cases on the dockets of the courts of appeals, and as chapter 1 indicated, almost one-fourth of all appeals court judges share one obvious source of expertise in criminal matters: previous service as a prosecutor. Several of the judges interviewed indicated that as former prosecutors themselves, they tended to self-assign many of the criminal cases that their panel heard. But in each case, they talked about that self-assignment in terms of their interest in criminal law rather than the need to entrust the opinion to the panel's expert on criminal matters. Unfortunately, not enough of the judges we interviewed discussed whether they favored former prosecutors when assigning criminal cases for us to be confident of whether or not this was a consistent theme across judges. Thus, to the extent that expertise influences the choice of an opinion author, it is most likely a reflection of the connection between the preferences of judges to write in a particular area and those preferences being related to expertise.

All the judges indicated that if the panel was split, one of the two judges in the majority would be asked to write the opinion of the court.[18] However, since more than 90 percent of published decisions of the courts of appeals are unanimous, most judges are eligible to be chosen to write the opinion of the court in most cases.[19] Dissenting judges usually wrote a separate opinion but on occasion simply noted for the record that they dissented, without filing an opinion that explained the basis of their dissent.

One consequence of opinion assignment by the presiding judge is the possibility that such judges assign the majority of the opinions in all cases or in the important cases to themselves. However, the interviews suggested that such a pattern does not occur. In general, there was agreement that a rough expectation of equality was the norm. Nonetheless, several judges indicated that they preferred to write opinions in particular areas of law and that when they were the presiding judge, they assigned the opinions in those cases to themselves. For instance, Judge S self-assigns a lot of criminal cases because he enjoys working through them, but he will usually assign corporate law cases to other members of the panel. On the other hand, Judge T prefers to write in economic cases; he doesn't like criminal cases, so when Judge T self-assigns, he doesn't take any criminal opinions. Judge V also self-assigns the cases he likes, but he doesn't define those in terms of a specific area of law. Instead, he takes the cases he finds to be personally the most interesting, which usually means he takes the most complicated and "messy" cases. Only two of the judges who specifically discussed their self-assignment preferences indicated that when they were the presiding judge, they would reserve for themselves the biggest or most important cases.

Most of the judges denied that political considerations, which are known to play a big role in the assignment of the majority opinion on the Supreme Court, routinely entered into the decision calculus of judges assigning appeals court opinions. But there were a few exceptions. After agreeing with his colleagues that balancing the workload was probably the most significant consideration in opinion assignment, Judge T went on to admit that there was some tendency to assign the opinion to someone who shared the assigning judge's views. And Judge V added that on occasion, a judge might make an ideologically based assignment in order to control the policy output of the court—but that this occurred in a definite minority of cases.

We did not systematically ask every judge interviewed whether more opinions were assigned to the most senior judges or whether visiting judges were disfavored in the opinion assignment process. Moreover, the judges who brought up either subject were not in agreement. Most judges admitted that there was some type of an "apprentice" period (Judge N said it took him five years before he felt his informal apprenticeship was over), but there was no agreement as to how long such an apprenticeship lasted or whether the "apprentices" received fewer opinions. Similarly, Judges I, W, and UU insisted there was no discrimination against judges sitting by designation in the assignment of opinion authorship, but Judge G complained that the workload of the regular judges was increased because the visiting judges were not given as many opinions to write.

The judges also noted that concerns about the equitable distribution of the opinion-writing chores and the desire to complete their work in a timely manner led presiding judges to be concerned about the workload of other judges on the panel. Judge V stated that this obvious workload pressure caused most presiding judges to take workload into account when deciding who should write the majority opinion. In fact, he argued that the biggest factor with regard to opinion assignment was workload considerations. He noted, "When I am presiding judge and assign cases the effort is to equalize the workload" because he recognized that if a given judge already had a backlog of opinions to write, he would not be likely to produce the next opinion in a timely manner. Judge T agreed, stating flatly that "opinions are often assigned based on workload." And he noted that the reason for this concern with workload was simply the great concern on their circuit for the need for efficiency, given the heavy caseload of the circuit.

While the comments cited above generally are broadly applicable to panels in all circuits, it should be noted that there is a practice unique to the Ninth Circuit that has a major impact on opinion assignment. As we described in chapter 1, as part of their preparation for oral argument hearings almost all judges ask one of their law clerks to write a "bench memorandum" describing the key issues in a given case, reporting research the clerk did on those issues and often including a recommendation on what to ask at the hearing or what the appropriate basis for the resolution of the case might be. These memos are considered to be confidential recommendations from the clerk to the judge employing them. But in the Ninth Circuit, for each case one law clerk is asked to write a "bench memorandum" that is circulated to all three judges on the panel. Often, before this memo is circulated to the other judges, the clerk and the judge discuss the conclusions of the memo, and the memo may be revised in light of these discussions before it is circulated to the other two judges. The Ninth Circuit judges whom we interviewed all said that the judge whose clerk wrote the bench memo would be asked to write the opinion, if he was in the majority. If that judge ended up dissenting, the majority opinion would be reassigned. Since the assignment of who is to write these memos is made in an essentially random manor, it means that the assignment of the opinion is unlikely to be influenced by either the interest or expertise of the judge or the ideological proximity of the judge to the presiding judge of the panel.

In summary, the interviews suggested that presiding judges make the effective assignment of who will write the opinion of the court even in circuits in which the formal power is lodged with the chief judge of the circuit. Judges occasionally volunteer to write a given opinion, but that is not the norm. There was a consensus that although the presiding judges sometimes assigned themselves opinion authorship in cases they had a special interest in, there was no general tendency of the presiding judges to take on more opinion writing than that given to the other judges, or for the presiding judges to take the most important cases. Some judges suggested that there was a pattern on the courts of appeals similar to what has been found on the Supreme Court of presiding judges favoring their ideological allies. But most of those we interviewed did not believe that such a practice was common. Additionally, judges were concerned with the relative workloads of potential opinion writers. Finally, the judges were divided about the influence of expertise on opinion assignment and about whether freshmen judges or those sitting by designation received less than their equal share of opinion writing. We decided to compare these observations of the judges to what has previously been written in scholarly treatments of opinion assignment on appellate courts, and then to test these observations of the judges with an empirical analysis of opinion assignment practices in a random sample of all appeals court cases with published opinions.

An Empirical Assessment of Opinion Assignment

Baum (1997) demonstrated that there is good reason to believe that judges may pursue a variety of goals, though some goals will be more relevant for some situations than others. Following up on this work, Klein (2002) concluded, based on both the empirical literature and his own interviews with judges on the courts of appeals, that they seek to pursue a variety of goals, including the promotion of policies consistent with their policy preferences, reaching decisions that are legally sound, and maintaining the coherence and consistency of federal law (11). Each of these goals may be relevant for decisions regarding the assignment of the majority opinion.

Many now accept that appeals court judges care about the policy consequences of their decisions (Klein 2002, 20–21). The judges we interviewed agreed with scholars that opinions form the "core of the policy-making" role of appellate courts (Rohde and Spaeth 1976). Thus, it would be natural to expect that, all other things being equal, the opinion assigner would be motivated to use his assignment power to bring about policy outcomes that are consistent with his own policy preferences (though as noted above, several of the judges we interviewed disagreed with this assessment). As Rohde and Spaeth noted, the primary responsibility for formulating the policy to be made in a case rests with the justice to whom the majority opinion is assigned (Rohde and Spaeth 1976, 172). The most straightforward way in which the assigner can ensure that the opinion reflects his own preferences is to self-assign the opinion. Alternatively, the opinion assigner might assign the opinion to the justice who is his closest ideological ally. These expectations have received strong confirmation from empirical studies of opinion assignment on the U.S. Supreme Court. Chief justices dramatically overassign to those ideologically closest to them and underassign to those furthest from themselves ideologically (Segal and Spaeth 1993, 268; see also Maltzman and Wahlbeck 2004; Rohde and Spaeth 1976). Similarly, when the senior associate justice has a chance to assign the majority opinion, he overwhelmingly self-assigns the opinion writing. Maltzman, Spriggs, and Wahlbeck (2000) hypothesize that because a senior associate justice has fewer institutional responsibilities than the chief justice, self-assignment of a majority opinion is more likely. The authors also show that, like the chief justice, the senior associate justice can be influenced by strategic concerns if his coalition is minimal or unstable. These considerations lead us to our first two hypotheses:

H1: The greater the ideological distance of the judge from the majority opinion assigner, the less likely it is that judge will receive the assignment to write the majority opinion in a case.

H2: Majority opinion assigners are more likely to assign opinions to themselves than to their colleagues.

Additionally, the tendency to assign to oneself or to ideologically proximate colleagues could be conditional on several factors. For example, the more important the policy under consideration, the more powerfully one would expect policy preferences to affect the opinion assignment (Brenner 1982; Brenner and Spaeth 1988). Consequently, this tendency toward self-assignment should be greatest in the most salient cases. Thus, it is unsurprising that Brenner (1993) found that on the U.S. Supreme Court, there is a strong tendency for the chief justice to assign himself the opinion in salient cases. Similarly, when Brennan, as the senior judge in the majority, was able to assign the opinion in important cases, he self-assigned in 40 percent of his opportunities. Ulmer (1970) examined how Chief Justice Earl Warren dealt with opinion assignments to ideological allies. Rohde (1972) more specifically tested the hypothesis that an opinion assigner would either self-assign the opinion or assign it to an ideological ally when the issue in question was politically important to him. This idea was repeated by Slotnick (1979a, 69), who mentioned at the conclusion of his study that there exist "self advantageous assignment patterns exhibited by Chief Justices in important cases." Finally, both Burger (Maltzman, Spriggs, and Wahlbeck 2000) and Rehnquist (Maltzman and Wahlbeck 2004) were more likely to assign Supreme Court opinions to ideologically proximate colleagues in politically salient cases.

While no comparable quantitative analysis exists regarding the tendency of assigners on the courts of appeals to assign salient cases to their political allies, one qualitative analysis suggests that on the crucial issue of civil rights in the 1960s, pro-rights judges who had the opportunity to assign overwhelmingly assigned the critical opinions to themselves or to their political allies (Howard 1981, 252). More generally, Judge Coffin of the First Circuit offered the observation that if an opinion is "to make a significant policy change," the presiding judge is likely to self-assign the opinion (Coffin 1994, 169). These considerations lead us to the following conditional hypotheses:

H3: In cases that are more salient, the judges are less likely to assign cases to ideologically distant co-panelists than in less salient cases.
H4: In cases that are more salient, judges are more likely to self-assign majority opinions.

The literature on Supreme Court majority opinion assignment suggests another conditional effect of ideology. Maltzman and Wahlbeck (1996) and Maltzman, Spriggs, and Wahlbeck (2000) contend that while majority opinion assigners are generally more likely to assign the opinion to ideologically proximate justices, in minimum winning coalition (MWC) cases they are more likely to assign the opinion to ideologically disparate justices to increase the probability of maintaining the initial majority coalition. This type of strategic decision making could also apply to the U.S. courts of appeals, though there is scant evidence that the judges indeed act strategically. While Kim (2009) found that three-judge panelists are influenced by the overall circuit ideology in sex discrimination cases, Lindquist and Martinek (2009) have challenged the finding. Moreover, the appeals court judges do not appear to dissent strategically (Hettinger, Lindquist, and Martinek 2004). This leads to the following hypothesis:

H5: In MWC cases, the judges are more likely to assign opinions to the judge who is closest in ideology to the median.

Beyond ideological concerns, Maltzman and Wahlbeck (2004) have suggested that the assigner considers what is best for the court as an organization. Along these lines, various studies have found evidence that experience or expertise, or both, influence U.S. Supreme Court majority opinion assignments (e.g., Brenner and Hagle 1996; Maltzman, Spriggs, and Wahlbeck 2000; Maltzman and Wahlbeck 1996, 2004; Slotnick 1979b). Presumably, substantive experts are more efficient, authoring "better" opinions in a more timely fashion (Brenner and Palmer 1988; Maltzman and Wahlbeck 1996).

The concept of substantive expertise is, of course, difficult to measure. Some studies (Brenner 1984; Brenner and Spaeth 1986; Maltzman and Wahlbeck 1996, 2004) operationalize expertise as the tendency of the justice to author separate opinions in cases in that particular issue area.

They find that U.S. Supreme Court justices are more likely to author majority opinions in cases involving their substantive expertise. At least two studies of the U.S. courts of appeals echo these findings (Cheng 2008; Howard 1981). Both found that some judges tend to specialize in certain issue areas.

Qualitative evidence also suggests that the personal experiences of the appeals court judges enhance expertise (e.g., Cohen 2002), which at least helps the judge appreciate the context of the case. Howard (1981) earlier found that court of appeals judge perceptions of colleague effectiveness are a function of, among other things, intelligence, expertise, and length of service. Howard's interviews also revealed that opinion assignment was not random, and that expertise was a factor in assignments. Several of the appeals court judges we interviewed made similar suggestions. Some of this experience may be quite idiosyncratic. For example, one judge indicated that on her circuit there was one judge who was such an outstanding golfer that he had on occasion been invited to the Masters Golf Tournament. Since everyone on the circuit recognized this experience, he was always assigned the opinion in any case related in any way to golf. Many of the sources of particular interest or expertise, such as this golf expertise, occur so infrequently or are so hard to document that it would be impossible to empirically test for them. But one source of expertise that was repeatedly mentioned by the judges interviewed was service as a prosecutor before being appointed to the courts of appeals. The judges suggested that such former prosecutors often expressed an interest in writing in criminal cases. Since the Gryski and Zuk (2004) database relied on to identify the backgrounds of judges for our analysis reliably indicates whether or not each judge had previous experience as a prosecutor, and since there is a sufficient number of criminal cases to permit analysis, we decided to test whether this particular expertise is related to the likelihood of receiving the opinion assignment in criminal cases. Specifically, we hypothesize the following:

H6: A judge who is a former prosecutor is more likely to receive the majority opinion-writing assignment in a criminal case than a judge who has no prosecutorial experience.

We also examined additional judge characteristics that should indirectly reflect substantive expertise. For example, Slotnick (1983) suggests that judges from a "prestigious law school" receive better legal training. Because these laws schools are more selective, we might also expect that their graduates would be, on average, more likely to absorb and comprehend legal information at a higher level than graduates of less prestigious schools. Moreover, even if graduation from a prestigious school does not reflect additional substantive expertise, if the majority opinion assigner believes that it does, then he or she might tend toward assigning majority opinions to graduates of elite schools. At least two different studies do indeed suggest that federal appellate judges use law school pedigree as a cue that reflects expertise. First, Landes, Lessig, and Solimine (1998) found some evidence that U.S. Courts of Appeals judges from certain elite law schools are cited more often than judges from other schools. Second, Johnson, Wahlbeck, and Spriggs (2006) contend that Supreme Court justices are aware of the pedigree of the litigators who argue orally before the court and use the pedigree as a heuristic for determining expertise. As such, we posit the following:

H7: A judge from a prestigious law school is more likely to be assigned the majority opinion in a case than a judge who is not from a prestigious law school.

To the extent that majority opinion assigners do want more efficient opinions (i.e., better opinions written in a shorter time period), the experience of the judge might be an additional cue that influences opinion assignments. On the Supreme Court, Brenner and Hagle (1996) and Maltzman, Spriggs, and Wahlbeck (2000) studied what is commonly referred to as the "freshman," "career," or "acclimation" effect (but see Slotnick 1979b). Freshman judges are often less likely to author opinions in general (Brenner and Hagle 1996). Presumably, experience leads to substantive expertise, as the judges would be expected to learn on the job. To the extent that majority opinion assigners perceive that experience reflects expertise, we posit the following:

H8: As a judge's tenure on the court increases, he is more likely to receive the majority opinion assignment.

We also examine another phenomenon that is unique to the federal appellate system: district court judges sitting by designation. We have reason to believe that majority opinion assigners are less likely to perceive that district court judges sitting by designation are experts, and therefore are less likely to assign them the majority opinion. As Slotnick (1983) found in his comparison of the backgrounds of U.S. appeals and district court judges, the former are more likely to graduate from prestigious schools, earn academic honors while in law school, serve as law clerks after law school, publish more scholarly works, and have higher ABA ratings during the confirmation process. In other words, as a result of the selection process, appeals court judges are, on average, more competent than their lower court colleagues. Additionally, by their very nature as "outsiders" to the process, district court judges by designation are less experienced (Cohen 2002) and are often viewed as "temporary" visitors by the other permanent panel colleagues (Collins and Martinek 2011). Collins and Martinek point out that "district court judges serving by designation, however, have the potential to undermine consistency in the law" (183). As one judge noted, "We have an unpublished rule that if a district judge is sitting by designation, they are not allowed to write an opinion that reverses another judge in the circuit (but this only applies to [circuit omitted] circuit judges—if the judge is from another circuit they are not restricted). There is often bitterness among some judges if the two regular appeals judges on a panel are split and it is the vote of the district judge that sets circuit policy."

Given the posited relative lack of expertise and experience of district court judges sitting by designation, in combination with the previously noted effects of both expertise and experience on opinion, we posit the following:

H9: A district court judge sitting by designation on a courts of appeals panel is less likely to receive the majority opinion assignment than his or her appellate judge counterparts.

In addition to designation status (Collins and Martinek 2011), scholars have also noted that two other characteristics of judges, race and gender, sometimes influence their behavior or affect the perceptions of other political actors about their competence (Agarwal et al. 2010; Alexander and Andersen 1993; Atkins and Zavoina 1974; Biernat and Kobrynowicz 1997; Boyd, Epstein, and Martin 2010; Peresie 2005; Sniderman et al. 1991; Songer, Davis, and Haire 1994; Walker and Barrow 1985; Wilson 1990). While we express no firm expectations about the ways in which race and gender may affect the assignment of the majority opinion, we include these judicial characteristics as controls in our models below.

Finally, prior studies suggest that majority opinion assigners attempt to distribute the authorship workload in an equitable fashion (e.g., Maltzman and Wahlbeck 2004; Slotnick 1979a). Additionally, Howard's (1981) descriptive analyses indicate that court of appeals majority opinion assignments are somewhat equitably distributed. Given this, we posit the following:

H10: Judges with higher workloads are less likely to receive the majority opinion assignment.

In summary, drawing on studies conducted on the Supreme Court and on the insights of the judges we interviewed, we developed the theoretical expectations outlined above. We would expect to find that on the courts of appeals, opinion assignments are likely to be influenced by equity, expertise (tenure, district court status, law school prestige, prosecutorial experience in criminal cases), ideology, and strategy (assigning the opinion to the median judge to maintain MWCs). Moreover, many of these relationships are theoretically conditional on case salience.

Data and Methods to Establish a Basic Model of Opinion Assignment

We analyzed a random sample of published, signed, three-judge panel decisions of the geographic circuits of the U.S. Courts of Appeals from 1971 to 2002 using data from the United States Courts of Appeals Database (Songer 2002) and its update (also available at http://www.artsandsciences.sc.edu/poli/juri/appealscourt.html). Additionally, we incorporated judge background data from the Multi-User Database on the Attributes of United States Appeals Court Judges, 1801–2004 (Gryski and Zuk 2004).[20] Following the strategy employed by Maltzman and Wahlbeck (1996, 2004), the unit of analysis is the judge in the majority in the case. In other words, for each case we have an observation for each judge that voted in the majority.

The dependent variable is a binary measure, coded one if the judge was assigned the majority opinion and zero otherwise. Because our dependent variable is dichotomous, we use a random effects probit model.

INDEPENDENT VARIABLES

Below we give the operational definitions of each of the independent variables included in our model. The descriptive statistics for each variable are presented in table 6.

*Equity**: A measure reflecting the relative number of unfinished assignments a given judge has compared to other judges in the circuit. Higher values indicate that the judge has relatively more assignments than his brethren.

Opinion Assigner: A binary variable, coded one if the judge was the longest-serving active, nondesignated judge in the final majority

TABLE 6 Descriptive statistics for model of opinion assignment

INDEPENDENT VARIABLE	MEAN	STANDARD DEVIATION	MIN	MAX
Ideological Distance	0.295	0.361	0	1.154
Distance from Median	0.214	0.308	0	1.124
Equity	8.612	0.061	6.008	9.041
District Court Judge	0.088	—	0	1
Law School Prestige	0.550	—	0	1
Prosecutorial Experience	0.390	—	0	1
Tenure	9.760	7.796	0	749
Opinion Assigner	0.337	—	0	1
Criminal Issue	0.306	—	0	1
MWC	0.015	—	0	1
Salience	−0.007	0.989	−0.454	10.335

coalition, as revealed in the published decision; it is coded zero if the judge did not satisfy all three requirements.

Ideological Distance: A variable indicating the distance between the ideology of the majority opinion assigner and that of the judge. The judges' ideologies were measured using a proxy measure of the mean ideologies of the primary actors in the selection of U.S. appeals court judges: the president and the senators from the president's party in the nominee's home state. We follow the same method described above in the model for predicting whether oral argument will be granted. The ideological distance variable is the absolute value of the difference between the ideologies of the judge and the opinion assigner. Lower values indicate higher ideological congruence between the two judges.

Distance from Median: The absolute value of the difference between the ideologies of the majority opinion assigner and the median panelist, computed using the same judge ideology scores discussed above.

District Court Judge: A binary variable, coded one if the judge was a U.S. district court judge at the time of the decision and zero otherwise.

Law School Prestige:* A variable coded one if the judge graduated from a prestigious law school, zero if she graduated from a nonprestigious school.

Tenure: The number of full years the judge was an active member of the U.S. courts of appeals at the time of the decision.

Salience:* A variable reflecting the political or legal importance of the issue in the case. Higher values indicate increased salience.

MWC (minimum winning coalition): A binary variable, coded one if there was an MWC (i.e., a 2–1 vote on the panel).
Prosecutorial Experience: Prior experience as a state or federal prosecutor (coded one for judges having such experience and zero for others).
Criminal Issue: Coded one if the issue in the case related to a criminal prosecution and zero for all other case types.

INTERACTION EFFECTS

As noted above, we posited several interaction effect hypotheses. As such, we included the following multiplicative terms in at least one model.

MWC × Distance from Median: Given the above hypotheses, we would expect a positive coefficient for the multiplicative term. Of course, we also note that there is limited support for the strategic model in studies of the U.S. Courts of Appeals.
Prosecutorial Experience × Criminal Issue: We tested one aspect of the general prediction that substantive experts are often assigned the majority opinion in cases relevant to their field of expertise by creating a multiplicative term between prior prosecutorial experience and the presence of a criminal issue in the case. We expect the sign of the interaction term Prosecutorial Experience × Criminal to be positive.

Results: The Basic Model of Opinion Assignment

The primary goal of this analysis was to develop a baseline model of opinion assignment on the U.S. courts of appeals. Most of the work (but see Atkins and Zavoina 1974; Hausegger and Haynie 2003) to date in this vein has focused on Supreme Court assignment. Studies of opinion assignment on the Supreme Court are severely limited by the very small number of different assigners—chief justices and the senior associate justice. In contrast, on the courts of appeals, with its twelve different circuits and constantly rotating panels, we were able to analyze overall patterns resulting from the decisions of hundreds of different appeals court judges who served as the presiding judge (and thus opinion assigner) during the thirty-three-year period we studied. Confidence can thus be high that the patterns discovered are not the result of the idiosyncratic preferences of one or two judges. We present the model coefficients and standard errors in table 7. The coefficient estimates generally corroborate the hypothesized effects of equity and expertise, while lending no support for the strategic hypotheses and mixed support for the attitudinal hypotheses.[21]

TABLE 7 Random effects probit model of majority opinion assignment, U.S. Courts of Appeals, 1971–2002

INDEPENDENT VARIABLE	COEFFICIENT	STANDARD ERRORS	CHANGE IN PREDICTED PROBABILITIES
Equity	−0.223⁺	0.136	0.01
Distance from Median	0.015	0.030	
MWC × Distance from Median	−0.293	0.236	
Ideological Distance	0.001	0.032	
Ideological Distance × Salience	0.016	0.029	
District Court Judge	−0.205***	0.034	−0.07
Law School Prestige	0.043*	0.019	0.02
Prosecutorial Experience × Criminal	0.078*	0.038	0.01
Prosecutorial Experience	−0.044*	0.021	−0.02
Tenure	−0.002	0.001	
Opinion Assigner	0.097***	0.027	
Opinion Assigner × Salience	0.089***	0.022	0.04
Criminal	−0.029	0.024	
Judge Race	−0.079*	0.041	−0.03
Judge Gender	0.017	0.032	
MWC	0.058	0.085	
Salience	−0.037*	0.017	
Constant	1.488		
N	23,356		
AIC	29,764.300		
Wald χ^2	120.090***		

Notes: Circuit fixed effects not reported.
⁺$P < 0.10$, *$P < 0.05$, **$P < 0.01$, ***$P < 0.001$.
Results are shown for one-tailed tests conducted for all but the moderator variables (Criminal, MWC, Salience). Discrete changes were calculated following the guidelines suggested by Long and Freese (2006). For the dichotomous variables, the statistics reflect the difference between the probability the judge receives the assignment when the variable is set to one or zero, all other covariates held constant at the appropriate measure of central tendency. For the interval-level variable (Equity), the changes reflect the differences in the probability the judge is assigned the majority opinion when the variable is set to one standard deviation above and below the mean, with the other covariates held constant at the center value.

In our analysis of the U.S. courts of appeals, we discovered a number of elements that are directly related to findings about the opinion assignment process on the Supreme Court. For instance, Segal and Spaeth (1993, 2002) and Rohde and Spaeth (1976) posited that ideology plays an influential part in the decision to assign the majority opinion on the Supreme Court level. We found mixed support for the attitudinal model as an explanation for opinion assignment on the courts of appeals. On both the U.S. Supreme Court and the U.S. courts of appeals, the most certain way the opinion assigner can ensure that the opinion writer shares the political preferences of the assigner is to self-assign. And on both courts, self-assignment is common. The results in table 7 show a strong, positive and statistically significant tendency of presiding judges on the courts of appeals to self-assign the majority opinion. More important, from the perspective of judges concerned with the policy output of their court, assignment of the opinion to an ideological ally is most critical in politically important cases. This takes on particular significance in the courts of appeals, which handle many cases that do not raise important political concerns. Consistent with this attitudinal expectation, our data show that on the courts of appeals, self-assignment is particularly likely in salient cases.

The statistical significance of the Opinion Assigner × Salience multiplicative term, however, suggests an even more complex conditional nature of self-assignment decisions. The graph of the conditional effects in figure 6 illustrates this relationship. The graph reflects the difference in the probability of assigning to self versus assigning to another judge as salience increases, with other variables held constant at their mean. The slope is strikingly positive. While judges are more likely to self-assign in low-salience cases, the difference is small. However, as salience increases, the tendency to self-assign increases dramatically: in the most salient cases, the presiding judge is more than 40 percent more likely to assign to self than to assign to another judge.

However, unlike on the U.S. Supreme Court, the data in table 7 show that presiding judges on courts of appeals are no more likely to assign to other judges who are ideologically proximate to the assigner. Moreover,

FIGURE 6. Discrete change in majority opinion self-assignment, by salience

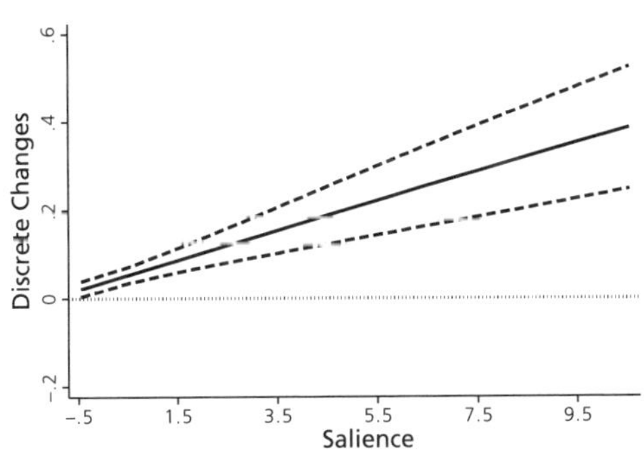

the failure to assign to the ideologically closer other judge is present both in salient cases and in cases with MWCs, situations in which the attitudinal model would predict an enhanced tendency of presiding judges to assign to their ideological allies.[22] In part, this finding may be a function of the relative sizes of the two courts. With at most only two colleagues from whom to choose an opinion writer in cases not self-assigned, and with equity norms that require that the opinion assigner not keep all the important opinions, the opinion assigner often may not have a true ideological ally on the panel. In contrast, chief justices on the Supreme Court will always have at least four colleagues from whom to choose when not self-assigning, and in many cases will have a choice among eight.

We found no evidence of strategic opinion assignment. If the active circuit court judge with the most seniority wishes to maintain the majority coalition in a 2–1 case, we would expect her to assign the majority opinion to the judge who is ideologically the most proximate to the median judge. This turned out to be not the case. Of course, we are not surprised by this result, given the mixed evidence supporting the applicability of the strategic model to the courts of appeals.

The coefficient for the Equity variable is negative and statistically significant, as expected. In other words, judges with more existing assignments relative to their colleagues are less likely to receive the opinion assignment. However, while statistically significant, the variable does not appear to have much substantive significance. The discrete change (see table 7), which, for continuous variables such as Equity is estimated as the difference in the probability a judge received the assignment when the independent variable is one standard deviation above and below the mean (while holding all other covariates constant at the appropriate level of central tendency), is –0.01. In other words, the two standard deviation increase in the variable only decreases the likelihood a judge receives the assignment by 1 percent, on average.

We found strong support for the theory that judges consider efficiency when making assignments, even though there was only ambivalent support for this theory among the judges we interviewed. Presiding judges are more likely to assign to expert judge. For example, the coefficient for the Law School Prestige variable in table 7 is positive and statistically significant, evincing a tendency to assign the majority opinion to graduates from elite schools in roughly average-salience cases. This result reaffirms the notion that although the courts of appeals are clearly understood to be important political decision makers, they remain at heart legal institutions, in which legal expertise and competence matter. It would appear, based on the discrete change of 0.02 in table 7, however, that the substantive effects of law school prestige are relatively small.

Substantive expertise also appears to affect opinion assignment. The significant Prosecutorial Experience × Criminal multiplicative term indicates a tendency to assign criminal cases to judges with prosecutorial experience in criminal cases. We note, however, that the substantive significance is relatively small: as presented in table 7, former prosecutors have only a 0.01 greater probability of receiving the assignment in criminal cases compared to judges with no former prosecutorial experience.

While the reduced likelihood that district court judges sitting by designation will receive the majority opinion-writing assignment may owe in part to their outsider status, the results are also consistent with the expectation that presiding judges favor assignment to more expert judges. The coefficient (see table 7) for the District Court Judge variable is negative and statistically significant. In other words, when other variables are set at their mean values, district court judges sitting by designation are less likely to receive the majority opinion than full-time courts of appeals judges. This effect also appears to be substantively significant, particularly compared to the other variables, at least when all of the covariates are held to the appropriate measure of central of tendency. The discrete change for the District Court Judge variable (for all dummies, the difference in the probability the judge received the assignment when the variable is set to one and zero, with covariates held constant at their central tendency estimate) is –0.07 (see table 7). Theoretically, this phenomenon could be attributed to the fact that most of the district court judges are indeed visitors and have not had a proper period of acclimation to the workload and culture of the host appeals circuit. Additionally, as Slotnick (1983) found, the district court judges are generally less competent, at least as reflected in proxy measures such as ABA ratings. This observation dovetails with our theoretical expectations, insofar as district court judges, who are both less experienced and less qualified, are not going to be burdened (or empowered) by being assigned important or complex opinions.

In light of the historical composition of the courts of appeals as a body composed only of white men, it is possible that newer categories of judges resulting from the racial and gender diversification of the courts might, like district court judges, be viewed to some extent as outsiders. The plausibility of racial and gender minorities being viewed as outsiders is increased by an assignment system based on seniority, which ensures that a large majority of those serving as the presiding judge on a panel continue to be white judges appointed to the court at a time of minimal racial and gender diversity on the courts. To assess whether this history affected opinion assignment in recent years, we added categories for race and gender to our model of opinion assignment. As can be seen from table 7, gender has no apparent effect on assignment of the majority opinion. There is virtually no difference in the likelihood that a male rather than a female judge will receive the majority opinion assignment.[23]

In contrast, race appears to be relevant for opinion assignment. Racial minorities were significantly less likely to receive the assignment to write the majority opinion even after we controlled for their tenure, gender, law school prestige, and ideological distance from the presiding judge. The probability the majority opinion is assigned to a Latino or an African American judge is approximately 0.03 less than the probability that the majority opinion is assigned to their Caucasian colleagues who possess similar attributes.[24]

In summary, the actual pattern of assignments discovered in our data is consistent with the opinion expressed by the judges that equity was an important consideration. While the pattern of assignment was not dominated by ideological considerations as much as previous studies have suggested it is on the Supreme Court, the desire to shape public policy appears to have more of an impact on the assignment of the majority opinion than was suggested by the interviews with the judges. But consistent with the views expressed by the judges, and differing from the results of studies of opinion assignment on the Supreme Court, strategic considerations appear to have virtually no relevance. Finally, both experience and expertise appear to have some impact on the assignment of the majority opinion, despite the doubts expressed by the judges, but the magnitude of these effects appears to be small.

The Special Case of Unpublished Opinions

Both the analysis above and most of the comments of the judges we interviewed were directed at those cases in which the majority opinion of the court was published in the *Federal Reporter* and made publicly available in a variety of electronic formats. Formal rules in each circuit suggest that these published opinions are the most important outputs of the courts from both a legal and a political perspective. These are the cases formally recognized as having precedential value, and because of their easy availability they are the opinions that have the greatest impact on legal policy. But in a substantial and growing number of cases, the judges write an opinion that is "unpublished."[25] Like published opinions, those assigned to an unpublished status are part of the public record; anyone desiring to see a copy can obtain it from the office of the clerk of court. Designation of an opinion as "unpublished" literally meant that it was not available in the official publication containing decisions of the courts of appeals, the *Federal Reporter.* Consequently, before the electronic reporting of cases, such opinions were not readily available to most people. We explore the trends in the use of such unpublished opinions as part of our more general treatment of the question of which opinions deserve publication status in the next chapter.

Conclusion

In this chapter, we have described the procedures that occur before the decision of the panel is made. The dramatic explosion in the caseload of the courts of appeals put increasing pressure on the courts to find ways to more efficiently handle their workload. As a result, all the circuits have increasingly relied on procedures to screen the flood of cases they receive and to dispose of the least important cases with less time-consuming processes. One consequence has been a sharp reduction in the number of cases receiving the full treatment of a merits decision following oral argument and the production of an opinion designated for publication. Our statistical analysis of the decision to grant oral argument is largely consistent with the more subjective assessment provided in the judge interviews. In this context, we found strong support for one aspect of our integrated model: the role of institutions. Specifically, both the formal federal procedural rules (FRAPs) and local circuit rules have a strong impact on the likelihood of a decision to grant oral argument. Additionally, as many of the judges suggested, case complexity and the substantive importance of the issues raised on appeal increase the likelihood of oral argument. Finally, we found some evidence that workload matters.

As explored further in chapter 5, who sits on each panel may potentially have an important influence on how the appeal is decided. Nevertheless, our interviews indicated that there is virtually complete satisfaction with the manner in which judges and cases are assigned to panels; the process in each circuit appears to be essentially random, and no judges raised any concern about the possibility that any panels were being "stacked" to achieve a particular political outcome.

After it has been determined, through the screening process, which cases will be the focus of the court's action, and those cases have been assigned to panels, detailed consideration begins with intensive study of a massive volume of written material by the judges themselves with the assistance of one of their law clerks. The oral arguments themselves were widely viewed as being a valuable part of the process, though many judges indicated that those arguments rarely changed the outcome. Once the hearings are over, a tentative decision is made by the conference of the three-judge panel, usually after relatively brief and collegial discussion.

The selection of the judge to write the opinion of the court is arguably one of the most important decisions of the court, but the process has received virtually no previous scholarly attention. Our interviews with the judges and our statistical analysis of the patterns of opinion assignment demonstrate that the actual pattern of assignments is consistent with the expectation expressed by the judges that equity is an important consideration. In contrast, contrary to expectations based on previous studies of Supreme Court opinion assignment (but consistent with the views expressed by our judges), ideological considerations appear to have only a modest impact, and strategic concerns appear to be largely irrelevant for the choice of the opinion author. Conversely, institutional factors such as experience and expertise appear to have some impact on the assignment of the majority opinion despite doubts expressed by the judges, but the magnitude of these effects appears to be small.

In chapter 3 we thoroughly incorporate the judicial perspective of the post-conference process and empirically examine various facets of the opinion-writing process. For example, the next chapter explores to what extent the judges negotiate over the content of the opinion of the court, and what factors affect the decision to publish the opinion in the *Federal Reporter.* Additionally, we investigate the amount of time it takes three-judge panels to decide cases and the lengths of the opinions—two aspects of the process that reflect the amount of deliberation taken to resolve the case.

THREE

Decision Making and Writing the Opinion of the Court

This chapter describes the process of decision making, particularly the important process of arriving at the opinion of the court. In contrast to the extensive literature on the patterns of votes of judges on U.S. appellate courts, much less is known about the process of arriving at the final decision of the appellate court.

We describe, from the judge's viewpoint, what happens after a tentative decision has been reached in the private conference proceedings. We also explain how judges use clerks to aid both preparation and opinion writing, and how the judges interact with each other on an informal basis. The picture that emerges suggests that the judges, in contrast to most officials in the government with comparable policymaking authority, work more independently, delegate fewer details to staff, and are more immersed in the day-to-day details. The interviews also suggest that judges often communicate informally with one another—a process that is largely invisible to the public. Opinions typically are released to the public only after going through multiple drafts and extensive negotiation and revision by the judges. These informal contacts appear to be characterized by extensive mutual respect, coupled with hard bargaining.

After characterizing the process of decision making, we turn to an empirical examination based on analyses of the decisions themselves. Simple descriptive statistics show that there is wide variation in both the time it takes to produce the opinion of the court and the length of that opinion. We close with a more systematic multivariate examination of the factors related to the length of time it takes to produce an opinion and final decision of the court, as well as factors related to the length of the opinion and the decision to report decisions. The analyses show how a number of characteristics of the case itself (e.g., its complexity and salience), the circuit (e.g., the extent of diversity, its size, and the nature of its docket) and the characteristics of the opinion writer and the other judges on the panel substantially affect both how long it takes to produce an opinion the panel can agree on and opinion length. Similarly, case and circuit effects play a significant role in the decision to publish.

The Process of Decision Making

As noted in chapter 2, appellate court judges usually meet in conference one or two (sometimes three) days after hearing oral arguments to discuss the cases. For each case, the conference typically results in a tentative decision as to whether the court will affirm or reverse the district court, and who will write the initial draft of the opinion of the court. But while that conference decision typically determines who wins and who loses in a narrow sense, it rarely defines the nature of the precedent that will emerge from the decision. That is, after conference it still remains to be determined how broad or narrow the "victory" of the winning party will be and what explanation will be given with respect to the meaning of the legal rules determined to be dispositive in the case. These matters await the release of the formal opinion of the court.

One of the first things we observed in all our interviews with judges is that there is no predetermined timetable for the release of any opinion of the court. The presiding judge may on occasion informally prod the opinion writer to finish the writing, but in general, the most that can be said is that the opinion will be announced whenever the three judges on the panel are finished with it. Opinion writing is one of the most time-consuming tasks of appellate judges. In our interviews, the judges indicated that in a typical year they wrote between fifty and eighty majority opinions. For some uncomplicated cases, the process may take only a couple of weeks, but for complex, controversial cases the time from conference to the announcement of the opinion may take more than a year. To flesh out these general comments on disposition times, we examined the distribution of the actual time opinion writing has taken over a quarter of a century. The results are presented in figure 7.

As can be seen from the graph, there has been considerable variation in average disposition times for the writing of the opinion of the court. Clearly, on average, producing a majority opinion for the court is a time-consuming process. Throughout the period examined, writing an opinion for the court and obtaining the agreement of the judges on the panel took

FIGURE 7. Mean disposition times (days) by year, U.S. Courts of Appeals published cases, 1971–1996

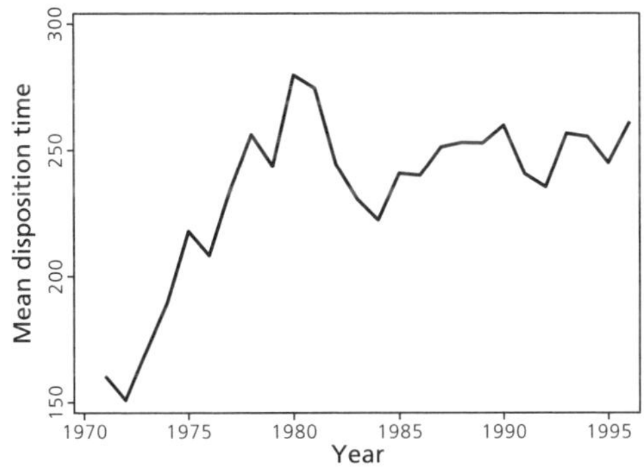

on average more than 150 days (i.e., at least five months). The actual disposition time varied substantially from year to year, rising from a low of just over 150 days in the early 1970s to a high of about 280 days in the early 1980s. However, there does not appear to be a clear linear trend toward either increasing or decreasing disposition times across the period examined.

Interviews with the judges indicated that a number of factors, including the type of issue and its complexity, the extent of disagreement on the panel and the circuit, and the use of outsiders (e.g., district judges or circuit judges from other circuits sitting by designation), can all affect the time required to reach agreement on the opinion of the court. Since these factors vary across circuits, it might be expected that average disposition times also vary across circuits.

Our examination of circuit trends confirms these expectations. Both the overall average and trends over time in mean disposition times vary considerably across the circuits. At one extreme, the First Circuit, the smallest and perhaps most homogeneous of the circuits, has consistently required less than 200 days on average to produce a majority opinion, and that time has remained essentially static across the years. In contrast, the Sixth, Ninth, and Tenth Circuits have shown great volatility across the two decades examined in the average length of time their panels take to produce a majority opinion. In the Sixth Circuit, the mean time to produce a majority opinion has varied from a low near 200 days in the mid-1970s to a high near 600 days in the 1980s. Perhaps the only generalization possible from an examination of these circuit trends is that in respect to disposition times, as in many other aspects of decision making on the courts of appeals, the circuits are different.

The judges interviewed indicated that cases involving some types of issues tend, on average, to be both more complex and more controversial than others. From the perspective of the judges, cases involving criminal issues tend to be both less complicated and less controversial than cases involving civil rights and liberties issues. Moreover, adjudicatory speed is normatively and legally more important in criminal cases, where defendants are entitled to a measure of swift justice. Indeed, this concern is reflected in the calendaring preferences expressly given to criminal cases in the Federal Rules of Appellate Procedure (e.g., FRAP 46(b)(2)), as well as in several circuit local rules (e.g., Fifth Circuit Rule 47.7 and Sixth Circuit Rule 34). Thus, one might expect criminal issues to be disposed of on average more rapidly than other cases. When we examined actual disposition times across issue types we found that this expectation was supported: criminal cases are decided faster than all other categories of issues. The mean criminal case is decided in approximately 180 days. The next fastest category is privacy cases, which are decided, on average, in just under 250 days. The mean times to decision in the other issue areas are all around 260 days.

As the judges' comments cited below on bargaining indicate, the more controversial the issues in a case, the more bargaining is likely to occur during the opinion-writing process. Presumably, such extended bargaining increases the time needed to produce a final opinion of the court. The absence of dissent, or of serious conflict that might pose a threat of an ultimate dissent, may thus promote the efficient administration of justice. Dissenting opinions mean more work not only for the dissenter, who must spend time to craft the separate opinion, but also for those in the majority, who may feel the need to counter the dissenter's arguments (Hettinger, Lindquist, and Martinek 2006, 20). Such conflict may result in opinions that not only take longer to write but also end up being much longer.

Opinions vary dramatically in terms of their length, complexity, and the clarity of the writing. Our analysis of the majority opinions of the courts of appeals released between 1993 and 2002 found that they averaged 8.7 pages in length, but varied in length dramatically (e.g., standard deviation of six pages). Nearly 10 percent of the opinions of the court were presented in three pages or less, and almost a third were less than six pages long. But the longest opinion in our sample of cases ran to 116 pages in the *Federal Reporter.*

Just as we discovered that the time to produce a majority opinion varied across issues, depending on the complexity and controversy associated with different issues, we anticipated that these same factors might influence the length of the opinion. However, examination of the actual opinion lengths in different issue areas indicated that at least for broad categories of issues, the variation across issues is modest. As shown in figure 8, the shortest opinions on average were written in prisoner petition cases (mean = 7.2 pages). But in all but one of the other issue areas, the average length of the majority opinion was under nine and one-half pages. Thus, the substantial overall variation in opinion length noted above appears to result from something other than the broad nature of the issue in the case.

One potential influence on the length of the opinion is the degree of controversy surrounding the issue. When issues are controversial, opinion writers may feel pressure to provide a more extensive justification and explanation of the majority's position. We took a preliminary look at this possibility by comparing the length of the majority opinion in cases that also included a dissenting opinion with the length of the opinion in cases decided unanimously. We found that majority opinions in divided decisions are in fact longer than opinions that are unanimously supported, but the differences are modest (eleven pages versus eight and one-third pages).

Similar to the U.S. Supreme Court's opinion-writing process, the opinion-writing process in the courts of appeals is conducted in secret. The final product will be publicly announced and easily available to anyone who is interested,[1] but until the court officially announces its decision, neither the litigants nor any other persons outside the court know what

FIGURE 8. Average opinion length for selected issues

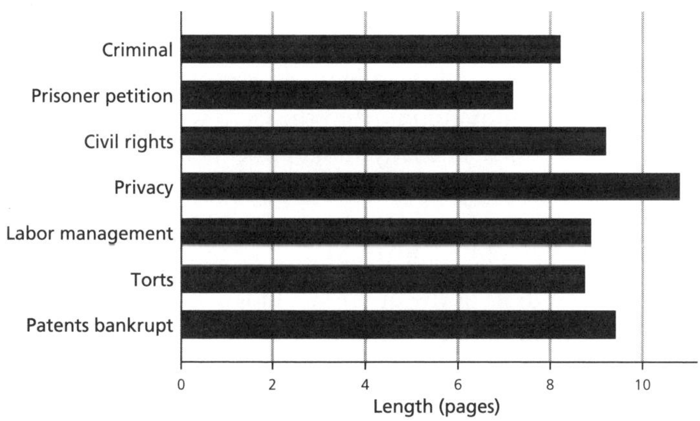

the decision will be or when it will announced. Only the three judges on the panel and their clerks are aware of the progress of the opinion writing. Compared to other government agencies, whose deliberations are frequently leaked to friendly reporters or political allies, the record of the courts of appeals in maintaining the secrecy of their opinion-writing proceedings is amazingly good. In fact, we cannot recall a single instance in the past decade of the content of an appeals court decision becoming public before the court was ready to announce its decision, and none of the judges we interviewed mentioned any instance in which an opinion they were working on was leaked to the press or the public.

The basic process of opinion writing is straightforward, and there was consensus among the judges we interviewed as to how it proceeds. Once the conference is over, the three judges return to their individual "home chambers," typically an office in a federal courthouse in their home state. Once in his home chamber, the judge assigned to write the majority opinion begins to work intensively on a draft with the assistance of a single law clerk (usually the clerk who wrote the memorandum of law on the case before conference). Often this stage begins with the judge and clerk sitting down together and discussing the main issues in the case and their ideas for how those issues might be resolved. The judge typically summarizes for the clerk the views expressed in conference and whether any consensus had developed on how to handle any of the more specific issues in the case. While both the judge and the clerk are intimately and intensively involved in the detailed work on the opinion, the precise way in which judges use their clerks varies from judge to judge and may also vary for a given judge, depending on the nature and difficulty of the issues in the case.

If the discussions between the clerk and judge or the judge's notes from conference uncover one or more areas in which the judge is uncertain about the meaning of the relevant law, the first priority becomes additional legal research. Most judges will assign such research to their clerk, expecting a memorandum from the clerk within a few days. Once that research is completed, many judges ask their clerk to write a first draft of the opinion, after providing guidance about the direction the opinion should take. As Judge V volunteered, "Most judges don't like to write a first draft. . . . They will give clear marching orders and then have their clerks write a draft of the opinion." Judge T concurred, saying that "clerks regularly draft opinions, and I use them for this purpose." But all the judges we interviewed were adamant that delegating the writing of a first draft to a clerk did not mean that the clerk simply decided the case according to the clerk's own preference. Clerks are typically given fairly clear indications of what was agreed to in conference and what their judge expects before beginning a draft. And all clerks appear to be aware that their draft is only a starting point. Once the draft is complete, it will be critiqued and edited by the judge, often followed by another detailed discussion between the judge and the clerk about the opinion, which may lead to the request by the judge for a revised draft. Judge XX noted that he "almost always" asks one of his clerks to write a first draft of the opinion, and then he "heavily edits" that draft. But if he plans to dissent, Judge XX always writes the opinion himself.

In contrast, Judge V thought it was a bad idea for the clerks to write the first draft of an opinion, and so he writes the first draft of all of his opinions. He uses his clerks to extensively edit his opinion draft, and then he sits down with the clerks for detailed discussions of their proposed edits before he undertakes a final draft. Thus, while judges' preferences vary about whether their clerks should actually write the first draft, in all chambers, both the judge and one of his or her clerks are heavily involved in the writing of the opinion, and often the writing is delayed until one of them (usually the clerk) has done further research on the case. In all judicial chambers, producing an opinion of the court typically involves multiple revisions and extensive interaction between the judge and the clerk. But until the opinion leaves the office of the judge writing the opinion, it would be rare for more than these two people to have substantial involvement. In this sense, writing judicial opinions is quite different from writing briefs in large law firms or producing decisions in many government agencies, in which a relatively large number of people may contribute to the decision.

Bargaining on Opinions

Once the opinion author is satisfied with the draft of the opinion, it is sent simultaneously to the other two judges on the panel. But this draft rarely emerges unscathed as the official opinion of the court. As all of the judges we interviewed agreed, the draft written by the judge designated to write the court opinion is viewed only as a starting point. Judge C articulated a widely held view when he said, "The first draft that is circulated almost always leads to extensive comments. Those comments then usually lead to a good bit of back-and-forth in which the writing judge will usually try to accommodate a colleague. Such accommodation is an *integral* part of the process; it is the core of the appellate process. I suppose the willingness to accommodate varies some by individual judge, but on our circuit every judge tries to accommodate if he can without violating a basic principle."

Judge A expressed a similar view more colorfully, noting that on his circuit, "We have a norm of 'messing around' with each other's opinions. We often make very substantive suggestions about the first draft opinion we receive—there is a very strong norm of accommodation." Judge A further noted that the consensus in his circuit was that they should try to "get the best opinion possible and . . . everyone [should] respect each other even when we disagree." More prosaically, Judge E noted that after a draft opinion was submitted, the judge would expect the other judges to write back with "extensive comments," and that in complicated cases, the judges might go back and forth with memos many times until everyone was comfortable with the final product. Judge J concurred, noting that there was typically "an awful lot of shaping of opinions" after the initial draft was circulated, with most opinions going through multiple drafts before winning acceptance from the panel.

From a social science perspective, the judges seemed to be suggesting that the final opinion of the court often involves extensive bargaining, and some judges were comfortable using the term "bargaining" to describe the process. For instance, Judge O said, "We negotiate during the opinion-writing process. There is often a back-and-forth." Judge M concurred, noting that "negotiation and bargaining goes on all the time at the opinion-writing stage." Judge F readily admitted that he engaged in bargaining with his colleagues. He said, "I have definitely written what you would probably call a 'bargaining memo' in response to a draft opinion from a colleague—something like, 'If you are willing to change X then I will not dissent.'" He noted that it doesn't work all the time, but often a colleague will accommodate that sort of response. And though Judge D suggested that some judges are reluctant to use the term "bargaining," he thought they all recognized that it was a normal part of the process, noting that "bargaining is often implicit, but sometimes it is quite explicit." For example, Judge D said that a judge might say, "There are only three points in your draft that I am not comfortable with, and I would be able to join if you are able to change . . . A, B, C." He said that all judges would recognize such a memo as offering an explicit deal in which the memo writer was promising to join the majority opinion if three specific changes were made but threatening to dissent if the changes were not made. Moreover, he noted that such a memo would often elicit a response from the majority opinion author suggesting a compromise that involved going partway toward incorporating the requested changes, but proposing alternative wording that might lead to further negotiations. How many such memos are ultimately exchanged on a given opinion will depend on how complicated the case is and the extent to which it involves an issue on which the judges have strong positions. Judge R made a very similar point. He said it was not at all infrequent for someone who had just received a draft of the opinion to write what we have characterized as a "bargaining memo": "Some of my colleagues might be offended by that label, but they all do it. By a bargaining memo I mean offering explicitly or implicitly to sign on to the opinion in return for some modification in it." Judge R noted that most writers are receptive to such memos most of the time—unless they think there is some strong principled reason to resist.

In contrast, Judge O didn't like the term "bargaining" but said that a judge might make suggestions to the draft of an opinion, and there was frequently "some back-and-forth" between the judges. Judge O saw this not as bargaining but as offering suggestions to improve the opinion and make it better—but admitted this type of back-and-forth was not uncommon. Judge Q also did not like the term "bargaining" but said, "We try to find common ground." And he added that frequently means he will write an opinion more narrowly than he might prefer if it were just up to him, to produce consensus. Similarly, Judge B was reluctant to use the term "bargaining" for what judges in his circuit did, though he admitted there was a lot of "give-and-take" as draft opinions were circulated. He added, "I would say that there is more of an effort at collective writing than 'bargaining'—a good analogy might be to the way academics write co-authored papers."

Central to this bargaining and negotiation in the courts of appeals is a general willingness to accommodate the views of colleagues on the panel unless one has a strong principled objection to the request. As Judge R put it, "We will usually try to obtain a unanimous court—we don't worry too much if we don't, but [we] try to accommodate the views of our colleagues if we can." Or as Judge V put it, "If you have a court that is collegial, then ideological tensions will be muted; there will be narrow opinions and there will be compromise." Beyond the obvious need to obtain a majority for one's opinion, many judges spoke more generally about respecting the views of their colleagues. Judge F said that one always considered the perspectives of one's colleagues on the panel: "Most of us have a strong sense that what we are to do is to produce a collegial decision. When I write, it is very different from when I was a district judge and was just speaking for myself. I always have in the back of my mind that I am writing for the court—for the three of us on the panel." Judge M agreed, saying, "The views of our colleagues are always important. We all take the approach of listening and considering carefully our colleagues' views and thus being open to persuasion; but in addition to persuasion, we will accommodate each other's views—compromise—if possible."

This seemed to be combined, in at least some judges, with a sense of humility, the recognition that they might be wrong and their colleagues might be right. Judge E agreed. He said there was definitely a norm of trying to reach consensus, for a judge's own thinking often would change as the judge interacted with his colleagues: "It comes from accepting that everyone is both bright and well trained, and when they have a different view from your original take it is worth considering . . . and even if you remain convinced that you are right, you may compromise if it won't violate some strongly held principle out of a sense of humility." After indicating that he thought every judge realized intellectually that the other guy was probably as likely as himself to be right, he noted that this meant that the best choice to make as a group was a compromise. Then, almost as an afterthought, Judge E said, "If you won't ever compromise it doesn't mean you are any more a man of principle—it just means you are arrogant." Judge F seconded these sentiments, noting that one of the good things about his circuit was the lack of ego: "Everyone acknowledges that there are a lot of smart people, and that the product of three people wrestling with an issue is more likely in the end to get it right than sticking to your own guns all the time."

One of the frequent outcomes of bargaining is to make the final opinion narrower than the original. Judge Q said that in trying to find common ground, "I frequently write an opinion more narrowly than I might prefer if it was just up to me, in order to produce consensus." Similarly, Judge L said, "Bargaining takes place frequently on the content of opinions; often you may narrow a holding in order to get agreement—or sometimes you . . . ask a judge to leave out a section to get agreement." Finally, Judge N indicated that in his experience, the most commonly used method to avoid a dissent in a case was to search for a way to solve a case without firmly addressing the issue on which there was disagreement.

But one form that bargaining never takes is log rolling. As Judge B said very emphatically, "There is absolutely NO bargaining across different cases; but there is some bargaining over how broad or narrow a given opinion will be." There seemed to be a consensus on this point.

While we did not directly ask any of the judges we interviewed about trading votes on different cases, several of the judges spontaneously clarified initial statements indicating that bargaining was common on their court by explicitly denying that the bargaining included trading votes or conceding on one opinion in return for a concession in a different case. And no judge who gave examples of bargaining in his or her court ever mentioned a trade that went across cases.

As the comments we have cited indicate, virtually all of the judges we interviewed understood the process of opinion writing to involve extensive feedback for the opinion author from the other panelists after the author circulated a first draft. Most of the judges indicated there was considerable give-and-take among the judges, with the final opinion often reflecting bargaining and compromise among the judges on the panel. The comments of the judges indicate that there are pervasive norms supporting a search for unanimity when possible, and a willingness to accommodate colleagues. Thus, opinions usually are not simply an expression of the preferences or approach of the opinion author but reflect to varying degrees input from everyone on the panel. But many of our interviews suggested that the influence of panel members on the shape of the opinion went beyond accommodating specific requests for changes in the original draft of the opinion. Many judges indicated that even when constructing the first draft of an opinion, they attempted to anticipate the preferences of the other two judges on the panel. As Judge A said, "We influence each other a lot, I think. . . . [We] have each other in mind almost from the first time I read the briefs in a case." Similarly, Judge O noted that judges get to know everyone on the circuit pretty well. Consequently, "When preparing for a case you are always thinking about what the others on the panel will do." And Judge K chimed in, "If you are assigned to write the court opinion you will always take into account what the preferences of your colleagues are." While these sentiments were widely shared, Judge J went even further, saying, "You are always thinking about the other judges on the panel. . . . There is an 'organic' relationship among judges on the same circuit." Thus, even before the first draft of an opinion has been written, accommodation of the preferences of the other judges on the panel has often begun.

Most scholars who have discussed the opinion-writing process on appellate courts (with most writing referring to the process on the U.S. Supreme Court) describe virtually all of the changes made in the initial draft of an opinion in terms relating to accommodation or bargaining. That is, the assumption is usually made that the opinion author privately retains his or her initial position on the issues in the case but may strategically make public changes to accommodate others. But our interviews indicate that persuasion may also account for some of the change. Judge H argued that persuasion is more important than compromise. He said, "I am always amazed at how much agreement there is among our judges, even on reversals. I was recently on a panel with two conservatives [Judge H describes himself as a liberal] and yet we only ended up disagreeing on one case during the week." He went on to note that some of those cases were tough, and that he changed his mind on several, but "we actually agreed in the end—they weren't cases of me just going along." Similarly, Judge E reflected that "When I stop to think about it, I am sometimes surprised at how often we end up agreeing on the result. A number of times we start off at least some distance apart—and I think those initial disagreements reflect our differences in opinions—I'm a bit more conservative than some of my colleagues, and that sometimes shows up in our initial assessments—but after we have talked the issue through, and especially after someone has worked through a first draft, and then I've worked on a possible concurrence or dissent—once I've worked through the whole process and tried to reason it all out, I usually end up in the same place as the opinion draft or possibly just slightly different in emphasis (but not on the other 'side' of the decision)."

Clearly, the bargaining process leads to some degree of voting fluidity—as when a judge switches sides (e.g., from supporting the appellant to supporting the appellee) after casting his or her initial conference vote. Judge O, for example, admitted that on several occasions he had switched sides on the outcome after feedback from the other judges on the panel. This usually happened, he noted, when one of the judges raised an issue that had not been argued by the lawyers on either side. He recalled one case in which after circulating the draft of the majority opinion, he received a draft of a dissent, and decided the dissenter was right and changed his position. Judge T had had a number of cases in which he changed his mind on the outcome, either while writing his initial draft of the opinion or after thinking about his colleagues' comments. "Often these were cases with an initial 2–1 split," he said, "so changing your mind changed the outcome of the case." Judge T said most of his colleagues had mentioned similar experiences of their own, and he thought that occasionally changing one's mind in such a fashion was not surprising. He suggested it was inevitable that "as you get into a case in detail—especially when trying to write an opinion—you sometimes change your mind. I think all of us have had cases where it was hard to write the opinion you started to write, and thus you reconsider your original position." Recalling his own experiences, Judge N made a similar point. He said that on a couple of times when writing the majority opinion for a unanimous decision he concluded that they had decided the case wrongly, and he therefore switched sides and wrote an opinion for the other side. Each time, he said, he wrote the other judges on the panel, and they agreed with his changed position, switching the outcome from a unanimous decision for the appellee to a unanimous decision for the appellant. Judge X agreed that every judge he had known had on occasion switched sides in the case they were on either after reading the draft of the majority opinion (when they were a dissenter in conference) or in response to the comments on a draft opinion by one of the other judges on the panel. He then volunteered an estimate that this voting fluidity occurred "in maybe 8 or 9 percent of the cases."

Overall, the interviews suggested that various types of strategic behavior occur during the opinion-writing process. Bargaining, negotiations, and accommodation appear to occur frequently. Voting fluidity, while rarer, still occurs in a nontrivial number of instances. Further, it appears that institutional norms of collegiality and consensus encourage this strategic behavior.

Disposition Times: Constructing a Preliminary Model

The judge interviews on panel conflict and bargaining on the opinion of the court suggest that the salience and complexity of the issues and the extent of conflict over the outcome all have a substantial impact on how many drafts an opinion goes through and how long it takes to reach agreement on the official opinion of the court (i.e., the opinion of the majority). We proceeded to test this theory derived from our interviews with a multivariate model of the time it takes to produce the opinion of the court.

Most political science studies of the U.S. Courts of Appeals focus on the nature of the outcomes in the case but ignore another important factor, how long it takes the courts to decide these cases. This gap in the literature is puzzling, in light of the amount of energy spent by law professors and judges in commenting on the effect of rising caseloads on disposition (e.g., Posner 1983; Richman and Reynolds 1988) as well as the normative importance of adjudicatory speed as an element of due process. Moreover, disposition times are likely proxy measures for the extent of the bargaining that occurs during the court's deliberation. While several studies have examined the extent to which U.S. Supreme

Court justices engage in bargaining (e.g., Brenner and Whitmeyer 2009; Maltzman, Spriggs, and Wahlbeck 2000; Spriggs, Maltzman, and Wahlbeck 1999; Wahlbeck, Spriggs, and Maltzman 1998), empirical tests of this phenomenon have relied on publicly available records kept by one or more justices. Since we did not have access to enough appeals court judge papers to construct direct measures of bargaining and negotiations, disposition times may be the best alternative proxy.

A few recent studies have attempted to fill some of this lacuna in our understanding of judicial adjudicatory speed (Binder and Maltzman 2009; Cauthen and Latzer 2008; Christensen and Szmer 2012; Lindquist 2007; Szmer, Christensen, and Kuersten 2012). Most of these studies examined the U.S. courts of appeals (but see the Cauthen and Latzer 2008 study of the state appellate capital cases). While Binder and Maltzman (2009) focused primarily on the impact of conflict in the confirmation process, Lindquist (2007) considered an array of factors (e.g., the effects of strategies such as nonpublication, the limited usage of oral arguments, and the use of judges sitting by designation). However, these pathbreaking studies are limited in that they analyzed only circuit-year aggregated data.

While the Christensen and Szmer (2012) and Szmer, Christensen, and Kuersten (2012) studies utilized case-level data, they also are subject to limitations. For example, as a consequence of comparing unpublished and published decisions, Szmer, Christensen, and Kuersten (2012) did not include judge characteristics. Finally, while Christensen and Szmer (2012) looked at one judge characteristic, gender, aggregated by panel, they did not examine other characteristics of the judges. We move beyond these earlier studies to provide an exploratory test of a theory of disposition time developed from the insights gained from the appeals court judges we interviewed.

In the absence of any existing theory of disposition times from previous studies of the opinion-writing process, we derive a proto-theory from the perceptions of the judges we interviewed. Most of the judges we interviewed did not directly address what factors might increase or decrease the time necessary to reach agreement on an opinion of the court. Instead, the judges focused on the characteristics of cases, judges, and circuits that led to more or less extensive negotiations among the panel members. Central to the way every judge we talked to understood the opinion-writing process was the idea that the opinion of the court is always a collective product. All judges understood that the person chosen to be the opinion author did not have carte blanche to write whatever he or she wanted. Instead, the opinion author's mandate is to produce a draft of an opinion that faithfully reflects the consensus of the panel. As the comments of the judges above indicate, everyone understands that an initial draft will be subjected to detailed examination by the two other judges on the panel and those judges will not be shy in suggesting changes to any aspects of the opinion that don't satisfy them. Moreover, strong norms of collegiality incline most of the judges to try to reach consensus. Thus, an opinion author expects to produce an initial draft of an opinion, receive feedback and suggestions from the other two judges, then produce a second draft that tries to meet the initial objections without doing serious damage to the preferences of the opinion author, and so on through as many drafts as are necessary to produce a version of the opinion that everyone can live with. As a result, we anticipate that a combination of two types of factors will determine the length of time it takes to produce a majority opinion.

Factors of the first type are those that influence the time it takes to produce the initial opinion draft. Perhaps most important, all the judges noted that the cases on their dockets vary tremendously in terms of the inherent difficulty of the issues presented for resolution. Nearly every judge referred to "easy" and "hard" cases on his or her docket. Cases that are more complex and cases that raise questions not previously decided by the circuit presumably require more time and effort by the opinion writer to figure out. Next, while on average appeals court judges have high levels of legal competence compared to the general public or even the general population of attorneys, there are clearly differences among judges in the competencies needed for the complex legal analysis required to produce strong opinions. Therefore, any factors that reflect the quality of the legal training or the extent of the experience on the bench possessed by different judges should affect the time it takes a given opinion author to produce a first draft. Finally, the political and legal salience of the issues in a given case are likely to influence how long it takes to produce the first draft. Most people take greater care and put more time and effort into "getting it right" on a task they hold important. We assume judges are not different.

The second set of factors influencing disposition times includes those that make it easier or harder for the panel to reach consensus. As the interviews made plain, much of the time between conference and the formal release of the court's opinion is spent on attempts at persuasion, negotiation, and bargaining over successive drafts of the opinion. Thus, factors that make bargaining more difficult should increase the total disposition time. The complexity and salience of the issues presumably increase the time needed for the negotiation phase, as well as for the initial writing of the opinion. On the other hand, the more the judges initially think alike, the easier the negotiation process should be. Consequently, ideological or political diversity on a panel is likely to slow down the process of negotiation. Similarly, conflict on a panel in the form of actual or threatened dissent could be expected to slow down the process of trying to reach accommodation. Finally, any characteristics of the panel or circuit that might impede efficient collegial relations, such as the presence of outsiders (e.g., district judges sitting by designation) or heavy caseloads, are likely to negatively affect the time it takes to produce a majority opinion.

From these more general theoretical perspectives, we developed the following specific hypotheses.

SALIENCE

Saliency is a measure of case importance. Presumably, when a case is more important, the judges will devote more time both to the decision-making process, including any possible bargaining and negotiations (for a U.S. Supreme Court example, see Spriggs, Maltzman, and Wahlbeck 1999), and to justifying the decision through the majority opinion (see our subsequent analysis of opinion length, as well as the Black and Spriggs 2008 study of the U.S. Supreme Court). As noted above, high-salience issues are likely to increase the time needed for the initial drafting of the opinion and to produce more contentious negotiations once the opinion draft is circulated. This leads to the following hypothesis:

H1: As case saliency increases, the number of days it takes the panel to decide the case will tend to increase.

COMPLEXITY

Courts should also spend more time resolving complex legal issues. As with case saliency, there is some reason to believe that judges on collegial courts negotiate more often in complex cases (see the study of U.S. Supreme Court bargaining by Wahlbeck, Spriggs, and Maltzman 1998). Most of the judges we interviewed spontaneously mentioned that more negotiation is usually required on "hard" cases. Also, intuitively, it seems reasonable that more time should be devoted to formulating justifications for outcomes in complex cases. This intuition is supported by the Black and Spriggs (2008) finding that the length of U.S. Supreme Court opinions tends to increase as case complexity increases. The judges we interviewed indicated that the same dynamic applies to cases heard by the courts of appeals. Most directly, Judge D observed that when a draft is circulated, the number of memos written "will depend primarily on how complicated the case is." Other judges agreed that there is a constant interchange on complicated cases, inevitably increasing the time that it takes to reach consensus. Complex issues take both more time to write and more time for negotiations. As such, we posit the following:

H2: As case complexity increases, the number of days it takes the panel to decide the case will tend to increase.

Similar to these first two hypotheses, prior publication of an opinion by the district court judge below is an indicator of both the salience and the complexity of the issue from the perspective of the district judge. Thus, we anticipate that cases coming to the courts of appeals with a published district court opinion will be associated with longer disposition times. Additionally, criminal cases frequently are both less complex and less salient than many other cases heard by the courts of appeals. Thus, we would expect disposition times on average to be less in criminal cases than in other case types.

CONFLICT AND DISPOSITION TIMES

There are several reasons to believe that both dissenting and concurring opinions extend the length of time it takes the panel to decide the case. Most obviously, the opinions take time to write. However, they also directly reflect substantive conflicts on the court. Presumably, time must be spent attempting to resolve these disputes. As Judge T noted, "On the difficult cases there is lots of give-and-take in the opinion-writing process—it may go through multiple drafts before you get an opinion that everyone is satisfied with." And he noted that a fair number of cases are open to conflicting opinions, with at least the possibility that someone will dissent. And since judges generally try to accommodate one another unless they perceive an important disagreement on principle, cases that engender conflict inevitably take longer to resolve with a majority opinion. In informal conversations, several judges attending the Second Circuit retreat noted that it was primarily in cases that initially split 2–1 in conference that judges, including opinion writers, are challenged in a serious way to consider whether to change their initial predisposition about how the case should be resolved. As one noted, "It is not surprising that as you get into such a case in detail—especially when trying to write an opinion—you sometimes change your mind—I think all of us have had cases where it was hard to write the opinion you started to write—and thus you reconsider your original position." And the more either the opinion writer or the other judges on the panel take time to reconsider the initial position they propounded in conference, the longer it takes to get agreement on a majority opinion. Similarly, Judge XX noted that on controversial cases—the ones that eventually result in a dissenting or concurring opinion—there is "more bargaining and back-and-forth" than in cases in which the panel is united as to the outcome. He continued that the back-and-forth can get quite substantive and take many rounds in the draft opinion process: "This is especially true when we start out further apart due to our differences in our jurisprudential concerns." And on most of the cases that end up with a dissenting opinion, there first was usually an extensive effort by all the judges to see if it was possible to produce an opinion that everyone could join. Given this apparent connection between conflict and the extent of the bargaining that ensues, we hypothesize the following:

H3: Cases with dissents or concurrences tend to take longer to decide than cases without dissents or concurrences.

IDEOLOGY

Following the attitudinal model, judicial conflict (dissent and concurrence) studies typically find that more ideologically diverse panels have higher levels of conflict (Hettinger, Lindquist, and Martinek 2006; Peterson 1981; Richardson and Vines 1970; Songer 1986). And, as noted above, a consistent theme in our judge interviews was that the time for negotiation over successive opinion drafts was greater the more diverse the political preferences of the judges. As such, we posit the following:

H4: The greater the ideological range of the panelists, the longer panels will tend to take to resolve cases.

Similarly, both attitudinal and strategic models theorize that the relationship between the ideology of the majority opinion writer (MOW) and that of the other panelists can lead to both increased conflict and bargaining, both of which can increase disposition times. Ideologically moderate (in relation to the other panelists) MOWs are more likely to build coalitions, thereby reducing the likelihood of conflicts (as manifested in dissents and concurrences). This leads to the following corollary of hypothesis H4:

H5: As the ideological distance between the MOW and the median panelist increases, the disposition time will tend to increase.

MOW JUDGE CHARACTERISTICS

As noted above, we theorized that some judges are more competent and have greater skill in legal analysis and writing, traits that should make them more efficient in producing the initial draft of the court's opinion when they are selected to write. Similarly, Maltzman, Spriggs, and Wahlbeck (2000) posit that expert judges are more likely to receive the majority opinion assignment because they are more efficient. In other words, they will more expediently produce a higher-quality opinion of the court.

While measures of judge expertise are often difficult to generate, and no standard exists in the courts of appeals literature, proxy measures include tenure, law school prestige, judge status (i.e., active, senior, visiting, or designated judge), and American Bar Association (ABA) ratings (see Slotnick 1983) Presumably, longer-serving judges, graduates of prestigious law schools, and those with higher ABA ratings are more expert (either in substance or process, or both), and therefore more efficient. We therefore suggest the following hypothesis:

H6: The more expert the majority opinion writer (as reflected in the length of experience serving as an appellate judge, ABA ratings, and prestige of law school alma mater), the faster the panel will tend to decide cases.

Unlike the other surrogate measures of expertise, employment status is more nuanced. Clearly, because of the higher standards in the selection process, combined with the appellate process expertise garnered from experience at that level, active judges will tend to have higher levels of expertise than district court judges. Moreover, when the opinion writer is a district judge sitting by designation, the interpersonal dynamics on the panel may be more difficult, resulting in increased time needed to reach agreement on the opinion. As Judge J noted, "You are always thinking about the other judges on the panel—it is so important to know the other judges. But you usually don't know judges sitting by designation, particularly if they are from the district courts. So judges sitting by designation make the process more difficult." He added that when he didn't know the opinion writer, it was more difficult and more time-consuming to reach accommodation on what the opinion should say. We therefore posited the following:

H7: When the MOW is a district court judge sitting by designation, the case disposition time will tend to be longer than when the MOW is an active, nonvisiting circuit judge.

The nuance comes in the difference between judges with appellate experience. Senior judges, for example, like active judges, are selected using similar expertise criteria. They also have similar appellate experiences, both in general and in the idiosyncracies of the specific circuit they serve. In fact, their longer service sitting as an appeals court judge may provide experience that enables them to perform their opinion-writing tasks more efficiently. However, unlike active judges, senior judges are not subject to the same level of workload pressures. Judges on senior status continue to draw their full salaries, but typically they are assigned to sit on only half as many panels as judges who remain on active status. As such, we hypothesized the following:

H8: When the MOW is a senior judge, case disposition times will tend to be shorter than when the MOW is an active, nonvisiting circuit judge.

The relevant distinctions between visiting and nonvisiting active circuit court judges are also less obvious. Both are selected using similar criteria and tend to have relatively comparable workload pressures (compared to senior judges) and experience. The only apparent difference is in the familiarity with the unique circuit-level characteristics and with the colleagues sitting on the panel. Cohen (2002) suggests that visiting active circuit judges therefore contribute to delays. In light of that, we posited the following:

H9: When the MOW is a visiting active circuit judge, the panel will tend to decide cases more slowly than when the MOW is a nonvisiting active judge.

CIRCUIT SIZE

Cohen (2002) also suggests that larger circuits are more inefficient. Size—in terms of both geography and personnel—can lead to increased levels of conflict. This primarily results from lower levels of collegiality in larger circuits (Cohen 2002). Small groups tend to be more cohesive. Moreover, more dispersed circuits have less personal interaction, which can decrease collegiality (Cohen 2002). While none of the judges we interviewed directly discussed the impact of circuit size on the efficiency of the opinion-writing process, there was frequent mention of the positive effect that high levels of collegiality and knowing the other judges on the panel had on the ability of a panel to quickly reach agreement on an opinion. Thus, as larger size would seem inevitably to reduce how well the judges know each other and is likely to reduce the extent of collegiality, circuit size may indirectly result in a less efficient opinion-writing process. This leads to the following hypothesis:

H10: Panels in larger circuits (large in terms of both circuit area and numbers of judges) tend to decide cases more slowly than panels in smaller circuits.

CASELOAD

Finally, much of the literature discussing disposition times tends to focus on caseload pressures (e.g., Binder and Maltzman 2009). Intuitively, panels on circuits with larger caseloads should be slower, as they try to balance more tasks. This suggests the following hypothesis:

H11: As circuit caseload increases, case disposition times will tend to increase.

While prior studies have examined the impact of circuit workload pressures, one might expect the caseload of the opinion writer to have an even greater impact on disposition times. The judges we interviewed generally appeared to recognize this basic dynamic. Given that, we posit the following:

H12: As the opinion writer's workload increases, the case disposition time increases.

Binder and Maltzman (2009) and others (e.g., Szmer, Christensen, and Kuersten 2012) find that judge vacancies put additional caseload pressures on circuits, even after controlling for the actual caseload per active sitting judge. Inevitably, as the number of vacancies increases, there is increased pressure on the circuit to recruit more judges sitting by designation, and, as noted above, reliance on such judges is likely to reduce the efficiency of the opinion-writing process. Additionally, while there is little hard evidence to establish this point, it seems reasonable to guess that as the number of vacancies increases, the circuit will feel increasing pressure to dispose of an increasing number of cases through the use of expedited procedures (e.g., denial of oral argument or the production of proportionally more opinions that are not designated for publication). While such processes may reduce the average time it takes to dispose of each case, the increasing reliance on these time-saving devices is likely to mean that on average, the remaining cases that still receive the full treatment, including a signed, published opinion, will disproportionally tend to be more complex and difficult cases that result in the longest times to agree on a majority opinion. As such, we hypothesize the following:

H13: As the number of circuit judge vacancies increases, the case disposition time will tend to increase.

Research Design for a Model of Disposition Time

We examined cases decided by three-judge panels in the United States Courts of Appeals Database (Songer 2002) sample that were decided between 1971 and 1996.[2] The dependent variable, Disposition Time*, is the number of days from the date the court received the last litigant's brief until the decision date. (Detailed descriptions of all variables followed by an asterisk are provided in the technical appendix.) We treated the dependent variable as a count, estimating the model parameters using a negative binomial regression (see the technical appendix for a description of the statistical method).

INDEPENDENT VARIABLES

Below we describe the measures of our independent variable. Unless otherwise noted, we expect the coefficients to be positive.

Salience:* The same measure of salience as discussed in chapter 2.

Complexity:* Higher values of the scale indicate a more complex or difficult case.

Criminal: The same measure—whether the case was criminal (one) or civil (zero)—as discussed in chapter 2. Given our hypothesis, the coefficient should be negative.

Prior Publication: A dummy variable, coded one if the lower court opinion was published and zero if it was not.

Concur: A binary variable, coded one if at least one judge authored a concurring opinion.

Dissent: A binary variable, coded one if a judge cast a dissenting vote in the case.

Panel Ideological Range: The measure is the absolute value of the difference between the ideology (see the section on chapter 2 in the technical appendix for a discussion of the ideology measure) of the most liberal and most conservative judges sitting on a panel.

Ideological Distance from Panel Median: The absolute value of the difference between the ideology scores for the majority opinion author and the panel median.

MOW Tenure: The tenure (number of years sitting as an active circuit court judge at the time of the decision) of the majority opinion writer. Based on our hypothesis, we would expect to find a negative coefficient.

MOW Law School Prestige: The quality of the MOW's alma mater, measured utilizing the same judge law school prestige construct discussed in chapter 2. Given our hypothesis, the coefficient should be negative (see the section on chapter 2 in the technical appendix).

MOW ABA Exceptionally Well Qualified: The ABA rates the federal judicial nominees based on their qualifications (Songer, Sheehan, and Haire 2000). The rating is ordinal, with judges receiving "extremely well qualified," "well qualified," "qualified," and "not qualified" ratings. We collapsed the variable into a dummy, coded one if the MOW was ranked in the highest category, extremely well qualified, and zero if the MOW received a lower ABA rating. Since we posit that exceptionally well-qualified opinion authors are faster, we would expect to find a negative coefficient.

MOW Judge Status (MOW Senior Judge/Visiting Active Appeals Judge/District Court Judge):* Three dummy variable, each coded one if that particular type of designated judge sat on the panel. The reference category is active judge on the circuit.

Circuit Active Judges: The total number of active judges on that circuit during the year the case was decided.

Circuit Area (per judge): The number of square miles of land in the circuit divided by the number of active judges during that year.

Circuit Docket Size:* Measured as the number of terminations per three-judge panel during the corresponding fiscal year by that circuit.

MOW Opinion Caseload:* Higher values indicate a more demanding caseload for the majority opinion writer.

Circuit Judge Vacancies: Using data compiled from the Administrative Office of the United States Courts Reports, we measured vacancies in terms of the number of months a judgeship was left open during the year the case was decided. For example, if a circuit had three positions open for the entire year and one position open for four months, the variable value for that circuit year would be 40.

Overall, the results of the model presented in table 8 support the theory of disposition time derived from the judge interviews. Most of the key elements identified by the judges as increasing or decreasing the time needed to write the initial draft of the opinion are strongly related

TABLE 8 Negative binomial model of days to decide cases, U.S. Court of Appeals published opinions, 1971–1996

		CHANGE IN EXPECTED COUNTS OF THE NUMBER OF PROCESSING DAYS[a]	
VARIABLE	COEFFICIENT	CONTINUOUS INDEPENDENT VARIABLES	DUMMY INDEPENDENT VARIABLES
Salience	−0.012 (0.010)	—	—
Complexity	0.054*** (0.009)	23.311	—
Criminal	−0.294*** (0.018)	—	−59.841
Prior Publication	0.052** (0.020)	—	12.594
Concur	0.215*** (0.034)	—	56.400
Dissent	0.243*** (0.024)	—	64.736
Panel Ideological Range	0.115*** (0.029)	16.045	—
Ideological Distance from Panel Median	0.015 (0.033)	—	—
MOW tenure	0.039+ (0.013)	15.513	—
MOW Law School Prestige	−0.037* (0.016)	—	−8.970
MOW ABA Exceptionally Well Qualified	−0.103*** (0.021)	—	−23.067
MOW Senior Judge	−0.074** (0.028)	—	−16.716
MOW Visiting Active Appeals Judge	−0.077 (0.054)	—	—
MOW District Court Judge	0.203*** (0.040)	—	52.960
Circuit Active Judges	0.022*** (0.002)	56.470	—
Circuit Area	−0.003 (0.004)	—	—
Circuit Docket Size	0.000*** (0.000)	28.114	—

(continued)

TABLE 8 *(continued)*

VARIABLE	COEFFICIENT	CHANGE IN EXPECTED COUNTS OF THE NUMBER OF PROCESSING DAYS[a]	
		CONTINUOUS INDEPENDENT VARIABLES	DUMMY INDEPENDENT VARIABLES
MOW Opinion Caseload	−0.006[+] (0.002)	−18.673	—
Circuit Judge Vacancies	0.002** (0.001)	10.059	—
Constant	5.003		
N	7,506		
Nagelkerke R^2	0.139		

Notes: Robust standard errors in parentheses; year fixed effects not reported.
*$P < 0.05$, **$P < 0.01$, **$P < 0.001$. [+]Significant at $P < 0.01$ level but sign is in opposite direction.
[a]See the discussion of changes in expected counts in the technical appendix, page <00>.

to the total time elapsing between the date the panel received the last brief submitted by the litigants and the date its decision and opinion were announced. Complex cases took substantially longer to decide than simple cases—the change in the expected count (described in the technical appendix), which estimates substantive significance, is over twenty-three days. Similarly, disposition time in criminal cases, which the judges thought were often less complex than other cases, was almost two months less than the time it took to resolve other types of cases. And an additional correlate of complexity, prior publication by the district courts, added more than twelve days to the expected disposition time compared to cases without a published district court opinion.

Judge characteristics are also strongly related to disposition times. As anticipated, judges who appeared to have higher levels of legal competence (as indicated by the prestige of their law schools, their ABA rating, and their experience on courts of appeals) were able to produce court opinions substantially more rapidly than their less qualified or less experienced colleagues. Most notably, opinion writers receiving the highest rating from the ABA of exceptionally well qualified were able, on average, to produce a majority opinion more than three weeks faster than those not as highly rated. On the other hand, when opinion authorship was assigned to a district judge sitting by designation, average disposition time increased by almost fifty-three days over that required if the opinion author was an active appeals court judge. The finding that four different measures of judicial competence and experience were all statistically and substantively significant in the ways predicted by the theory lends strong support to the more general theoretical proposition that judge competence is a vitally important part of the explanation of disposition time on the courts of appeals.

The main departure of the results from our theoretical predictions is the failure of our measure of salience to achieve statistical significance. However, two other variables that appear to tap into issue salience to some degree, prior publication by the district court and whether the case involved a criminal issue, are both statistically significant at the 0.01 level. Thus, the overall findings in regard to political and legal salience remain mixed.

We theorized that conditions that increase the difficulty of negotiations in reaching agreement on a majority opinion also increase the total disposition time. There seemed to be a consensus among the judges that the primary determinants of the time required for negotiation and the number of opinion drafts needed to reach final agreement were the complexity of the issues in the case and the degree of conflict on the panel. As noted above, complexity was strongly related to increased disposition times. In addition, several measures of conflict were also strongly related to the time necessary to finalize the decision and opinion of the court. Most notably, cases involving a dissent by one member of the panel required slightly more than two months longer, on average, to produce a decision. Similarly, cases with a concurring opinion had an average disposition time more than fifty-six days longer than cases with no judges who wrote separately. Both the existing social science literature and the comments of the judges in our interviews suggest that the biggest cause of conflict on the courts of appeals is ideological diversity among panel members. In accordance with our theory, wide ideological differences among the panel members led to significantly longer disposition times.

Finally, though not the focus of most of the observations of the judges we interviewed, circuit characteristics also were related to average disposition times. In particular, circuits with large dockets and circuits with judicial vacancies had longer disposition times than other circuits.

Opinion Length

Other things being equal, writing a longer opinion would normally be expected to take more time than writing a short opinion. Moreover, we expected that many of the factors that increase the time needed to write and reach agreement on the majority opinion would also tend to increase the ultimate length of the opinion. Certainly, it could be anticipated that the resolution of complex issues would take longer to adequately explain than the resolution of simple issues, and that opinion authors would go into more detail and thus produce longer opinions on salient than on nonsalient issues. Similarly, as several of the judges noted in the interviews, opinion writers often take more time and produce more detailed majority opinions when they feel the need to respond to alternative perspectives presented in concurring or dissenting opinions by their colleagues.

The results, displayed in table 9, largely confirm the expectation that many of the same factors that increase the disposition time for the writing of the majority opinion also increase the average length of the majority opinion. Both the direct measure of salience and the indirect measure (i.e., prior publication of an opinion by the district court) were associated with significantly longer opinions, though the magnitudes of the effects were modest. Using the changes in expected counts to estimate substantive significance (see the technical appendix), majority opinions in cases with previously published opinions by the district court averaged less than half a page in additional length compared to opinions in cases without a district opinion (a 5 percent increase in opinion length). Similarly, as cases increased in complexity, their opinions became longer. Compared to cases of average complexity, those that were a standard deviation greater in complexity were about 25 percent longer (a length increase of more than two pages, on average).

As the judge interviews suggested, when one judge on the panel decides to write separately, producing either a dissenting or a concurring opinion, the majority opinion requires more time and more pages to produce a satisfactory opinion for the court. On average, majority opinions in cases with a concurrence were slightly more than a page longer and those with a dissenting opinion were about a page and a third longer (i.e., about a 15 percent increase in length) than opinions in cases in which no one wrote separately.

Circuit characteristics were also related to changes in the length of the average opinion, though none of the judges we interviewed suggested any rationale for why circuit characteristics might affect opinion length. Both increases in the size of the circuit's docket and increases in the number of judicial vacancies on the circuit were associated with longer opinions, though the changes were modest in both instances. Increases

TABLE 9 Negative binomial model of opinion length, U.S. Courts of Appeals published opinions, 1971–1996

		CHANGE IN EXPECTED COUNTS OF THE NUMBER OF PAGES	
VARIABLE	COEFFICIENT	CONTINUOUS INDEPENDENT VARIABLES	DUMMY INDEPENDENT VARIABLES
Salience	0.067*** (0.008)	2.242	—
Complexity	0.232*** (0.008)	2.244	—
Criminal	−0.016 (0.015)	—	—
Prior Publication	0.073*** (0.017)	—	0.402
Concur	0.187*** (0.034)	—	1.084
Dissent	0.221*** (0.026)	—	1.309
Circuit Active Judges	−0.001 (0.001)	—	—
Circuit Docket Size	0.000*** (0.000)	0.455	—
Circuit Area	−0.057+ (0.004)	1.394	—
Circuit Judge Vacancies	0.003*** (0.001)	0.394	—
Panel Ideological Range	0.023 (0.027)	—	—
MOW Tenure	0.012 (0.012)	—	—
MOW Law School Prestige	−0.024* (0.014)	—	−0.124
MOW ABA Extremely Well Qualified	−0.023 (0.018)	—	—
MOW Senior Judge	−0.064** (0.023)	−0.326	−17.006
MOW Visiting Active Appeals Judge	−0.081* (0.040)	—	—
MOW District Court Judge	−0.029 (0.037)	—	—

(continued)

TABLE 9 *(continued)*

VARIABLE	COEFFICIENT	CHANGE IN EXPECTED COUNTS OF THE NUMBER OF PAGES: CONTINUOUS INDEPENDENT VARIABLES	DUMMY INDEPENDENT VARIABLES
MOW Opinion Caseload	−0.043*** (0.002)	−2.919	—
Ideological Distance from Panel Median	0.032 (0.030)	—	—
Constant	−2.009		
N	7,506		
Nagelkerke R^2	0.082		

Notes: Robust standard errors in parentheses; year fixed effects not reported.
*$P < 0.05$, **$P < 0.01$, ***$P < 0.001$; $^{+}P < 0.01$ level but sign is in opposite direction.

of one standard deviation in either the circuit's docket or its vacancies were associated with increases in the length of the average opinion of less than half a page.

Opinion writing is the most time-consuming aspect of most appellate court judges' jobs. Thus it is not surprising that increases in a given judge's workload result in shorter opinions. For a one standard deviation increase in the caseload of the opinion writer, the average length of the majority opinion written decreases by almost three pages. Finally, more experienced and more competent judges appear to write slightly shorter opinions than other judges. Both judges on senior status and those who graduated from prestigious law schools wrote opinions that were shorter to a statistically significant degree than other judges' opinions.

Overall, then, complexity, salience, and the presence of dissenting and concurring opinions result in opinions that are both longer in absolute length and take more time to write than opinions in the typical case heard by the courts of appeals. Additionally, both circuit and individual judge characteristics appear in general to influence the length and disposition times in similar ways.

Anticipation of Action by Judges outside the Panel

The process of arriving at a majority opinion (and possible dissenting and concurring opinions) is roughly the same in all circuits. But once the panel has completed its own work on the opinion, the practices of the circuits diverge substantially. In seven circuits, the panel immediately proceeds to decide whether or not the opinion will be published in the *Federal Reporter,* and then simultaneously releases the opinion to the parties in the case and the general public. However, in the remaining circuits there is an intermediate step. In the Third, Fourth, Sixth, Tenth, and District of Columbia Circuits, before the decision and opinion are released to the parties and the public, it is circulated among all the active judges in the circuit who were not on the panel. The judges outside the panel then have a limited amount of time to comment on the opinion draft.

As Judge P explained, "When complete, the draft opinion of the court is sent to everyone in the circuit at the same time it is sent to the other two judges on the panel. Every judge is supposed to respond within ten days or the opinion can be filed. If a judge (not on panel) disagrees with something in the opinion, [that judge] will write a letter to the opinion author, and sometimes the opinion author will respond back. When a judge responds to a draft opinion, that response goes to all members of the circuit." Thus, the circuit can often work out potential differences before the opinion is formally filed. Judge E (on a different circuit) observed a similar process on his circuit. He noted that if there were no comments within eight days, the opinion author could file the opinion for publication. But "alternatively, one or more judges may comment and send their comments to the full circuit, [and] sometimes this leads the panel to revise their opinion before it is filed." Judge E argued that this process tended to reduce considerably the need for en bancs and helped keep circuit law unified. Judge Q noted that he "frequently" got comments from nonpanel judges, and that while these were often just "helpful details," they sometimes led to substantial change in the opinion. He thought this practice of circulation was very good for the circuit because it gave the author useful feedback on potential objections from other judges, and also indicated whether there was a chance for en banc review. Judge Q felt this practice helped eliminate many potential en bancs because very often the author would make revisions in response to the expressed concerns. However, he noted—and all the other judges we interviewed agreed—that the ultimate decision about whether to accommodate the suggestions made by judges off the panel was in the hands of the panel itself. Judge X agreed that this practice "often avoids problems." For instance, he said, "someone will point out a precedent that you didn't consider—so then you can go back and look at it—and this may prevent you from being embarrassed when your opinion is published." He also noted that although the norm was to wait ten days, if he hadn't heard from someone after two weeks he would "just give them a call."

While support for this informal norm of prepublication circulation of opinions is nearly universal in the circuits that have the practice, one judge raised doubts about its efficacy. Judge N said there are so many opinions it is hard to keep up. He admitted that as a result, often he merely scanned the opinion, and read it closely only if it appeared to be relevant to some case that was on his docket. But if something in the opinion seemed to be a problem at first glance, he would usually give it to a clerk and ask for a memo of law on the problem. Then, if he was convinced, he would write a letter to the panel. As a result, "sometimes—more than rarely but not frequently—the panels will change their opinion in response to these comments." Despite not giving full attention to all the opinions, Judge N joined the rest of his colleagues in approving of the practice. He noted that the intent of this system was to reduce the need for formal en banc proceedings, and thought that on the whole, it accomplished that purpose. However, when we asked judges in other circuits that do not have a similar norm, we didn't find a single judge who thought that such a practice of circulating opinions was a good idea.

The Decision to Publish

Once work on an opinion has been finalized, the only remaining decision is whether to release it as a published opinion.[3] The decision to publish is important if only because the circuits generally do not treat unpublished cases as precedents.[4] Most studies examining publication focus on the differences in the factors that affect decision making in published and unpublished cases (e.g., Keele et al. 2009). A handful of studies try to explain the decisions to publish, though most are either descriptive (e.g., Hoffman 1981) or purely qualitative (e.g., Wasby 2004). Merritt and Brudney (2001) have offered the most systematic test of the decision to publish, and even then they focus only on unfair labor practice suits arising out of a single statute. We begin with a description of the process, informed by many of our interviews, and follow with an empirical analysis of the decision to publish.

Substantial use of the practice of nonpublication began in the 1960s as an additional strategy for dealing with rising caseload pressures. Unpublished opinions were typically much shorter than published opinions, and because they were not intended to be cited as precedent, they could be written quickly, without as much concern for the implications of the opinion for future cases. As shown in figure 9, beginning in the mid-1970s there was a steep decline in the proportion of cases receiving a published opinion. The trend temporarily bottomed out in the early 1980s, followed by a brief recovery around 1985. But since 1985 there has been an additional steady decrease in the proportional use of published opinions. In the last two decades, the courts of appeals have made increasing use of this tactic for handling caseload pressure. As table 10 shows, in recent years more than four-fifths of all merits terminations by the courts of appeals have been accompanied by an unreported opinion. The trend over time to decrease the number of opinions designated for publication is one of the steps taken by the judges to deal with their increasing caseloads. As Judge UU noted, "When you decide to publish, a lot more work goes into the opinion." Therefore, reducing the number of published opinions has helped the judges process more decisions per year.

The FRAPs are silent with respect to the criteria for publication.[5] As such, the precise rules for determining which cases should be designated for publication versus nonpublished status vary across circuits, and are usually implemented through local rules or internal operating procedures. As we have seen with respect to other procedures, such as the decision to hear oral arguments, the circuit rules vary in specificity. Some circuits, such as the Second, do not have expressed criteria for determining which decisions are not published (what the Second Circuit local rules refer to as "summary orders"). By contrast, Fifth Circuit Local Rule 47.5 lays out a list of factors that are to be applied when determining whether to publish a decision. These are whether the decision:

FIGURE 9. Proportion of U.S. Courts of Appeals published decisions per year, 1976–2002

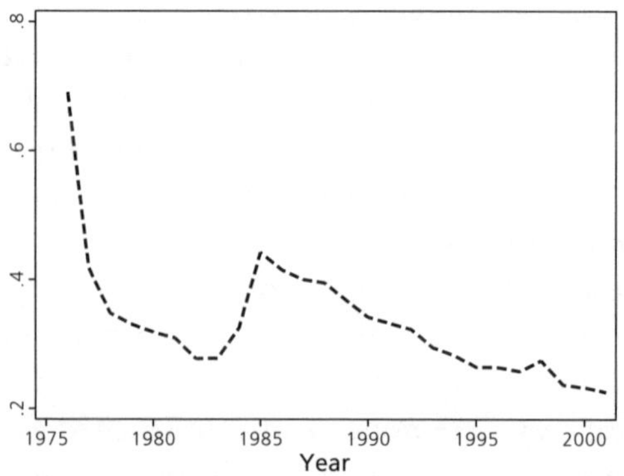

Source: Federal Judicial Center (2005), Federal Court Cases, Integrated Database, 1970–2000.

TABLE 10 Change over time in use of unpublished opinions: Cases terminated on the merits after oral hearing or submission on briefs

FISCAL YEAR	TOTAL CASES	WRITTEN, SIGNED OPINIONS		TOTAL UNPUBLISHED	PERCENT UNPUBLISHED
		PUBLISHED	UNPUBLISHED		
1990	21,022	6,008	2,374	14,204	67.6
1995	27,772	6,118	3,814	20,984	75.6
2000	27,516	5,099	4,281	21,895	79.6
2005	29,913	5,043	5,211	24,411	81.6
2008	29,608	4,949	5,870	24,231	81.8

Source: Annual Report of the Director of the Administrative Office of the United States Courts.

(1) establishes a new rule or modifies an existing one, (2) applies a rule in a novel way, (3) explicates or critiques an existing rule, (4) resolves an intra- or intercircuit conflict, (5) concerns an issue of "significant public interest," or (6) involves a case previously remanded by the Supreme Court (those six are mandatory). Additionally, the panel has the discretion to publish opinions that are accompanied by a dissenting or concurring opinion, that reverse the lower court, or that affirm the lower court decision applying alternative legal grounds. Beyond the formal rules, the circuits also appear to have informal norms that influence whether or not a given opinion is published.

The effects of the variation in formal and informal institutions governing publication can be seen in table 11. In all but one case, fewer than half of all merits decisions receive a published opinion. Still, while all circuits make extensive use of nonpublication, there is considerable variation across the circuits. In the Fourth Circuit, which has one of the more rigid rules governing publication (Local Rule 36(a), which resembles the Fifth Circuit rule discussed above), more than 92 percent of all cases terminated on the merits in 2008 resulted in an unpublished opinion. Conversely, the Seventh Circuit, which, like the Second, does not expressly delineate criteria for publication, publishes slightly more than half of all merits terminations.

Of course, given the virtually identical publication rates (above 86 percent) for the Second and Fifth Circuits, the specificity of the publication rules is not dispositive. Indeed, the criteria are still such that the judges will always have some discretion. In general, in all circuits, unpublished opinions are those thought to be less important, especially those that are thought to have no precedential value. That is, cases decided with an

TABLE 11 Variation in use of unpublished opinions by circuit, 2008: Cases terminated on the merits after oral hearing or submission on briefs

CIRCUIT	TOTAL CASES	WRITTEN, SIGNED OPINIONS: PUBLISHED	WRITTEN, SIGNED OPINIONS: UNPUBLISHED	OTHER UNPUBLISHED	PERCENT UNPUBLISHED
District of Columbia	557	220	0	325	58.3
First	1,020	411	24	569	58.1
Second	2,859	313	2,472	06	86.7
Third	2,300	232	1,336	726	89.7
Fourth	2,581	195	301	2,081	92.3
Fifth	4,121	459	67	3,514	86.9
Sixth	2,569	440	634	1,476	82.1
Seventh	1,338	670	0	654	48.9
Eighth	1,922	665	7	1,204	63.0
Ninth	5,800	721	84	4,938	86.6
Tenth	1,473	386	921	151	72.8
Eleventh	3,068	237	24	2,717	89.3
Total	29,608	4,949	5,870	18,361	81.8

Source: Annual Report of the Director of the Administrative Office of the United States Courts.

unpublished opinion are those in which the judges on the panel decided that the issues could be resolved by a straightforward application of existing law. Deciding whether a case has any precedential value is by its nature a judgment that cannot be objectively determined by circuit rules. Our interviews indicated that the judgment of the judge who wrote the opinion was generally accepted by the other judges on the panel and thus determined whether or not a given opinion would be published. Thus, the rate of publication varies across individual judges, as well as circuits.

Formally, the decision to publish is a decision of the panel, governed by majority vote. However, regardless of the formal circuit criteria, the common rule of thumb that appears to have been adopted by most panels is that the judge assigned to write the opinion has the main responsibility to decide whether to designate the opinion for publication. But as Judge A indicated, "We still follow the informal rule that a decision will be published if any one of the three judges wants it published." This appears to be a widespread informal norm. Judge FF explained, "If one of my colleagues pressed for publication, even if I didn't think it warranted publication I would relent and publish the decision. This doesn't happen often, but it is part of working in a collegial environment." Or, as Judge X noted, "The decision to publish or not is usually left to the judge writing an opinion, but if the judge writing the majority opinion initially slates the opinion to be unpublished and the judge writing the dissenting opinion wants it published, then the majority opinion will also be published."

All the judges we interviewed agreed in a general sense with circuit rules limiting publication to those opinions that in some sense were politically or legally important, but expressed their sense of what made a case publishable to them in slightly different ways. According to Judge AA, "The most important factors for me are significance of the issue and novelty. Is it a new issue? I will take that into consideration when deciding whether or not to publish. Usually if it is the first time a particular issue has been addressed, I will publish the opinion—not always, but more often than not." Judge CC had an only slightly different take on publication criteria, saying, "Freshness of the case is a big reason." Similarly, Judge TT explained, "I am less likely to publish a decision if it is a routine matter that we deal with—often lots of criminal appeals fall into this category. Now if there is something unique in the case—well, I would be more apt to encourage publication." Judge WW clarified that a reversal of the district court almost always indicates that there is some ambiguity in the existing law, so the concern with publishing opinions with precedential value usually leads him to recommend publication any time he is reversing a published district court decision. Beyond the concern to limit publication to new or unique issues, Judge FF added that his circuit wouldn't publish if the issue dealt with state law, but then quickly amended his statement by adding, "Well, sometimes we do, but most of the time we do not or I do not." Nevertheless, after listening to the judges talk about when and why they would publish, we were left with the sense that circuit criteria reserving published decisions for those with precedential value take different concrete meanings in the minds of different judges and that as a result, which decisions are actually published depends a lot on which judge wrote the opinion.

Building on the somewhat ambiguous circuit standards suggesting that publication should depend on the importance of the opinion or its precedential value, we sought to identify a series of more objectively defined criteria that in practice were related to the probability that a given opinion would be published. A first indicator of the probability that the resolution of a given case will have precedential value is whether or not the case was granted oral argument. As noted above (see chapter 2), the judges we interviewed indicated that oral argument is usually reserved for those cases whose outcome is in doubt because the cases raise new issues or are particularly complex or salient. Thus, we hypothesize the following:

H1: Cases with oral argument are more likely than cases decided solely on the briefs to result in a published opinion.

Another prominent indicator that the legal issues are not straightforward is the occurrence of dissensus among the judges, either on the appellate court or between judges at different levels of the judicial system. Indeed, there are formal criteria in some circuits (e.g., the Fifth and Sixth) that mandate publication in cases that exhibit horizontal (e.g., dissents) or vertical (reversal of the lower court) dissensus. Given this, we hypothesize the following:

H2: When a judge dissents or concurs, the case is more likely to result in a published opinion.
H3: When the decision reverses or vacates the decision of a lower court, the case is more likely to result in a published opinion.

The judge interviews also indicated that certain types of issues are less likely to be considered worthy of published opinions. Prominent among those issue types are cases that deal only with rather technical procedural rules. Additionally, several of the judges indicated that while some criminal issues raise new and important legal and political issues, many criminal appeals are "slam dunks" because criminal defendants, with nothing to lose following conviction in the trial court, and represented by appointed counsel (with the result that an appeal has no cost borne by the defendant), will appeal even when the issues raised by the appeal are frivolous. Thus, we hypothesize the following:

H4: Criminal decisions are less likely to be published than civil decisions.
H5: Panels are less likely to publish cases that raise procedural issues.

Finally, circuit characteristics may also be expected to influence the likelihood of a published opinion. As the number of judicial vacancies on a circuit increases, the corresponding workload of the remaining judges increases. As noted in chapter 2, one of the increasingly popular devices for handling workload pressures is to increase the use of unpublished opinions (because the judges interviewed indicated that it takes substantially less time to write an opinion designated as not for publication than it does to write one that will be published). Thus, as the number of vacancies increases, we would expect the number of published opinions in the circuit to decrease. Increasing docket size puts similar workload pressures on the judges. Thus, we also anticipate that as the size of the docket in a circuit increases, the number of published opinions will also decrease. Similarly, as we found in our earlier analysis, circuits with more judges are generally slower. Presumably, larger circuits will then compensate for the resulting inefficiencies by publishing fewer cases. Thus, we hypothesize the following:

H6: As the number of judge vacancies increases, the likelihood of publication decreases.
H7: As the workload of the circuit increases, the likelihood of publication decreases.
H8: Cases decided by circuits with more judges are less likely to be published than cases decided by circuits with fewer "less active" judges.

Research Design for a Model of Publication Decisions

We tested these expectations with an analysis of the Federal Court Cases: Integrated Database, created by the Federal Judicial Center (FJC). We included all cases terminated on the merits (for which we had no missing data) from 1977 to 2002. The dependent variable is binary, coded one if the opinion was published and zero if it was not published. Given the nature of the dependent variable, we estimated the model coefficients using logistic regression. To account for possible correlated errors within circuits, we included circuit-level fixed effects and robust standard error estimates.

Many of the independent variables included in the model—Dissent, Concur, and Criminal, as well as Circuit Judge Vacancies, Docket Size, and Circuit Active Judges—were incorporated into models discussed earlier in the chapter. Additionally, we included three case-level dummy variables: Oral (whether the case was orally argued), Reverse (whether the panel reversed the decision of the immediate lower court), and Procedural (whether the outcome of the case hinged on the court's application of a threshold doctrine, such as standing or mootness).

It should be noted that while the publication model includes nine independent variables, it is significantly more parsimonious than the other multivariate models discussed in this chapter. Unfortunately, the FJC's database does not include many of the variables found in the other analyses. As such, the model is subject to claims of underspecification. In response, we note the exploratory nature of the model.

The results of our analysis largely confirm the expectations derived from the circuit rules governing publication and the views of the judges

TABLE 12 Logistic regression of U.S. Courts of Appeals' publication decisions, 1977–2002

		DISCRETE CHANGES IN PREDICTED PROBABILITIES	
VARIABLE	B	CONTINUOUS INDEPENDENT VARIABLES	DUMMY INDEPENDENT VARIABLES
Oral	2.570*** (0.008)	—	0.31
Dissent	1.712*** (0.026)	—	0.15
Concur	1.456*** (0.028)	—	0.11
Reverse	1.353*** (0.008)	—	0.10
Procedural	−2.402*** (0.035)	—	−0.03
Criminal	0.013 (0.032)	—	0.00
Circuit Judge Vacancies	−0.007*** (0.000)	−0.01	—
Circuit Docket Size	−0.002*** (0.000)	−0.01	—
Circuit Active Judges	−0.073*** (0.002)	−0.10	—
Constant	−0.688		
N	627,812		
Nagelkerke R^2	0.516		

Notes: Robust standard errors in parentheses; circuit fixed effects not reported.
$*P < 0.05$, $**P < 0.01$, $***P < 0.001$.

as to what makes a case worthy of a published opinion. Cases that were granted oral argument were much more likely than those without oral argument to result in a published opinion. In fact, after setting all the covariates at the appropriate measure of central tendency, the probability of publishing an orally argued case is 0.31 higher than the probability of publishing a case decided based solely on the briefs (see the discrete changes presented in table 12 and discussed in the technical appendix). Put another way, those with oral argument were 780 percent more likely to have their opinions published than those without oral argument (see the technical appendix for a discussion of percent changes).

As expected, we also found that disagreement among the judges profoundly increased the likelihood that the opinion would be published. Cases with a dissent were more than 368 percent more likely to receive published opinions than cases in which all the judges at both levels were in agreement. Concurring opinions on the court of appeals or the decision of the panel to reverse the decision of the lower court also led to large increases in the likelihood of a published decision. Specifically, decisions with a concurrence were almost 278 percent more likely to have a published opinion than cases in which all three judges joined the opinion of the court, and reversals were 247 percent more likely than affirmances to result in publication.

Characteristics of the nature of the issue or the circuit had much smaller impacts on the likelihood of publication. Surprisingly, criminal cases were not less likely than noncriminal cases to result in a published opinion. While procedural decisions were less likely than others to receive a published decision, the magnitude of the difference was small. Circuit characteristics also exerted only small effects on the likelihood of a published opinion. As expected, published opinions were less likely in circuits with multiple vacancies or large docket sizes, but the magnitude of both effects was minute compared to the impact of dissensus among the judges or the prior decision to grant oral argument to the litigants.

Who Has the Last Word?

In the final section of this chapter, we explore two analogous questions: how frequently do the courts of appeals disturb the decisions of the courts below, and how frequently are their own decisions disturbed by subsequent review? We first examine how successful the appellants are in overturning the decision of the trial court and whether their success varies by issue or circuit.

For losing litigants in the federal district courts, an appeal as of statutory right exists. That is, each litigant is guaranteed the right to have an adverse district court decision reviewed by the courts of appeals.[6] One would expect as a result that there might be many litigants, especially criminal defendants, who have very weak grounds for appeal but, feeling they have little to lose, will appeal anyway. Such a phenomenon would presumably result in a low rate of success for appellants in the courts of appeals. But as we noted in chapters 1 and 2, the courts of appeals have devised a number of procedures to deal with the increasing workload of the circuit courts that have the practical effect of screening out many of these weak appeals from the group of cases that receive the full treatment of oral argument followed by a published opinion. Thus, we limited our examination of the success of appellants to those cases receiving the "full treatment." In such cases, the courts of appeals reverse the decision of the lower court in slightly less than one-third of their decisions (30.9 percent). That is, review by the courts of appeals is not pro forma. While the decision of the lower court is affirmed in most cases, appellants are successful in a substantial minority of their appeals.

The rate of reversal varies significantly across different type of issues. The decision below was disturbed most often in civil rights cases, which had a reversal rate of 42 percent. Criminal defendants, who frequently have little to lose from an appeal, had the lowest rates of success as appellants, succeeding in slightly less than one-fourth of their appeals. But overall, the variations across issues in the rates of reversal (vertical dissensus) are substantially less than the variations in the rates of dissent (horizontal dissensus).

The rate of reversal also varies substantially across circuits. In part, this difference may reflect variations in the mix of cases across circuits (e.g., a circuit with a large number of civil rights cases on its agenda might therefore have a higher rate of reversal than a circuit whose agenda is more heavily dominated by criminal appeals). Additionally, variations in the proportion of cases granted oral argument in different circuits might also influence the rate of reversal. One might expect that the smaller the percentage of cases granted oral argument, the higher the rate of reversal. There is some support for this conjecture. The two circuits with the highest rates of reversal, the Third and the Eleventh, both have very low rates of granting oral argument. In contrast, the Seventh Circuit and the Eighth Circuit, which have the lowest reversal rates, have relatively high rates of granting oral argument.

Finally, we note from figure 10 that beginning in the early 1970s, the overall annual rate of reversal appears to have increased substantially. While the cause for this increase remains somewhat unclear, the rising rates are consistent with the reasons proffered for the variation in the rates of reversal across circuits. That is, since the early 1970s the proportion of civil rights cases on the docket of the courts has increased while the proportion of appeals granted oral argument has tended to decline. In summary, the district courts still have the final word (in the sense that their decision is not disturbed on appeal) in the majority of cases, but the courts of appeals overturn their decisions in a nontrivial number of cases.

Turning to the frequency with which published decisions of the courts of appeals are overturned, previous studies of decision making

FIGURE 10. Rate of reversal on the U.S. Courts of Appeals, 1960–2002

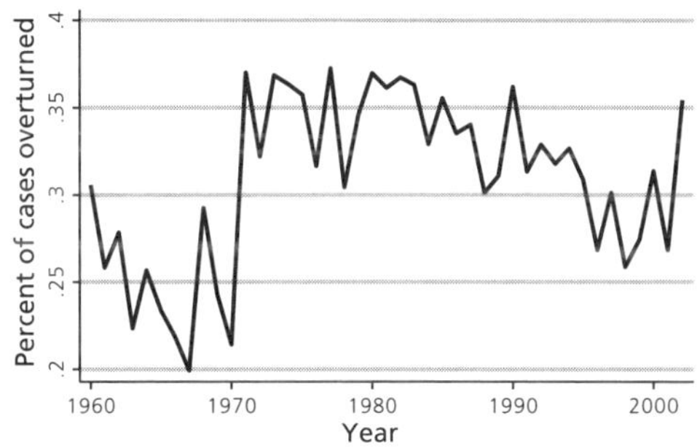

on the U.S. courts of appeals have made the point that in practice, the courts of appeals should be viewed as the court of last resort for most litigants (see Howard 1981; Songer, Sheehan, and Haire 2000). A quick look at the raw numbers of cases decided at different levels of the federal judiciary underscores the reality of this observation. In recent years the courts of appeals have disposed of roughly 60,000 cases per year. In contrast, in most years the Supreme Court hears and gives full treatment to fewer than sixty appeals from those decisions of the courts of appeals. Up to one hundred additional petitions from the courts of appeals may be disposed of by summary decisions of the Supreme Court. Consequently, the rate of review is less than three-tenths of 1 percent. In this context, a proclamation by litigants or their lawyers that they will "fight this all the way to the Supreme Court" is rarely more than bluster. Of course, as noted earlier, the courts of appeals have increasingly devised techniques for handling the large number of appeals that do not raise any legitimate issues of national importance. Such decisions (e.g., those made on procedural grounds or those disposed of without oral argument or without a published opinion) rarely result in controversy among the judges, and few if any are viable candidates for appeal. In this chapter the focus has been on the exceptional cases—those that raise substantial issues and as a result receive the full treatment of a merits decision by a panel of three judges, who issue a published opinion explaining their decision after full briefs, oral argument, and substantial negotiation and bargaining among the judges on the panel. Only around five thousand cases per year receive such full treatment.

We close this chapter by examining what happens to this small subset of the legally and politically important cases that receive the full treatment of the courts of appeals, resulting in the publication of a formal opinion. How frequently do the three-judge panels of the courts of appeals have the final word in these important cases?

To answer that question, we examined all the cases included in the last four years of the United States Courts of Appeals Database, 1997–2002 (Haire and Kuersten 2007). *Shepard's Citations* was used to trace all the subsequent appeals and revisions in this stratified random sample of 1,440 cases. Several mechanisms are available for the review of decisions of appeals court panels. First, the losing litigant in the court of appeals may petition the U.S. Supreme Court for review. While filing such a petition for certiorari (or "cert," for short) is a matter of right for all litigants, granting the writ (and thus agreeing to review the appeals court decision) is at the discretion of the Supreme Court. Alternatively, the losing litigant may petition the whole circuit for a review en banc of the panel's decision. Such a petition will result in an argument before all active (i.e., those not on senior status) judges in the circuit, but only if the petition is supported by a majority of the active appeals court judges in the circuit.[7] Alternatively, any one of the judges in the circuit may petition for a review en banc of the panel decision. This petition also requires a majority vote of the circuit to institute the review.

Most panel decisions, even those from the important cases receiving published opinions, are not challenged. Litigants filed cert petitions in only 25 percent (364) of the cases in our sample.[8] But success in challenges to panel decisions of the courts of appeals was rare. As can be seen from table 13, only fifteen of the 1,400 panel decisions were unambiguously reversed by the Supreme Court, and only seven were reversed by the circuit sitting en banc. Even when we add together all decisions partially overturned by either court or vacated by a summary decision of the Supreme Court, only forty panel decisions (2.8 percent of the 1,400 cases in the sample) were disturbed by subsequent review of the panel decision. Thus, the courts of appeals appear to have the final word for most litigants, even on the most substantial and controversial cases they decide.

As noted above, the judges from five circuits indicated that all panel decisions are circulated to all appeals court judges in the circuit before the opinions are officially released. The judges in these circuits were convinced that this process of vetting draft opinions in the whole circuit helped produce better opinions and reduced the need for en banc review. To test this idea, we reexamined the data in table 13, looking separately at what happened to cases from circuits employing this form of whole-circuit review and those that did not circulate panel decisions to the whole circuit. So while we understand that en banc review is highly

TABLE 13 Review of panel decisions of the U.S. Courts of Appeals, 1999–2002

	TOTAL CASES	PERCENT OF PANEL DECISIONS
PETITIONS FOR REVIEW BY THE U.S. SUPREME COURT		
Cert denied	328	22.8
Cert granted, affirmed*	7	0.5
Cert granted, reversed in part*	2	0.1
Cert granted, vacated or reversed*	15	1.0
GVR+	12	0.8
Total no. of cert petitions	364	25.3
Total no. of panel decisions	1,440	
REVIEW BY CIRCUIT EN BANC		
Panel affirmed	6	0.4
Reversed in part	5	0.3
Reversed or vacated	7	0.5
Total no. of panel decisions	1,440	

*After submission of briefs and oral argument.

+Grant, vacate, and remand: Cases in which cert was granted, the decision of the panel was vacated in light of a named case, and the case was remanded to the circuit in a summary decision of the Supreme Court.

unlikely in the first place, we decided to examine whether circulating panel opinions to all judges within a circuit reduces the number of rehearing en bancs for those circuits.

The results, presented in table 14, suggest that the practice of circulating panel opinions to all others in the circuit had no effect on the number of en banc hearings in the circuit. In all circuits, the number of cases reviewed en banc was small, but the difference in the proportion of cases reviewed in circuits using the practice of circulation in advance of publication and those not circulating panel decisions was insignificant. Similarly, the practice of circulation of panel opinions to the whole circuit had no impact on either the proportion of panel decisions that were disturbed by the circuit en banc (i.e., those reversed, vacated, or reversed in part) or that were disturbed by review by the Supreme Court. In both cases, differences between circuits with and without prior circulation were statistically not significant (calculations not shown). Thus, our analysis found no evidence in support of the belief of the judges in the five circuits using the practice of circulation of panel decisions that the practice either reduced the number of en banc rehearings or improved

TABLE 14 Effect of circulation prior to publication on review of panel decisions of the U.S. Courts of Appeals by the circuit en banc, 1999–2002

	EN BANC REVIEW		
OPINION CIRCULATED IN ADVANCE	NOT GRANTED	GRANTED (%)	TOTAL
No	831	9 (1.07)	840
Yes	590	9 (1.5)	599

$\chi^2 = 0.526$, $P = 0.468$, $\varphi = 0.019$.

the quality of the opinions. One possible explanation for this finding suggests that even in circuits that do not circulate their opinions prior to publication, some sort of informal monitoring still occurs prior to publication, either through requests to rehear the case by the same panel or by the panel make-up itself (i.e., the whistleblower effect).

Conclusion

In this chapter, we examined the various aspects of the opinion-writing process, perceived to be at the heart of the job of appeals court judges. It is the stage at which concerns about getting the law right and making good policy intersect. It is also the most time-consuming activity undertaken by judges on the courts of appeals. Given the importance of the process, we explored it from a variety of angles, some of which have rarely, if ever, been explored. Among other things, we examined the opinion-writing process, the time it takes to release published opinions, the length of the opinions, and the decision to publish them. Once again, based on our findings, the judges' behavior in these contexts appears to be a function of a variety of factors, including attitudes, judge backgrounds, institutional factors, and strategy.

For example, opinion writing is a task characterized by extensive interactions between the writing judge and the judge's clerks, and by extensive input from other judges and negotiating and bargaining among judges on the panel. The individual qualities of the judge initially assigned to write the opinion of the court matter, with the most highly qualified judges producing opinions more efficiently than their colleagues. But more important, the degree of conflict among the judges on the panels has a major impact on both the eventual length of the opinion and the time it takes to produce an opinion. Once the panel has reached agreement, however, the legal policy announced by the opinion is rarely disturbed either by the circuit sitting en banc or by Supreme Court review.

Both the interviews with the judges and the results of our statistical analyses indicate the importance of disagreement on the panel resulting in either concurrences or dissent. In the next chapter we follow up on these insights by exploring the causes of such dissensus, especially the extent to which attitudinal differences drive public disagreement on the courts of appeals. Then, in chapter 6, we extend the analysis of the extent to which the courts of appeals are the court of last resort in practice for most litigants by examining the extent to which this limited possibility of review of panel decisions influences the deliberation and the voting of the judges on the cases before them. That is, chapter 6 explores the degree to which the judges behave strategically, anticipating the possible reactions of other political actors to their decisions.

FOUR

Separate Opinion Writing on the Courts of Appeals

It has been said repeatedly within the legal culture that unanimity is to be preferred to dissent. This view of dissent was also expressed by the judges we interviewed and seems to fit what one Canadian scholar has called the "'American model,' where unanimity is desirable but not required and where judges can, at their discretion, either sign on to the reasons of a colleague or write their own" (McCormick 2003, 90). Unanimity is thought by many judges to enhance the legitimacy of the appellate courts. As an example, Goldman and Lamb (1986) have written that unanimity "reinforces the judicial myth that there is always an objective legal solution which is dictated by the law and principles of legal reasoning" (1). The public expression of dissent "may shake the public confidence in the judiciary by bringing into question the certainty of the law" (Wahlbeck, Spriggs, and Maltzman 1999, 491). Similarly, Judge Learned Hand of the Second Circuit said that a dissent "cancels the impact of monolithic solidarity on which the authority of a bench of judges so largely depends" (Hand 1958 72). Thus, avoiding dissent may help mobilize political or public support behind controversial court policy, making it easier to secure compliance with the court's decisions. Consensual decision making may help legitimate the decisions of courts because it helps promote the perception that the law is not political in nature but rather is uniformly and impartially applied (Hettinger, Lindquist, and Martinek 2006, 19).

The absence of dissent may also provide benefits to the legal system as a whole. Unanimous decisions help citizens and their lawyers better predict the outcome of future legal disputes and thus may lead more potential litigants to settle their disputes before trial. In other words, unanimous decisions promote consistency and predictability of court decisions and legal outcomes. Posner (1996) has argued that greater dissention within the Supreme Court not only reduces the efficiency of the Court but, more critically, reduces both the consistency and the long-run stability of decisions. Dissents, and especially decisions with "razor-thin majorities," reduce certainty about fundamental rules of the game for a wide variety of decision makers. Goff (2006) finds evidence at the macrolevel that supports these inferences that increased dissent reduces both the consistency and the stability of the Supreme Court's legal policy pronouncements.

On the other hand, whereas the judges we interviewed rarely described dissent as a desired outcome, other legal commentators have seen positive benefits from dissent. The expression of dissent can provide judges with the satisfaction derived from directly expressing their preferences. "To be able to write an opinion solely for oneself, without the need to accommodate, to any degree whatever . . . the views of one's colleagues . . . that is indeed an unparalleled pleasure" (Scalia 1994, 42). Dissents may also contribute to the independence of individual judges, "as it allows them to express their disagreement through a legitimate channel" (Hettinger, Lindquist, and Martinek 2006, 18). Similarly, dissent enhances the mental comfort of judges by reducing their "cognitive dissonance" (Peterson 1981, 428).

In addition to the important normative concerns raised by dissent on appellate courts, Goldman and Lamb (1986) suggest there are also important social scientific reasons to study patterns of consensus and dissent. They argue that since courts in the common law world exercise important political power, an examination of conflict on courts may tell us about the ways in which that power can be exercised. Moreover, patterns of dissent may enhance our knowledge of the individual attitudes and values of judges who are reluctant to openly discuss their political preferences (Goldman and Lamb 1986, 4–5).

Attitudinal Diversity as a Cause of Dissent

Empirical studies of decision making now provide extensive evidence that dissent on many appellate courts is strongly related to the divergent ideological preferences of the judges (Goldman 1975; Ostberg and Wetstein 2007; Ostberg et al. 2009; Peck 1969; Robertson 1998; Schubert 1965; Segal and Cover 1989; Segal and Spaeth 2002; Smyth 2005; Songer 2008; Tate 1981; Tate and Sittiwong 1989). In this "attitudinal model," the high degree of political independence enjoyed by the judges, combined (on the Supreme Court) with nearly complete docket control, means that a large number of cases present judges with difficult questions of law, giving them substantial discretion to decide the outcome in conformance with their personal political preferences. In such a general model of decision making, dissent is most frequently explained as the result of political or ideological conflict among the judges. Hettinger, Lindquist, and Martinek (2006) note that a review of the literature on dissensus in the United States leads to the conclusion that "our most robust finding is the effect of attitudes on horizontal dissensus" (111). As Goldman (1969) put it some decades earlier, "ideological differences are at the heart of dissensus" on the U.S. courts of appeals (218; see also Atkins 1973 for a similar view). Similarly, the two foremost scholars of decision making on state supreme courts contend that "dissent is the product of ideological disagreement among the justices" (Brace and Hall 1993, 918).

While ideological differences may be at the heart of dissent, the literature suggests that such differences are particularly likely to manifest on issues that are particularly important or salient. As Hettinger, Lindquist, and Martinek (2006) found on the courts of appeals, dissent is more likely "where the issue is of profound importance to the judge, society and/or the development of the law" (39). The reason for this finding is relatively straightforward: judges are much more likely to be willing to use their scarce resources of time and energy to produce separate opinions when a case is salient to them. Thus, indicators of case salience should be associated with higher rates of dissent. The appeals court judges interviewed by Howard (1981) reported that it was primarily constitutional issues that were most often important enough to justify taking the time to dissent (209). Furthermore, Songer (1986, 133) found statistical evidence in an analysis of appellate court voting from 1953 to 1975 that supports Howard's interview findings that salience matters in the decision to dissent.

Strategic Influence on Dissent

Like attitudinal explanations of appellate decision making, strategic models often posit that judges wish to achieve certain goals, such as developing policies that are consistent with the judges' policy preferences (e.g., Cross and Tiller 1998; McNollgast 1995; see also chapter 6 for a thorough discussion of the strategic model in appellate court decision making). However, while the attitudinal model assumes judges behave sincerely—that is, that their behavior is consistent with their preferences—the strategic model assumes judges will behave in the manner most likely to result in an outcome that is maximally consistent with the judge's preference (Baum 1997; Brenner and Whitmeyer 2009). Typically, this means factoring in the preferences of other actors and the institutional setting.

There is some evidence that appellate court judges strategically dissent. For example, Wahlbeck, Spriggs, and Maltzman (1999) found that judges with higher levels of past cooperation with the majority opinion writer (i.e., the rate at which the majority opinion author joined separate opinions authored by the judge) were less likely to dissent. According to Wahlbeck and his colleagues, this stems from a judge's strategic decision to reward or punish the majority opinion assigner, depending on the prior level of cooperation.[1]

In our context, a strategically minded judge could dissent to signal courts that have the authority to review the decisions. Since three-judge U.S. courts of appeals panel decisions are reviewable by the circuit en banc and by the U.S. Supreme Court, judges sitting on the panel could signal the circuit as a whole and the Court by filing a dissent. As Hettinger, Lindquist, and Martinek (2006) note, when the judge's preferred outcome is closer to the potentially reviewing court's preferences (i.e., closer to the preferences of the median judge) than the preferences that are likely to be incorporated into the panel decision, the strategic judge should cast a dissenting vote. Interestingly, Hettinger and her colleagues found no evidence of strategic dissents.

Institutional Influences on Dissent

The importance of institutional variation on judicial decision making is now widely recognized. Particularly in studies of state supreme courts in the United States, the impact of institutional rules relating to the degree of docket control possessed by appellate courts or the existence of an intermediate appellate court that can filter which appeals make it to the docket of the top court has a profound effect on the differences observed among the courts of different states. Many studies of state supreme courts report that the presence of an intermediate appellate court results in significantly higher levels of dissent (Atkins and Glick 1976; Beiser 1974; Brace and Hall 1990; Canon and Jaros 1970; Glick and Pruet 1986; Glick and Vines 1973; Handberg 1978). Similarly, strong empirical evidence from a variety of appellate courts in the United States supports the conclusion that increases in the degree of docket control exercised by the court are likely to result in higher rates of dissent (Atkins and Green 1976; Glick and Pruet 1986; Halpern and Vines 1977; Peterson 1981; Songer 1986).

An additional institutional characteristic that may substantially affect rates of dissent is the workload of the court. Workload may affect the dissent rate "because it is influential—if not determinative—of the time judges have to articulate disagreement with their peers" (Hettinger, Lindquist, and Martinek 2006, 40). Howard (1981) reported that the judges he interviewed on the courts of appeals cited heavy workloads as the main cause of the low dissent rate. Empirical confirmation of this suggested relationship has been reported by Kagan and colleagues (1978) and by Wold and Caldeira (1980) in studies of separate samples of state appellate court decisions. However, neither Songer (1986) nor Hettinger, Lindquist, and Martinek (2006) found any effect of the size of the court's workload on the rate of dissent in the U.S. courts of appeals.

Additionally, some scholars (e.g., Gerber and Park 1997) have suggested that informal norms influence dissensual behavior. Norms may develop within circuits such that some circuits become more consensual than others. Hettinger, Lindquist, and Martinek (2006) note that some institutional variations across circuits, such as the number of judges serving on the court, can affect the level of collegiality. Larger groups are generally less collegial (see Gerber and Park 1997). While Hettinger, Lindquist, and Martinek (2006) found evidence that intracircuit norms of consensus do indeed affect the decision to dissent, they found no evidence that circuit size plays a role.

Legal Factors Affecting Dissent

As both scholarly studies of the courts of appeals and interviews with the judges indicate, appellate courts remain courts of law as well as being political courts. Even early empirical work on the courts of appeals characterized them as ones whose decision making is subject to pushes and pulls from both the "legal subculture" and the "democratic subculture" (Richardson and Vines 1970). Thus, legally relevant factors such as the legal complexity of the case and the degree of ambiguity of the law are likely to affect the probability of dissent in a given case.

As a result, it should be expected that any easily identifiable factors that are likely to be highly correlated with the degree of ambiguity in a given case should be associated with higher rates of dissent. In studies of dissent, there is a consensus that reversal is one of the clearest indicators of ambiguity in the law. As Hettinger, Lindquist, and Martinek (2006) put it, "Arguably, reversal of the lower court reflects legal ambiguity because it represents a situation in which presumably reasonable federal judges, considering the same case, have come to different conclusions as to its appropriate resolution" (59). Similarly, Lamb (1986) argues that reversal may be interpreted as reflecting the presence of "meaningful choice points" at which the appropriate outcome is far from clear (183). Judge Newman (1992) of the Second Circuit went so far as to say that in his experience, the "overwhelming proportion of reversals" arose from disagreements among the judges "on a reasonably debatable point of law" (638). One might therefore hypothesize that reversals will be associated with substantially higher rates of dissent than are present in affirmances.

Another indicator of the presence of ambiguity in the law might be the degree of complexity of the issues. To the extent that a case is complex or the relevant rule of law is ambiguous, the opportunities for disagreement multiply; thus, "in complex cases, more opportunities exist for judges to part company as to the appropriate resolution and/or legal rationale" (Hettinger, Lindquist, and Martinek 2006, 59). Additionally, the relationship between complexity and increased dissent may reflect a simple statistical fact of life: where multiple issues are presented, judges have greater choice concerning both reasoning and case disposition, and thus, all other things being equal, the chances that there will be complete agreement go down.

In summary, past empirical studies of appellate courts suggest that dissent is a function of at least three kinds of considerations: (1) political factors, including attitudinal differences among the judges and the presence of politically salient issues; (2) institutional structures, including the court's workload; and (3) the legal characteristics of the issues, including the extent of ambiguity (especially as reflected in reversals of the lower court) and the complexity of the issues.

Judge Background Characteristics

Prior studies have also examined the effects of a variety of judge background characteristics on dissenting behavior. We group them into three categories: prestige, institutional status, and demographics (e.g., gender and race).

Presumably, prestigious judges have a greater incentive to write dissenting opinions because they are more likely to influence their peers. Indeed, appellate court judges are more likely to cite opinions written by prestigious fellow jurists (Landes, Lessig, and Solimine 1998).

Institutional status also varies across judges. Although most U.S. courts of appeals judges participating on three-judge panels are active appellate court judges from that circuit, as discussed in chapter 1, a significant proportion of the judges participating in such cases do so by designation. They are typically district court judges, active court of appeals judges from another circuit, or senior judges. District court judges are presumably less assertive as a result of their lower status when they sit by designation. Indeed, there is some evidence they are more likely to defer to sitting judges (Collins and Martinek 2011) and therefore are less likely to dissent (Brudley and Distlear 2001). Also, while the visiting judges (the first two categories) likely have their own workload pressures, senior judges have a lighter workload than active judges. Moreover, senior judges do not feel the same status-based pressure to conform. As such, they may dissent more than active court of appeals judges.

Chief judge status may also affect dissensual behavior. As the putative leaders of the circuits, they may value collegiality more than their fellow judges. Also, they are burdened with additional workload responsibilities (Hettinger, Lindquist, and Martinek 2003). As such, they may be less likely to write dissenting opinions.

Following a long line of research in a variety of contexts, the length of the circuit court judge's tenure could influence his decision to dissent. Specifically, like district court judges, less experienced judges may not feel that it is appropriate to challenge their more experienced peers. With respect to the U.S. courts of appeals, Hettinger, Lindquist, and Martinek (2006) found that freshman judges are less likely to write dissenting opinions.

Finally, to the extent that race and gender affect the viewpoints of judges (e.g., Peresie 2005), we might expect that women would tend to reach different outcomes than men and that members of racial groups would tend to reach different outcomes than members of other racial groups. Both women and ethnic minorities will on average have quite different socialization experiences than their white male colleagues, and these different experiences may lead them to perceive some issues differently from their colleagues who are in the majority. The organizational behavior literature suggests that such diverse groups are more conflictual than homogeneous groups (Pelled 1996), and the corollary of this observation is that female and minority judges are individually more likely to cast dissenting votes than their colleagues who share the cultural experiences common to the majority.

These two causal mechanisms suggest several relationships. First, when a judge is in the racial or gender minority on a panel, that judge is likely to prefer a different outcome than the majority, and is therefore more likely to dissent. Second, when the panel is diverse, judges are more likely to dissent. While no one has explored the latter, Hettinger,

Lindquist, and Martinek (2004) found mixed support for the former: women judges are no more or less likely to dissent than men, but racial minority judges are more likely to dissent than white judges.

Judges' Views on the Causes of Dissent

Listening to judges talk about their commitment to accommodating the views of their colleagues and their willingness to compromise, one might think that all the decisions of the court were unanimous. In fact, if only the decisions of the court with published opinions were examined, this guess would not be too far off the mark (and using the data analyzed in the publication model in chapter 3, we found that judges dissent in less than 0.5 percent of all unreported decisions).[2] Analyzing all the decisions in the United States Courts of Appeals Database, 1925–1996 (Songer 2002), for the years 1960–2002 shows that judges were divided on the final outcome in only 8.7 percent of their decisions. One or more judges wrote a separate concurring opinion in only 4.2 percent of cases. Combining the number of times any judge wrote separately (either to dissent or to concur with the majority on the outcome but not all the reasoning in the majority opinion), the majority opinion received unanimous support in 87.7 percent of all cases with a published opinion.

There was considerable variation in the rate of dissent across circuits. As can be seen in figure 11, for the entire forty-three-year period examined, the First Circuit had the lowest rate of dissent (4.1 percent), while three other circuits, the Third, Fourth, and District of Columbia Circuits, had dissent rates three times as high as those in the First Circuit.

FIGURE 11. Dissent rate by circuit, U.S. Courts of Appeals, 1960–2002

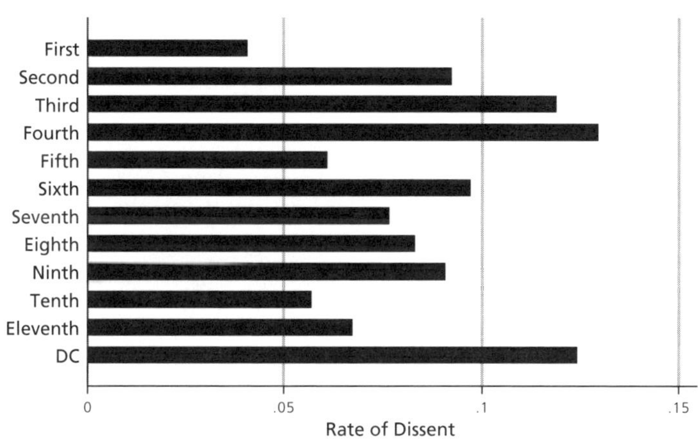

Further analysis indicated that the First Circuit had maintained its low rate of dissent across the entire time period examined and the District of Columbia Circuit had a relatively high rate of dissent for more than thirty years, which dropped off somewhat in the last decade. Other circuits have undergone substantial change. For instance the Fourth, Sixth, and Eighth Circuits have had substantially higher rates of dissent in recent years than they did in the 1960s.

Overall, the trends over time in both the rate of dissent and the proportion of cases having at least one concurring opinion have been upward, though as figure 12 indicates, there has been considerable fluctuation over time. The biggest increases in both dissents and concurrences in reported decisions occurred in the 1960s and early 1970s. Since the mid-1970s the annual rates of dissent have oscillated between 8 and 12 percent, while the rates of concurrence have oscillated between 4 and 6 percent.

After noting the empirical frequency, we turned to the interviews to discover the judges' views on the causes of the failure of panels to reach unanimity despite the existence of norms favoring efforts to accommodate judges with divergent views. It is somewhat more difficult to spell out the reasons for dissent because when asked about when or why they would dissent, many judges answered with fairly vague generalities. As noted in the judges' comments above on the process of bargaining and accommodation, many qualified their willingness to compromise or accept the changes proposed by their colleagues with language like "unless it was an important matter of principle." This sort of qualification was so common that it appears that a basic threshold for a dissent has to do with the saliency of the issue: most judges seemed to be saying that they would reserve their dissents for issues they thought were especially important or issues they cared most about. One aspect of this is whether the case raises

FIGURE 12. Rates of dissent, U.S. Courts of Appeals, 1960–2002

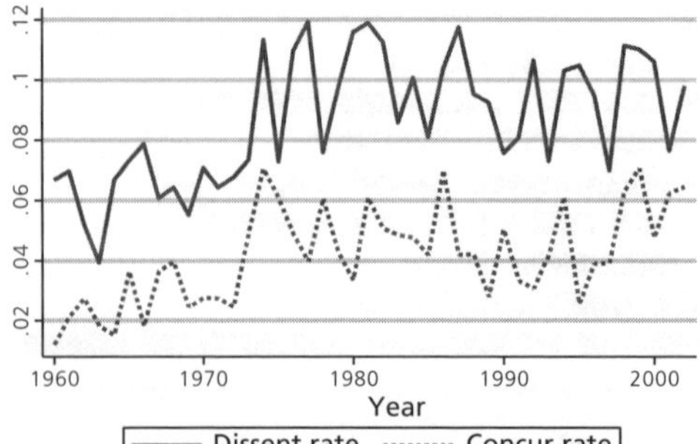

a significant legal issue that will be important in a number of other cases beyond the specific litigants in the current case. As Judge HH said, "If there is a significant issue of law that I disagree with the majority about, I always write a dissent. If it is a factually driven case that concludes on sufficiency of evidence, I usually don't dissent, even if I disagree with the majority. There really isn't much point in those circumstances." Other times it is simply the magnitude of the differences. As Judge F noted, "Of course, it depends on how great the differences are. . . . It is easier to compromise on the less important issues." Judge XX agreed: "If it is a case I feel strongly about as a gut matter, I will write a dissent. . . . But sometimes I go along with the majority even if I don't agree. I won't dissent in these cases because it is often on an insignificant issue." And Judge H expressed a similar perspective with a more colorful flair, saying, "I use a gag rule—if it doesn't make me gag, I'll go along with it. If I can live with a decision, I won't dissent."

As described above, a large number of empirical studies firmly establish that divergent political and ideological values among the judges are a principal cause of dissent. We expected the judges we interviewed to be reluctant to talk about the role of ideology in divisions of their court, and as it turned out, many were shy about using the actual words "ideology" or "political attitudes" when discussing the divisions on their court. Nonetheless, though some preferred phrases like "judicial philosophy," it was striking how many of the judges we interviewed both understood and were willing to admit that when their court divided, divergent political views were behind the splits. And we were struck by the fact that none of the judges denied that political views ever had an impact on decisions. Instead, the differences that emerged from our interviews related to how frequently political preferences determined judicial outcomes.

Our impression is that between one-third and one-half of the judges admitted that political preferences and ideology sometimes divided their court, but that such splits were relatively infrequent. Judge Q was typical of these judges, though more willing to quantify his impressions of how often political differences among the judges were decisive. He opined that fundamental differences in "judicial philosophy" were responsible for split decisions on the court in "perhaps 5 percent of their cases." While not willing to provide a numerical estimate, Judge OO seemed to agree with Judge Q, saying that although liberal versus conservative splits sometimes mattered, "most cases we hear invoke established precedent, so even if you have a panel that consists of differing judicial philosophies, we often all reach the same decision because the precedent is clear and established." Similarly, Judge P acknowledged that his court was "somewhat split between 'liberals' and 'conservatives,' but the courts of appeals really do not have much discretion in many cases." Thus, he thought the division did not make a significant difference "most" of the time.

Other judges were more forthright in acknowledging the impact of political values. Judge X provided a good illustration of the position of many of the judges. He said, "We all know we disagree on some issues, and those lead to dissents." Among those judges who were more willing to admit the ideological divisions on their court, there was still a strong sense that in many cases, precedent constrained the expression of those differences. For instance, Judge B said, "We sort of all know where the others stand—some just have different views about their conception of what justice is, and of course that comes into play when the law isn't too clear." But he hastened to add that he was only talking about those relatively few cases "where precedent isn't so clear." Judge R expressed a similar view in a slightly different way: "There will be some cases where the issues are so obviously ideological and there is an absence of clear precedent that the decision will of course follow ideological lines—but in our court those are a very small number." Similarly, Judge II recognized that the political composition of the panel was sometimes decisive. He noted that often, before conference, "I think about the make-up of the panel and how this will influence the opinion of the case. It can sometimes make a difference, not so much when precedent is clear, but when it is not: panel make-up counts for something." And many judges agreed with the way Judge T summed up the difference between the Supreme Court and the courts of appeals: "Political preferences certainly do not make as much difference on the court of appeals as on the Supreme Court. Most judges are conscientious about sticking to the clear demands of the law. But of course, political preferences do affect the outcome in the cases in which the law is unclear. I think we all recognize that."

Few of the judges offered more analytical perspectives on the institutional or contextual factors that led to or increased the incidence of dissent. But those few who did largely echoed the conclusions of the previous empirical studies discussed above. Judge H highlighted the heavy workload of the courts of appeals as a major suppressor of dissent. He said, "Time also limits dissent—it takes a tremendous amount of time to write a dissent, and since dissents don't change the law, given how heavy your workload is it often isn't worth the time." Judge V cited the impact of the increasing number of judges sitting by designation. As he noted, such judges "are often reluctant to dissent—they sometimes see themselves as an 'outsider,' and thus don't think it is their place to dissent." And finally, several judges indicated that dissent was often tied to reversals—judges felt freer to dissent when they were siding with the judge below, and thus not having to appear as a lone voice. Judge O asked rhetorically, "Why do we all agree? Well, I would have to speculate that it is because the lower courts are doing a good job." Judge TT elaborated that one reason why there is often a low dissent rate is because the district court judges seem to know what they are doing. "It's an index of competence of the trial courts, and when there is [a] lot of agreement at the appellate courts it is often an indication that things are going okay in the district courts—this of course when we affirm a lower court ruling. Which we tend to do often."

In summary, there was a high rate of agreement among the judges we interviewed that decision making on their panels was usually characterized by high degrees of collegiality. This led most opinion writers to actively attempt to accommodate the views of their colleagues on their panels. The high rate of unanimity suggests that these efforts were successful; dissent in panel decisions is rare. Nevertheless, those instances in which panels are publically divided often contain many of the politically most important issues decided by the courts. The judges suggested that when they are divided, it is often the result of substantial differences among the judges in ideology or political preferences on highly salient issues. In the next section, we test this perception of the judges with an empirical analysis of the covariates of dissent on the courts of appeals.[3]

Hypotheses

Considering the views of the judges themselves on the causes of dissent in conjunction with the suggestions on the nature of dissent in previous studies of appellate courts described at the beginning of this chapter, we identified twenty-one specific hypotheses to test with recent empirical data on decisions by the courts of appeals. As noted earlier, most theories about dissent locate the cause of dissent in one of five main categories: attitudinal differences on the panel, strategic concerns of the judges, legal constraints, institutional characteristics of the circuits, and the effects of diversity in the backgrounds of the judges on the panel. We group our specific hypotheses into these five main categories.

ATTITUDINAL HYPOTHESES

H1: The greater the ideological distance of the judge from the panel median, the more likely the judge is to dissent.

H2: The higher the level of case salience, the more likely the judge is to dissent.

STRATEGIC HYPOTHESES

H3: Judges who are more ideologically proximate to the circuit median than to the panel median are more likely to dissent.
H4: Judges who are more ideologically proximate to the Supreme Court median than to the panel median are more likely to dissent.

INSTITUTIONAL HYPOTHESES

H5: Judges with higher opinion caseloads are less likely to dissent.
H6: Judges serving on circuits with higher caseloads are less likely to dissent.
H7: Judges serving on circuits with more judicial vacancies are less likely to dissent.
H8: Judges serving on circuits with more active judges are more likely to dissent.
H9: Judges deciding cases on circuits with higher rates of dissent in the past year are more likely to dissent in the case.

LEGAL HYPOTHESES

H10: Judges are more likely to dissent as case complexity increases.
H11: Judges are more likely to dissent in reversals than in affirmances.
H12: Judges are less likely to dissent in criminal than in civil cases.
H13: Judges are more likely to dissent in cases in which the lower court decision was published.

JUDGE BACKGROUND HYPOTHESES

H14: Graduates of prestige law schools are more likely to dissent than graduates of less prestigious law schools.
H15: Judges who have received the highest available ABA rating are more likely to dissent than judges who have not received the highest rating.
H16: Chief judges are less likely to dissent than non-chief judges.
H17: The longer the judge's tenure, the more likely the judge is to dissent.
H18: District court judges sitting by designation are less likely to dissent than active appellate court judges from that circuit.
H19: Senior judges are more likely to dissent than active appellate court judges from that circuit.
H20: Female judges are more likely to cast dissenting votes than male judges.

H21: Female judges are less likely to dissent than male judges when they are sitting on a panel with at least one other female judge.

H20: African American judges are more likely to cast dissenting votes than white judges. (*Note:* We chose not to examine other racial minority groups because of the scarcity of judges from other minority groups, which we discussed in chapter 1.)

H21: African American judges are less likely to dissent than white judges when they are sitting on a panel with at least one other African American judge.

Dissent: An Empirical Analysis

We close with a more systematic examination of the causes of dissent that sheds light on the different rates of dissensus in the various circuits. The analysis shows how the extent of diversity on a given circuit, in terms of both judge characteristics such as gender and race and the political background of the judges, is the primary contributor to the rates of dissensus.

DATA AND METHODS

Once again, we utilized the Songer (2002) United States Courts of Appeals Database. As we noted in chapter 1, very few women or racial minorities served on the U.S. courts of appeals until 1979. Since we are in part interested in observing the effects of race and gender, we limited our estimation sample to those three-judge panel cases decided between 1979 and 2002. Once again, the unit of analysis was the judge's participation in the case. The dependent variable, Dissent, was coded one if the judge cast a dissenting vote, zero if he or she did not. Since Dissent is a binary variable, we estimated the model coefficients using logistic regression.

VARIABLES

We measured two attitudinal measures. The first, Ideological Distance from Panel Median, conceptually reflects the ideological distance of the judge from the median panelist: the greater the distance, the higher is the probability of dissent. (The measurement definition of ideology used to construct the Distance from Median, and the variable itself, are discussed in detail in chapters 1 and 2, respectively. Also, as previously noted, based on the attitudinal model, dissents are more likely to occur in salient cases.) The Salience variable operational definition is discussed in chapter 2. (See the technical appendix for details on these variables and those followed by an asterisk below.)

We also generated two strategy measures: Signal En Banc Review* and Signal SCOTUS Review*. The former reflects the degree to which a judge would prefer to have the panel's decision overturned by the circuit sitting en banc. In other words, the preferences of the circuit as a whole are closer to the preferences of the judge than to the preferences of the panel, such that en banc review is more likely to reflect an outcome that is closest to the judge's ideal preference.

Since three-judge panel decisions are also reviewable by the U.S. Supreme Court (or SCOTUS), we also constructed the Signal SCOTUS Review* variable to account for the possible tendency to signal the High Court.

We included a variety of measures that should reflect workload to some degree, including the caseload pressures of the individual judge—Judge Opinion Caseload—and the circuit—Circuit Docket Size. The former variable, described in greater detail in the first two chapters, reflects the number of majority opinions assigned to the judge in the previous two months relative to the number assigned to other judges on the circuit. The latter variable, Circuit Docket Size (see chapter 1), measures the number of cases per active judge decided by the circuit during that year. We also included an indirect measure of circuit workload pressure, Circuit Judge Vacancies (see chapter 1). Binder and Maltzman (2009) posited, and found, that vacant judgeships both create workload pressure and lead to increasing levels of dissent.

We included two measures of circuit norms. The first, Circuit Active Judges (see chapter 1), is the number of active judges on the circuit during the year. As previously discussed, smaller groups are more likely to develop consensual norms, while larger groups are more likely to develop norms of conflict. Additionally, borrowing from Hettinger, Lindquist, and Martinek (2006), we incorporated Circuit Opinion Rate, or the proportion of cases in the circuit during that year in which a judge cast a dissenting vote. This variable reflects the overall culture of consensus (or dissensus) within the circuit.

We included four variables that at least in part reflect legal factors. Complex cases, as well as those that are legally ambiguous, are expected to lead to more dissent. The first variable, Complexity*, is an index. Larger values of the index indicate greater complexity. Also, following Hettinger, Lindquist, and Martinek (2003), we included a measure of legal ambiguity, Reverse (a dichotomous variable, coded one if the court voted to reverse the lower court/administrative agency decision). Additionally, we included two proxy variables that reflect complexity and salience to some degree: Criminal (a binary variable, coded one if it was a criminal case) and Prior Publication (a binary variable, coded one if the lower court decision reviewed by the panel was published).

As previously discussed, we posited that prestigious judges are more likely to cast dissenting votes. Judge Law School Prestige (coded one if the judge graduated from an elite law school; see chapter 2 and the technical appendix) and Judge ABA Extremely Well Qualified (coded one if the judge received the highest possible rating from the ABA) tap into aspects of prestige.

We also included five different measures of institutional status: Judge Tenure (the total number of years served as an active judge prior to the decision) and three dichotomous variables indicating the official role of the judge if he or she was not an active judge sitting on the circuit that decided the case (District Court Judge, Senior Judge, and Visiting Active Appeals Judge). The Chief Judge variable (coded one if the judge was the chief judge of the circuit during the year the case was decided) is introduced because the chief judge has added administrative duties, which create workload pressures (Hettinger, Lindquist, and Martinek 2003).

Finally, we estimated the effects of race and gender. The two judge-level variables (Judge Gender, Judge Race) were coded one if the judge was a member of the minority group (female, African American) and zero if the judge was a member of the majority group (male, white). (Of course, while women are not a minority in the general population, as we noted in chapter 1, they are a minority in this context.) The two panel-level variables, Panel Gender and Panel Race, were coded one if at least one of the co-panelists serving with the judge on the case was a member of the respective minority group (female, African American) and zero if none of the co-panelists was a member of that minority group. Additionally, to account for the possible interactions between panel- and judge-level race and gender, we included two multiplicative terms: Judge Gender × Panel Gender and Judge Race × Panel Race.

ANALYSIS AND DISCUSSION

The logistic regression results are presented in table 15. Overall, we found strong support for attitudinal and legal theories of the causes of dissent, but no support for the strategic perspective. Institutional hypotheses and hypotheses based on judge characteristics received mixed support. As expected, the Ideological Distance from Panel Median coefficient is strongly positive and statistically significant. In other words, the more ideologically dissimilar the judge is from the median judge on

TABLE 15 Logistic regression model of judge casting a dissenting vote, U.S. Courts of Appeals, 1979–2002

HYPOTHESES	INDEPENDENT VARIABLE	COEFFICIENT	STANDARD ERRORS	PERCENTAGE CHANGE
Attitudinal	Ideological Distance from Panel Median	1.080***	0.275	72
	Salience	0.194***	0.038	43
Strategic	Signal En Banc Review	−0.048	0.339	
	Signal SCOTUS Review	0.087	0.250	
Institutional	Judge Opinion Caseload	0.514	0.891	
	Circuit Docket Size	0.124	0.176	
	Circuit Judge Vacancies	0.003	0.003	
	Circuit Active Judges	−0.004	0.010	
	Circuit Opinion Rate	9.178***	0.569	233
Legal	Complexity	0.154***	0.045	34
	Reverse	0.195*	0.095	21
	Criminal	0.221+	0.107	24
	Prior Publication	0.182*	0.103	19
Judge background	Judge Law School Prestige	0.174*	0.100	19
	Judge ABA Extremely Well Qualified	−0.175	0.137	
	Chief Judge	−0.423*	0.209	−34
	Judge Tenure	0.015*	0.009	24
	District Court Judge	−0.203	0.208	
	Senior Judge	−0.035	0.186	
	Visiting Active Appeals Judge	−0.519	0.416	
	Judge Gender	0.297*	0.167	
	Panel Gender	−0.039	0.136	
	Judge Gender × Panel Gender	−0.919*	0.547	−46#
	Judge Race	−0.094	0.219	
	Panel Race	0.115	0.139	

(continued)

TABLE 15 *(continued)*

HYPOTHESES	INDEPENDENT VARIABLE	COEFFICIENT	STANDARD ERRORS	PERCENTAGE CHANGE
	Judge Race × Panel Race	0.165	0.620	
	Constant	−10.499		
	N	16,778		
	McKelvey and Zavoina's pseudo-R^2	0.159		

Note: Robust standard errors clustered by case.
One-tailed hypothesis tests: *$P < 0.05$, **$P < 0.01$, ***$P < 0.001$. ⁺$P < 0.05$ but the coefficient sign is opposite that hypothesized. Percentage change reported as discrete changes.
#This is not the percent change for the multiplicative variable, which is of little interpretational utility. Instead, this is the percent change for Judge Gender when the moderator, Panel Gender, is set to zero.

the panel, the more likely the judge will dissent. There is also a greater likelihood a judge will dissent as Salience increases. Both findings are consistent with the attitudinal theories of dissent and with the views expressed by the judges in our interviews.

We found strong evidence that case complexity and legal ambiguity affect the decision to cast a dissent. As expected, judges were significantly more likely to dissent in cases that reversed the lower court, when the lower court decision was published, and as case complexity increased. Only the Criminal variable did not conform to our theory. While we had anticipated that judges would dissent less in criminal cases, which are often less complex than civil cases, we actually found evidence to support the opposite contention: judges are significantly more likely to dissent in criminal cases.

We found weak evidence that institutional factors influence dissents. Our direct measures of workload pressures (Judge Opinion Caseload, Circuit Docket Size), as well as one of our indirect measures (Circuit Judge Vacancies), were not statistically significant. Similarly, one measure of dissensual norms, Circuit Opinion Rate, was statistically significant and positive (as anticipated), while the other measure, Circuit Active Judges, was neither statistically significant nor in the posited direction.

We also found mixed support for our judge characteristic hypotheses. We expected to find that judges who had graduated from a prestigious law school and had received the highest ABA rating would be more likely to dissent. We found evidence supporting the former hypothesis but not the latter. We also found limited evidence supporting our judge status hypotheses. While chief judges are less likely to dissent and judges with more tenure are more likely to dissent, designated judge status had no effect on dissensual behavior.

Similarly, we found mixed evidence that minority status influences the decision to dissent. While judge and panel race apparently have no effect on dissenting votes, gender does. The coefficient for Judge Gender is statistically significant and positive. In other words, when the moderator variable, Panel Gender, is set to zero (the judge is not sitting with a woman co-panelist), a woman judge is more likely to dissent than her male counterpart. This is consistent with one of the key theories about women and politics (though one that has not received much support in this context): women and men often have different policy preferences, and are therefore more likely to disagree about outcomes.

It also appears that the effects of judge gender are moderated by panel gender. The coefficient for the multiplicative term, Judge Gender × Panel Gender, is negative and significant, as posited. In other words, the tendency for women to dissent is much lower when the woman judge is joined by another woman on the panel.

To get a better sense of the nature of the interaction, as well as of the substantive effects of the statistically significant variables, we generated discrete changes in predicted probabilities (the difference in the probability of a dissent when the specific independent variable is set to two interesting values while the covariates are held constant at the appropriate measure of central tendency; see the technical appendix for the specific values of the discrete changes and for additional descriptions of the methodology used in this process). Overall, the discrete changes are very low. Some are less than 0.01 in magnitude, and the largest, for Circuit Opinion Rate, is only 0.03. At first glance, this suggests that our variables have little substantive effect on the decision to cast a dissenting vote in U.S. courts of appeals cases. However, given the generally low baseline probability of causing dissent (approximately 0.02 when all independent variables are held to the appropriate measure of central tendency), combined with the nature of logistic regression models, the discrete changes are very conservative measures of predicted probabilities (see King and Zeng 2001).[4] As such, we also present the percent changes in predicted probabilities resulting from the discrete changes in the final column of table 15 (see the technical appendix for an interpretation of percent changes).

The percent changes for Judge Gender are presented when Panel Gender is equal to zero and one. When there are no other women co-panelists, a female judge is 33 percent more likely to dissent than a male judge sitting on a three-judge panel with two other men. Conversely, when a woman judge is sitting on a panel with at least one other woman judge, she is 46 percent less likely to dissent than a similarly situated male judge. In other words, when a woman judge is in the gender minority, she is more likely to disagree with the male majority; when she is in the gender majority, she is more likely to join that majority than a male judge sitting with at least one woman co-panelist. This suggests a particular causal mechanism: that, to some degree, male and female judges do indeed have different views on judicial outcomes.

The percent changes also give us an insight into the substantive effects of the remaining statistically significant variables. Among the continuous variables, Circuit Opinion Rate has the most dramatic effect on the probability of a judge dissenting in a case. A judge sitting on a circuit with a dissent rate one standard deviation above the mean has a 233 percent higher likelihood of dissent than a judge sitting on a circuit with a dissent rate one standard deviation below the mean. This implies that circuit institutional factors (beyond those we directly measured), such as norms and formal rules, play a significant role in the decision to dissent. Similarly, the percent changes suggest attitudes play a prominent role, as Ideological Distance Distance from Panel Median and Salience have two of the four highest values. Judges whose attitudes are one standard deviation more or less liberal than the ideology of the median judge on the panel are 72 percent more likely to dissent than their more moderate colleagues, and increasing salience leads to a 43 percent increase in the likelihood of dissent by a given judge even after controlling for the ideology and gender of the judge and other statistically significant variables.

Conclusion

An important finding that emerged from our analysis of dissenting behavior on the courts of appeals is that when one considers all cases disposed of by the courts (instead of limiting the analysis to just those cases that survive the various screening practices described in the first two chapters), dissent is rare. Less than one half of 1 percent of all appeals court cases result in public disagreement among the judges. This finding provides an important corrective to most of the existing studies of appeals court behavior, which typically report much higher rates of dissent with little acknowledgment that their analyses are based on a sample of cases (those with published decisions) that are highly unrepresentative of the universe of cases decided by the courts of appeals.

An important consequence of this corrective about the frequency of dissent is that it resolves what otherwise appears to be an anomaly in the results. Many previous studies have argued that attitudinal or ideological disagreement among the judges is a principal correlate of dissent on appellate courts and that up to 10 percent of appeals court decisions are characterized by dissensus. From these results, the apparent conclusion is that the judges split along ideological lines in one out of every ten of their cases. However, the judges we interviewed argued that almost all the differences in political preferences among the judges failed to manifest themselves in public dissent. Politically based dissent was rare, the judges maintained, because initial differences in political perspective gave way to a common understanding of what the law required in a given case or were resolved through persuasion, negotiation, or compromise. The finding of our statistical analysis, that the attitudinal distance of a judge from the court median is strongly associated with the likelihood of dissent, appears at first glance to support the conclusions of previous empirical analyses and to refute the claims of the judges. But when one realizes that less than 1 percent of all appeals court cases result in dissent from any cause, the statistical analyses are more properly seen as providing strong support for the position advanced by the judges. Our measures of judge ideology suggest that there are substantial differences in the political preferences of the judges on many appeals court panels. Nonetheless, those panels end up with a unanimous disposition almost all of the time. This corresponds very nicely with what the judges said in our interviews. Most of the judges were aware that some of their colleagues had quite divergent personal preferences and acknowledged that when the court did issue a divided decision, the divisions often fell along predictable differences in approaches to the law that, they understood, social scientists would label "political" differences. Yet the judges stressed that in a very large majority of their cases, judges with quite different political or jurisprudential preferences ended up in agreement on how the case should be decided. In sum, both the judges themselves and our empirical analysis of their actual behavior agree that dissent of any kind is a rare event, but when it does occur, the divisions on the panel often reflect the underlying division in political preferences.

Our empirical analysis also reinforced the position articulated in virtually every judge interview, that clear law was a major influence on the behavior of the judges. The judges emphasized that in most cases the judges on a given panel were able to agree on a common understanding of what the relevant law required in the context of the given facts of the case and that this common understanding led to a unanimous decision. The judges further maintained that judicial political preferences became important, and thus the likelihood of a divided decision became high, only when there was some ambiguity or lack of clarity in the law. Our statistical analysis of dissent provided strong confirmation of this position articulated in the interviews. Three measures that one might reasonably conclude captured to some degree the extent of ambiguity in the law were strongly associated with an increased likelihood of dissent.

Strategic approaches have become increasingly popular in recent years among social scientists studying the behavior of judges on appellate courts around the world (see chapter 6 for a further discussion of the strategic approach). But in our interviews and in other reported interviews, judges on the courts of appeals almost unanimously rejected the validity of these strategic interpretations. Our statistical analyses of dissent in cases with published opinions strongly support the position voiced by the judges. We found no evidence that strategic concerns motivated dissent.

The results of the analysis of the impact of institutional characteristics were mixed. Perhaps the most interesting finding was that there do appear to be differences in circuit-based cultural norms regarding the importance of collegiality and accommodation. Even after controlling for legal factors, ideological differences, and key judge personal characteristics (e.g., gender and race), the previous history of the overall frequency of dissent in a given circuit is strongly related to the likelihood that a given judge will dissent in a given case. But contrary to the expectations derived from previous studies, neither individual nor circuit workloads, nor judicial vacancies on a circuit, nor the size of a circuit have any measurable impact on the likelihood of dissent.

Likewise, there were mixed results as to the significance of the personal characteristics of the judges. The status of a judge on a given panel (e.g., whether a "regular" circuit judge rather than a senior judge or a visiting judge) was not related to the propensity to dissent. On the other hand, there was some evidence that the more prestigious or qualified judges dissented more frequently than their colleagues. And women judges, especially when on panels with two male colleagues, were more likely than their male colleagues to dissent. In contrast, racial diversity did not appear to be related to dissent.

Overall, the qualitative and quantitative evidence supports our integrated model of the behavior of judges on the U.S. Courts of Appeals.

Consensual norms appear to dampen public manifestations of disagreement. Moreover, to the extent that dissenting votes are cast, it is often a function of legal, attitudinal, and judge background factors. In the next chapter, we further focus on these three factors, though our attention shifts to more directly consider what influences the direction or nature of the outcomes supported by either united or divided panels. That is, in chapter 5 we no longer ask what causes a judge to disagree with whatever outcome is supported by his or her colleagues and instead turn our attention to what leads judges to support a liberal rather than a conservative outcome in the case before them.

FIVE

Explaining Attitudinal and Legal Influences on Decisions

Since at least the Clinton administration, there has been steadily increasing conflict in the U.S. Senate over the confirmation of nominations for service on the courts of appeals (Binder and Maltzman 2009). With the increasing polarization of politics in the United States, the courts, including the intermediate appellate courts, have increasingly been seen by partisans in Congress as important players in the game of national politics. The core belief among politicians behind the growing controversy is that the political values of judges are strongly related to the way they decide cases and thus influence national policy. Judicial scholars agree. For the past ninety years, they have argued that attitudes play a significant role in how judges make decisions at all levels of the federal judiciary, including the courts of appeals.

Attitudinal Influences

To this point in the book, we have suggested that many factors influence the behavior of judges throughout the decision-making process, including political ideology. Students of judicial behavior regularly credit Pritchett (1948) for noticing dependable patterns of judicial attitudes in Supreme Court voting behavior. Since Pritchett's classic work, several studies have empirically linked political ideology to the decision making of Supreme Court justices (Rohde and Spaeth 1976; Segal and Spaeth 1993, 2002; Tate 1981; Ulmer 1973). This view, in recent times labeled the "attitudinal model," holds that justices possess policy preferences and "want the outcomes [of their legal decisions] to approximate as nearly as possible to those policy preferences" (Rohde and Spaeth 1976, 72).

Notwithstanding the overwhelming research focus on the Supreme Court, scholars have also examined the influence of attitudes on lower court decision making. Although the disincentives to promoting one's policy preferences at the Supreme Court level are few, the same may not be true for lower circuit court judges. As Hettinger, Lindquist, and Martinek (2006) succinctly explain, "At the U.S. Courts of Appeals—unlike the Supreme Court—circuit judges are faced with mandatory dockets, and their decisions are subject to review by a higher court," thus decreasing the opportunities for lower court judges to vote attitudinally (32). However, despite the institutional differences, the overall consensus, dating back to Goldman (1966, 1975) and Richardson and Vines (1970), is that appeals court judges are jointly influenced by both legal constraints and their own attitudes. For example, using party ideology as a proxy for judge preferences, scholars analyzing voting behavior on both district courts and courts of appeals have found that judges appointed by Democratic presidents make more liberal decisions than judges appointed by Republican presidents (the converse is also true) (Carp and Rowland 1983; Cross 2007; Goldman 1975; Pinello 1999; Songer 1982; Songer and Haire 1992; Stidham and Carp 1982; Zorn and Bowie 2010).

While there is a strong basis supporting the influences of ideology, scholars have also found that precedent influences lower court decision making too. Baum (1994) argues that since lower federal appeals court judges do not have docket control, they overwhelming tend to hear cases where there is only one decision that is correct under the law (see also Sunstein et al. 2006). For example, numerous studies analyzing various issue areas such as economic policy (Stidham and Carp 1982), patents (Baum 1980), labor and antitrust (Songer 1987), obscenity (Songer and Haire 1992), search and seizure (Songer, Segal, and Cameron 1994), employment discrimination (Songer, Davis, and Haire 1994), and review of administrative agency decisions (Humphries and Songer 1999) have all consistently shown that law and precedent, coupled with policy preferences, influence appeals court decisions. In fact, over the past forty years, the mainstream view has been that circuit judges' decisions are based on a combination of legal and attitudinal considerations (Cross 2007; Hettinger, Lindquist, and Martinek 2006; Howard 1981; Klein 2002; Richardson and Vines 1970; Songer, Sheehan, and Haire 2000). As Songer, Ginn and Sarver (2000) aptly conclude, "Thus, there seems to be a consensus that in the lower federal courts, at least some judicial decisions are influenced by the policy preferences of the judges, but that the exercise of discretion to advance one's policy preferences is constrained by statute, precedent, and other manifestations in the law" (138).

Building on these earlier studies on voting behavior in the federal courts, Zorn and Bowie (2010) in their research, which incorporates all levels of the judicial hierarchy, argue that policy preferences will become more pronounced as one moves up the federal judicial hierarchy because of various institutional constraints and judicial goals. They point out that prior studies largely centered on only one level of the judiciary rather than examining ideological influences at each level simultaneously. Utilizing Baum's (1997) pyramid metaphor, Zorn and Bowie put forth the hierarchy postulate, which simply states, "The influences of judges' policy preferences on their decision making increases as one moves higher up the judicial hierarchy" (Zorn and Bowie 2010, 1214). For example, they argue that district court judges would possess the widest range of goals while Supreme Court Justices would possess the narrowest, and appeals court judges would fall somewhere in between (Baum 1997; Zorn and Bowie 2010). Zorn and Bowie (2010) analyzed cases decided at each level of the federal judicial hierarchy, which allowed them to examine whether the influence of judges' policy preferences increased as one moved up the judicial hierarchy while controlling for case-specific factors. They found broad support that the policy preferences of judges exert a larger influence at higher levels of the judicial hierarchy.

In addition to recognizing institutional constraints, more recent research has tried to explain when a judge's policy preferences might play a greater role in the decision-making process. To untangle this question, scholars have suggested that it is important to distinguish between "easy" cases, where the law—precedent, statutes, and the Constitution—is clear and presumably ideological influences will play a lesser role, and "hard" cases, where the relevant legally provisions are ambiguous, not as obvious, or nonexistent, thus allowing more discretion in the interpretation of the law (Atkins and Green 1976; Cross 2007; Howard 1981; Klein 2002; Songer 1982). While many have conceptualized the idea of legal clarity, it is much more difficult to devise a measure of it. Therefore, few scholars have been able to test the theory that judges are more ideological in hard cases. That said, Randazzo, Waterman, and Fine (2006) developed a measure that is similar to legal clarity: statutory constraint. They suggest that legal clarity in statutory cases is a function of the length of the statute. Longer statutes are presumably clearer, while shorter statutes are more ambiguous. Consistent with the larger theory, Randazzo and his co-authors (2006) found evidence, at least in some limited contexts (e.g., Democratic appointees in criminal cases, Republican appointees in discrimination cases) that appeals court judges are indeed less ideological when they interpret longer statutes.

To understand these case differences, judicial scholars have looked at ideological influences in non-unanimous opinions. For example, Hettinger, Lindquist, and Martinek (2006, 133) found that as the ideological distance between a judge and the panel majority gets larger the likelihood of writing a dissent increases. They argue that their findings support the attitudinal view of decision making rather than the strategic model in the courts of appeals (see chapter six for more on strategic decision making).

In a similar vein, Sunstein and colleagues (2006) looked at judicial decision making with a view to understanding the extent to which the ideology and political values of the judges shape court outcomes and judicial votes. While their findings reinforce the earlier reports of partisan differences on the courts, the authors' more important contribution is the finding that panel composition matters. For example, unified Republican panels (three judges appointed by Republican presidents) produce liberal votes in 36 percent of their cases, while panels made up of three judges appointed by Democratic presidents vote liberally 62 percent of the time. The authors also found that mixed panels can dampen the ideological voting effects, such as when there are two Democrats and one Republican judge or two Republicans and one Democrat (Sunstein et al. 2006; see also Kastellac 2010; Revesz 1997). More recently Kastellac (2011), in an analysis of panel effects, found that over the past twenty years there has been a growing polarization within three-judge panels (387). As noted below in the description of our interview data, much of the work by Sunstein and colleagues (2006) and Kastellac (2010, 2011) is consistent with findings from our judge interviews.

Finally, ideological differences among judges can also develop in response to differences in socialization related to race and gender, and these judge-based differences may potentially affect judicial decision making. Scholars have examined whether gender or race can influence three-judge panel decisions, such as a nonwhite judge on a panel with two white judges (Cameron and Cummings 2003) or a female judge on a panel with two male judges (Boyd, Epstein, and Martin 2010; Farhang and Wawro 2004; Peresie 2005). Additionally, some suggest that race and gender cannot be examined separately. Instead, they argue, researchers should look at the intersectionality of both. For example, Collins and Moyer (2008) did not find differences in the tendencies of women and minorities to support criminal defendants. However, they did find that female minorities are more likely to support criminal defendants than minority males, Caucasian males, and Caucasian females. While the general race and gender findings are mixed (see Peresie 2005 for a discussion), there is some evidence that on some types of issues, judge gender and race can influence decision making on three-judge panels.

It is clear from prior work that ideology plays a role in influencing the decisions made by courts of appeals judges, but it is only one of many influences. We raised these findings and conjectures with the judges we interviewed.

Judges' Views of Precedent and Attitudes

So far we have explained that while ideology is an important influence on decision making, it is but one of several factors—and our interviews confirmed the empirical findings. We were struck by how much the judges spoke of their decision making in terms of following precedent. Not surprisingly, most of the judges felt more comfortable discussing their decision making in terms of precedent rather than ideology, and when the judges did discuss ideology they tended to present the concept as "judicial philosophy." Within the context of precedent and ideology, the judges spoke to the importance of following precedent, the differences between easy and hard cases, and what happens when there is no precedent or the precedent is unclear. We begin by explaining the role precedent plays in the decision-making process from the perspective of the judges.

Role of Precedent

We asked the judges why precedent matters when deciding cases. Many of the judges explained that it matters because it is part of how the judicial system works, suggesting that it is important to maintain consistency in the interpretation of the law and legitimacy in the courts. The judges explained this idea in several different ways. We highlight a few of their responses. For example, Judge A responded, "We follow precedent just because it is part of the generally accepted constraints under which we operate." Judge I provided a more nuanced response, noting that people expect judges to follow precedent: "I never thought my role would allow me to do anything else than to follow clear precedent—it is what we do—right or wrong is what is set by the law. Additionally, you have to keep remembering that people organize their affairs in the confidence that you will follow precedent—business can only work if there are 'settled expectations'—it is sort of a social contract." Similarly, Judge N suggested, "We believe in the chain of command here—our view is that even the dicta of the Supremes [are] to be viewed as highly persuasive. Following precedent is just what we do—we are all judges." Judge N went on to explain that he would expect all his colleagues to reach the same decision an overwhelming percentage of the times when the precedent is clear or, as he put it, a "slam dunk." Finally, Judge I simply stated, "No one would ignore precedent. You just don't do that."

A common theme that emerged from our discussions with the judges was the distinction between clear and unclear precedents. The judges noted that when precedent is clear, it is much easier to follow, and there is little room for extralegal factors to influence decision making. But when precedent is unclear or nonexistent, disagreements are more likely to occur over the interpretation of the precedent(s) and how to decide the case. Judge B commented, "When precedent is really clear, everyone will follow it. Now of course there are some cases where precedent isn't so clear, and on those cases there are differences among us—we sort of all know where the others stand—some just have different views about their conception of what justice is, and of course that comes into play when the law isn't too clear." Judge C explained how ideology can influence the decision-making process when precedent is not clear: "Of course, everyone would follow precedent if it was really completely clear—I don't think you would even think about doing anything else—but often precedent isn't so clear. And on those cases we all have our views about what good law should look like—I suppose you political scientists would call that political views—and in those cases you know your colleagues and can predict what their views will be, and I suppose that the less guidance there is from the law, the more our views about what the law should be, matter." Likewise, Judge J explained, "But in most cases it isn't a matter of the precedent tells me what to do or there is no precedent—there are almost always some precedents that are relevant to some degree—the more relevant they are the more weight I give them, and the more distant they are the more I think about what I think the right result would be." Judge X, who was more comfortable in talking about ideology, stated the following: "Everybody follows precedent, that is just a given. The key question is what happens when precedent isn't clear, or when there are conflicting precedents. That happens more often than you would think. In those cases, of course, a judge's philosophy or preferences are going to matter."

Judge D made two interesting comments. First, he suggested that clear precedent would be followed, unless it was old. For example, Judge D commented that if precedent was clear, "around here, everyone would follow it," but then added, "unless, perhaps, the precedent was old, and you wanted to invite the Supreme Court to reconsider—but that sort of thing would be pretty rare." Judge D followed up this comment by suggesting that when precedent is unclear, judges may think about where the Supreme Court is headed on the issue (see chapter 6 for more discussion on this area of research): "When there is no clear precedent, you will think about the way the Supreme Court is headed, but if you think they are headed in the wrong direction, you may think that my voice will help to move the Court or make them reconsider the implications of where they are going. But the way you think they [the Supreme Court] will decide will generally count for something. Life is hard enough without people suspecting that the appeals courts are going the wrong way. But it is definitely a matter of degree—you wouldn't feel bound by your impression of the direction the Court is moving in the way you would be bound by an actual precedent. Ultimately, when the law is unclear you have to rely on your own basic ideas of what constitutes justice."

Judges Q and E were more methodical in their approach in deciding cases with unclear precedent. Judge Q offered:

> I try to draw on what precedents there are even in an unclear case, and often have to work it out as I write the opinion. The "right" answer often emerges in the process of opinion writing and discussions with colleagues. Even when the precedents aren't completely clear you follow legal norms about how to arrive at a "right" answer. Now of course in those unclear cases your legal philosophy affects how you eventually work things out, but even then judges with different philosophies may come to conclusions that are fairly close.

Judge E also explained how he approached these types of cases:

> Our job is to "get it right," and part of that means following precedent. Of course, everyone would follow precedent if it were clear; those are the cases that we wouldn't have to spend much time discussing and probably wouldn't even have an oral argument. If there were no clear Supreme Court precedents, then the next thing I would look for is whether other circuits have decided this issue. If there is no precedent that is very clear at all, we can sometimes get some rough ideas from the general direction the Supreme Court is going, but there isn't the sort of pressure to follow such "hints" or trends as there is when the Court has provided a clear precedent.

A few judges noted that sometimes disagreements center on whether precedent is even clear. They pointed out that while most of the time the clarity of the precedent is obvious, sometimes that is not the case. When the latter occurs, the judges will debate whether a precedent is clear or not, and sometimes a judge's judicial philosophy plays a role in how he reaches a decision. Judge H simply noted, "I don't have any doubts that everyone would follow clear precedent if it really is that clear." Judge L described it more completely:

> We would all follow clear precedent—I can't even think of any exceptions. Of course, different judges may disagree on whether the precedent is in fact clear. And if it is not clear, then of course your judicial philosophy influences the way you decide. But even then it is a matter of degree—there is almost always some law—so you rarely just ask what outcome would I like, but the less law there is or the more ambiguous it is the closer you come to deciding the case based on your judicial philosophy.

While there are disagreements at times on the clarity of the precedent, the judges still try to work together and compromise. It was evident from our conversations that compromise was an important aspect of the decision-making process. Judge G provided the following explanation:

> All judges would follow the precedent if it was really clear—of course, we don't always agree which precedent is most relevant—that is what a lot of the attorneys are arguing about in their briefs. Still, there are quite a few cases where you can see through that pretty easily, and we all agree which precedent should control the case and what it means. And once we reach that point, then everyone is going to agree on the outcome. And even when we disagree—I may say that precedent X is the most important for this case, while one of my colleagues says no, it is precedent Y—and probably that is because precedent Y is more in line with my colleague's general philosophy—we almost always will agree that X and Y both have some relevance and that both of us will take both precedents into account to some degree, and both precedents will shape our thinking about the right outcome to some degree. We will end up at somewhat different final positions, but we won't be as far apart as we would be if we could both just decide the case according to our own general sense of justice.

Ideological Influences

We also asked the judges about political ideology and decision making. Many judges were less comfortable discussing whether ideology influenced their own decision making. However, they felt freer in discussing ideology in general terms (with respect to when ideology may come into play), patterns they noticed in their circuit, patterns they noticed in other circuits, and finally ideology and the Supreme Court. Reiterating several of the comments above, the judges were quick to point out that the clearer the precedent, the less likely it was that ideology would influence decision making. It is those hard or unclear cases that make it harder for extralegal factors to remain to the side. Several judges also mentioned that the type of case or issue would influence the relative strength or weakness of judicial attitudes.

When we asked Judge R about ideological influences, he spoke in terms of his circuit versus other circuits. For instance, he stated:

> Some courts of appeals are highly ideological and very divided ideologically. Our court is traditionally not ideological—and our judges socialize the new judges into that orientation—we lead new judges not to expect . . . how a given colleague will react to a case to be based on who appointed them. And maybe we've just been lucky to some degree that the ideological splits haven't developed to the degree they have in other circuits. But you develop expectations about how you and your colleagues should and will approach cases, and maintaining the respect of your colleagues is important, especially because we are such a small community, and we all expect to be working together for a long time. But there will be some cases where the issues are so obviously ideological and there is an absence of clear precedent that the decision will of course follow ideological lines—but in our court those are a very small number.

Judge H pointed out that much of how philosophies or attitudes pressure the decision-making process depended on case type. He said, "Whether judges' attitudes come out varies a lot with the type of case. The cases that are most likely to see divisions along ideological grounds are habeas corpus cases, civil rights, and any sort of constitutional issue." Judge J simply pointed out that "judges with different judicial philosophies end up agreeing on case outcomes all the time, but it is mainly [in] those few really hard cases that our philosophical differences matter."

Judge V, who felt more comfortable speaking about judicial attitudes and who described the various ideologies of judges on his circuit, asserted that he did not think the percentage of cases influenced by the political values of the judges was very large. He noted that there are vast areas of law, from corporate to contract, bankruptcy, and labor relations law, where one might not find any political differences in the ways judges decide cases. Additionally, he mentioned that most commercial cases are not influenced by the political preferences of the judges in recent decades. He noted that the role of ideology was remarkably diminished from earlier decades, when these economic cases excited ideological responses from the judges. Finally, he pointed out that there were few ideological disagreements on jurisdictional matters or procedural rules. However, Judge V also pointed to areas where "ideological tensions," as he put it, were relevant:

> The areas where there are still significant ideological tensions [include] immigration, particularly asylum requests, as some judges are just more sympathetic to immigrants. Our circuit's reversal rate of the immigration board is about 34 percent, but the Fourth Circuit rate is about 2 percent, and you can't explain that difference by anything except values. This may not be the traditional liberal/conservative dimension, but the differences are certainly not legal. How much credence you give to foreigners in general will largely affect how much credence you give to claims when good evidence is in short supply. Some judges are clearly more hostile to white-collar criminals than others. Judges also clearly disagree about the death penalty and abortion, in part due to differences in their religious backgrounds. More recently there have been sharp disagreements in terrorism cases.

Judges P and VV spoke more about ideology and their own circuits. For instance, Judge P said, "The court is somewhat split between 'liberals' and 'conservatives,' though I don't like to use those terms." Judge VV explained that he did not think the ideological difference mattered much. "There are ideological differences on our court, but I found in most case they tend to wash out."

Two other judges mentioned that the Supreme Court was more ideological than their respective circuits, in part because of the issues that confront each court. For example, Judge XX claimed, "We are less ideological than the Supreme Court, but part of that reason is we deal with more technical issues than the Supreme Court does." Judge T further explained, "Political preferences certainly do not make as much difference on the court of appeals as on the Supreme Court. Most judges are conscientious about sticking to the clear demands of the law. But of course, political preferences do affect the outcome in the cases in which the law is unclear. I think we all recognize that."

Judge AA, one of the few judges who talked about ideology in the types of appointments each political party likes to make, had this to say:

> Presidents like to appoint like-minded judges; it is a big deal to make appointments. Republicans care more about this than Democrats. I say that because Republicans like to appoint far right individuals, where[as] Democrats will appoint more middle-of-the-road liberals; they are not as ideologically driven. Clinton didn't care much about far left judicial philosophies, he wanted moderate judges. But Republicans care about putting in tough conservatives not only at the Supreme Court but [on] the courts of appeals too. Since I was appointed and since Justice Stevens was appointed every subsequent appointment has been more conservative on the Republican side. But getting back to your question, I do believe attitudes play a role. For example, as a general statement Democrats tend to be more sympathetic to human beings.

Several judges tried to minimize the idea of judicial ideology in their responses. For example, Judge WW argued, "It is not always about ideological voting. People are motivated by their likes and dislikes." Judge HH questioned how scholars categorize liberal and conservative, and spoke about the differences in terms of "divisions" rather than ideology. He stated, "I don't know what it means for the Supreme Court to be categorized as liberal [or] conservative. The division is whether one gives more deference to individual rights versus law enforcement. There are divisions, I suppose. If you have an environmental case, some judges will put the government to task where others don't. I guess there are divisions on how the issue should be handled."

Judge M also minimized the effects of ideology on his circuit. He observed that because of the collegial nature of his circuit, these influences were not so apparent. He explained:

> The main reason is that even though the judges on our circuit were appointed by four different presidents, and we vary quite a bit in terms of our political preferences, everyone takes their job very seriously and accepts the rules that govern our decisions even when we do not agree with the policy implications of those precedents and rules. There is always a major effort to work together through the implications of those rules, and even when the case is complex, after we have gone through all the arguments of both sides and batted ideas back and forth, we end up agreeing on what the correct legal outcome should be. Second, our court is very collegial, and people listen to each other; and we are all aware that we have to give guidance to the lower courts and administrative agencies, so we are usually willing to compromise in order to be able to send a message that is not confusing.

In similar fashion, Judge E was critical of the concept of ideology in decision making, noting how much his court was in agreement, and suggesting that the reason his circuit comes to an agreement is because of the judges' ability to compromise:

> When I stop to think about it, I am sometimes surprised at how often we *end up* agreeing on the result. A number of times we start off at least some distance apart—and I think those initial disagreements reflect our differences in opinions—I'm a bit more conservative than some of my colleagues, and that sometimes shows up in our initial assessments. But after we have talked the issue through, and especially after someone has worked through a first draft, and then I've worked on a possible concurrence or dissent—once I've worked through the whole process and tried to reason it all out, I usually end up at the same place as the opinion draft, or possibly just slightly different in emphasis (but not on the other "side" of the decision). Usually when I first see a general overview of the issues in the case, I have a first reaction about which side should win, but then the further I get into the legal arguments of both sides, the more my initial view gets pulled one way or the other by the more persuasive argument.

Judges' Views of Race, Gender, and Attitudes

Finally, we also asked the judges about gender and race effects. We explained some of the research findings political scientists and law professors have put forth and asked whether the judges noticed any differences in decision making by women and minorities, both generally and on the panel. Judge R provided one of the most thoughtful and candid responses to our question. He eloquently explained:

> In general, different backgrounds are very important [to] how we judge—whether academic career versus career judge versus political background makes a big difference. The fact that I am an immigrant—especially a political refugee—undoubtedly colors the way I view the many immigration cases we get. Then, obviously, gender is another part of our background that has a big impact on the type of experiences and socialization we have received—so it certainly influences the way we think—but I'm not sure that it is more important than a number of other characteristics and background experiences. So it is important, but is it dominant? The female judges in our circuit are different in many other important ways from each other, and gender itself does not necessarily produce the same effects in everyone. For example, being born poor and having to work hard to later become rich affects people different ways—for some, the experience of be-

ing poor gives them a deep empathy for others who are struggling to try to climb out of poverty, but for others the similar experience makes them say, "Well, I was able to rise up without any help, so why should these poor people now expect a handout?" So gender certainly has an impact on the way we judge, but I suspect that its influence is quite complex; certainly, all . . . women are not the same and don't have similar views or approach decision making the same way—and of course, the same can be said for the men—we are different from each other.

Judge S assumed that gender has something to do with the way a judge views life in general, and that sometimes might influence a judge's view of a particular case. He noted, "Judges inevitably look at some factual issues differently because of differences in life experience—and gender is one of the things that may influence those life experiences—but certainly [it] is not the only relevant life experience, and I'm not sure that gender is even the most important influence." Judge S also explained that in his experience on panels, he had not seen consistent gender differences in the way judges approach legal issues.

Judge XX put it another way when discussing gender and race effects: "It is easier for three white judges to dismiss and marginalize a race discrimination case than if you have two whites and one black judge. The same can be said for sex discrimination. Women are not necessarily more empathetic—there are hard-nosed women and men, and bleeding heart men and women. Gender does change how men may view the case. For example, in the schoolgirl strip search case[1] the men are like, 'What is the big deal, men are naked in the locker room,' but [it] would become harder for men to dismiss an issue like this when a woman is on the panel. I guess what I would say is it matters but isn't blatant. Over time it [gender effects] is less overt and noticeable than it once was." Judge YY also explained, "We are all products of our life experiences. Different people have different experiences. If I was on a panel with a woman and she said this really happens (an issue related to sex discrimination or some women's issue), I'll listen to that."

A handful of judges expressed with more certainty that gender and race play a role. Judge AA best encapsulated these judges' responses: "Gender and race absolutely play a role in decision making. Women and minorities tend to be more sympathetic and compassionate, although sometimes I thought it would play a role with certain woman and it hasn't, but overall it does influence decision making."

A few other judges made the same observations but also suggested that ideology probably influenced decision making more than gender or racial differences. For example, Judge Q said, "Gender is probably one of many background characteristics that affect who a judge is and how they think—but one of many such factors, and I do not think that gender affects all judges in the same way. I can't think of any issue in which gender is the main basis of cleavage, but which president appointed you more frequently makes a difference." Judge V agreed but did point out that at one time, gender influence was more noticeable: "No major difference on how female judges approach cases—[it] was true at one time but not anymore. There was an amusing difference in sexual harassment cases. Male judges had a higher tolerance level for annoying comments men would say, women judges were more sensitive, but now this has disappeared. Men have become more sympathetic to the woman's point of view."

Finally, a small number of judges believed there were no major gender or race differences. Judge P presented the extreme version of this view. When we raised this topic with him, he could not think of any issues to which women as a group seemed to have a different approach that reflected the different socialization they may have had. Moreover, he was not convinced that there was a difference even on so-called women's issues. Judge P, however, noted that "judges' differences in the way they approach issues depends more on who appointed them than [on] their gender." Likewise, Judge WW stated, "No difference there either [referring to race and gender]. But what makes a difference is judicial philosophy, this makes a difference. There is much room for philosophy to play a role in the decision making of cases, not as much [for] race and gender." Finally, Judge T noted that women may have more compassion for litigants or certain issues, but there are no major differences between men and women judges generally. He clarified: "A substantial number of female judges tend to be more sympathetic in general—they often have more 'milk of human kindness'—but I have not noticed any extreme differences between male and female judges. Some female judges appointed by conservative presidents are not as conservative as males appointed by the same president."

The overall consensus we compiled from the judge interviews is that many factors influence decision making, from precedent, institutional constraints, ideology, gender and race (at times, but perhaps not as relevant today), panel make-up, and the circuit norms of collegiality, to name a few. The picture that emerges is that decision making includes a complex set of factors. In other words, it is best represented by an integrated model.

Ideology and Decision Making: An Empirical Perspective

We begin our empirical examination by presenting a series of descriptive statistics. Table 16 reports the difference in the proportion of liberal votes cast by judges on the U.S. Courts of Appeals from 1993 to 2002. We report the percentage of liberal votes cast by courts of appeals judges for all cases and separately for non-unanimous cases. We found that judges appointed by Democratic presidents supported the liberal position in 38 percent of their votes, while judges appointed by Republican presidents voted for a liberal outcome in only 30 percent of their votes (The results are similar when a longer period is scrutinized. From 1960 to 2002, Democratic judges supported a liberal outcome in 42 percent of their votes, compared to 36 percent for Republicans.). Although the ideological difference between the two groups is not overwhelming, when we turn to non-unanimous votes the differences are substantially more striking. Judges appointed by Democratic presidents voted liberally in non-unanimous cases approximately 58 percent of the time. In contrast, judges appointed by Republican presidents voted in the liberal direction only 28 percent of the time.

Most of the findings reported in table 16 are supported by the judges themselves. Most of the judges noted that because of the respect for precedent and collegiality, they ended up agreeing a majority of the time, regardless of their differences in ideology. More specifically, our results, which are derived from published opinions (as discussed in chapter 3, this

TABLE 16 Party differences in proportion of liberal votes cast by judges on the U.S. Courts of Appeals, 1993–2002

PARTY OF APPOINTING PRESIDENT	ALL VOTES		NON-UNANIMOUS VOTES	
	PERCENTAGE OF LIBERAL VOTES	NUMBER OF LIBERAL VOTES	PERCENTAGE OF LIBERAL VOTES	NUMBER OF LIBERAL VOTES
Democratic	37.8	3,193	58.4	344
Republican	30.4	5,073	28.4	518
Party difference	07.4		30.0	

$\chi^2 = 47.75$, $P < 0.001$. $\chi^2 = 75.55$, $P < 0.001$.

is arguably a set of cases that includes the most important issues, given the judges' tendency not to publish opinions where the law is perceived to be clear), support this assessment. However, as the judges pointed out, the large ideological differences are most prevalent in divided decisions. Again, our results are consistent with the judges' perspective that in hard cases—those where precedent is not clear or is nonexistent—differences in judicial philosophy and attitudes matter (but divided decisions represent less than 5 percent of all of the reported cases).

Goldman (1975) noted that beginning with President Roosevelt, presidents have made an effort to appoint like-minded individuals to the federal bench. Table 17 provides a breakdown of the proportion of liberal votes cast by judges based on appointing president. The patterns are clear: from President Roosevelt through George H. W. Bush, judges appointed by Democratic presidents all voted more liberally than judges appointed by Republican presidents. In non-unanimous cases the percentage of liberal votes by judges appointed by Democratic presidents increases substantially. These results also suggest that in hard cases, or cases

TABLE 17 Differences in proportion of liberal votes cast by judges on the U.S. Courts of Appeals by party of appointing president, 1960–2002

	ALL VOTES		NON-UNANIMOUS VOTES	
PARTY OF APPOINTING PRESIDENT	PERCENTAGE OF LIBERAL VOTES	NUMBER OF LIBERAL VOTES	PERCENTAGE OF LIBERAL VOTES	NUMBER OF LIBERAL VOTES
DEMOCRATIC				
Roosevelt	41.5	771	61.5	65
Truman	42.3	1,200	55.5	119
Kennedy	43.5	2,343	61.2	206
Johnson	42.3	5,079	62.2	468
Carter	41.9	4,759	61.1	486
Clinton	39.7	1,454	62.7	142
REPUBLICAN				
Eisenhower	38.9	4,825	40.3	350
Nixon	39.4	4,340	39.4	467
Ford	35.9	1,032	42.4	106
Reagan	33.0	5,511	34.3	537
Bush 41	29.6	1,888	24.5	204

$\chi^2 = 227.05$, $P < 0.001$. $\chi^2 = 214.32$, $P < 0.001$.

in which precedent is ambiguous, there is more room for ideological interpretation of the law. The table also reflects the cleavages that existed among presidential administrations. For example, Kennedy and Johnson appointments tend to vote more liberally than the judges appointed by other Democratic presidents. Reagan and George H. W. Bush appointments have tended to vote most conservatively when compared to other judges appointed by Republican presidents. Nevertheless, the big differences are related to party. The differences among judges appointed by different Democratic presidents or the differences among judges appointed by different Republican presidents pale in comparison to the general differences between Democrats versus Republicans.

We also looked at the impact of race and gender (from 1960 to 2002), and our findings are consistent with the perspective presented by the judges. For example, African American judges supported the liberal position in approximately 46 percent of their votes, while Caucasian judges supported the liberal position in 39 percent of their votes and Hispanic judges in 35 percent of their votes. Additionally, male judges voted liberally in 39 percent of the cases and female judges supported the liberal position in 41 percent of their cases. While the differences among judges are statistically significant, the magnitude of those differences, especially for gender, is quite modest, indicating that as suggested in the judge interviews, neither gender nor race divides the judges on most issues most of the time.

Although these descriptive statistics provide a view of the nature of conflict on the courts of appeals that is generally consistent with the views of the judges interviewed, a more complete understanding of the influence of attitudinal differences on judicial decisions requires a more nuanced, multivariate analysis.

A Model of Attitudinal Influence on Courts of Appeals Decisions

As noted above, numerous studies over the years have found attitudinal differences among appeals court judges related to the party of their appointing president associated with the voting choices of the judges, especially on politically salient issues such as civil rights and liberties. As figure 13 illustrates, these partisan differences have maintained their impact for half a century, continuing to the present. Thus, we examined whether these attitudinal factors continue to be related to judicial decisions after we controlled for the presence of other factors that either previous studies or our judge interviews had identified as influencing the decisional calculus of the judges.

FIGURE 13. Party voting differences versus party composition of the Courts of Appeals, 1960–2002

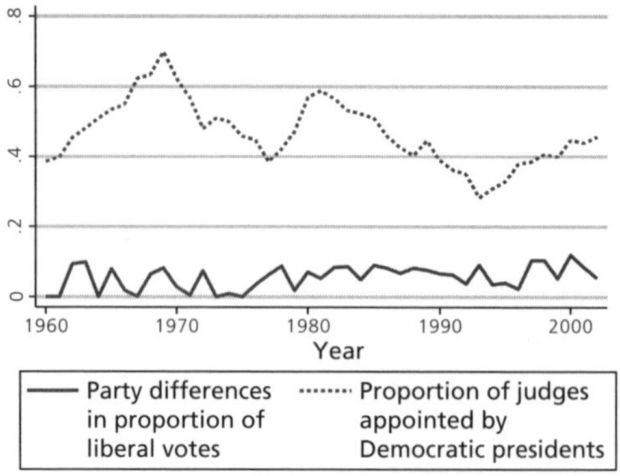

Our data come from the (Songer 2002) United States Courts of Appeals Database, and we limited our analysis to the last decade of that data (i.e., 1993–2002) to preserve a focus on contemporary trends in the courts of appeals. Since the data are limited to the decisions of the courts of appeals in cases decided on the merits that resulted in a published opinion of the court, it includes only those cases that the judges deemed most important from a legal and political perspective.[2] Thus, it would be incorrect to generalize from the finding below that partisan preferences continue to influence judges' votes in these most salient cases (i.e., those with published opinions) to conclude that political preferences influence the resolution of most cases decided by the courts of appeals.[3]

The primary hypothesis investigated is that the political preferences (or ideology) of appeals court judges have a significant impact on the nature of the judicial outcomes. Nonetheless, both the judge interviews and previous scholarship on the courts of appeals lead to the expectation that the magnitude of these ideological impacts on judicial votes will be relatively modest. To determine whether there is a statistically significant impact of judicial political preferences on their voting choices, we developed a multivariate model that includes controls for other variables that previous studies have suggested may also influence judicial votes.

The dependent variable in the analysis below is whether each vote of each judge participating on three-judge panels in cases decided with published opinions supported a liberal outcome. Liberal outcomes are coded one and conservative outcomes are coded zero. Cases whose outcomes could not be unambiguously categorized as either liberal or conservative (e.g., contract disputes between two corporations, or civil rights disputes in which the court supported in part the plaintiff and in part the defendant) were excluded from the analysis. Since the dependent variable is dichotomous, we used logistic regression with robust standard errors clustered on individual judges.

The primary independent variable of interest is the political preferences of the judge, using the political party of the appointing president (coded one for Democratic and zero for Republican) as a surrogate for whether those preferences are liberal or conservative. The attitudinal model of judicial decision making leads to the expectation that the relationship between preferences and voting outcomes will be positive and significant.

As both the previous studies referenced above and the comments of the judges we interviewed indicate, the political preferences of the judges are most likely to influence the resolution of the small number of hard cases in which there is no clear law or precedent. To capture the significance of these hard cases, we added a variable denoting the presence or absence of dissent—whether the decision of the panel was unanimous (coded zero) or divided (coded one). We then added a multiplicative term (Dissent × Party of Appointing President) to capture the interactive effect of political preference and the presence of a hard case in which the panel was divided. If political preferences do have particular relevance for the resolution of cases without clear precedent or other manifestations of law, this multiplicative term should be strongly positive and statistically significant.

As the review above of other studies of judicial voting behavior suggests, there is some indication in the literature that the perspectives judges acquire through differences in socialization related to gender and race may also influence judicial votes. While the existing evidence is mixed, some studies have found women to be more likely than their male colleagues to support liberal outcomes and for judges from racial minorities to be more likely than Caucasian judges to support liberal outcomes. To test these expectations, we added control variables to our model to indicate whether the judges were female, African American, or Hispanic (with Caucasian as the reference category for the race dummy variables).

Our judge interviews indicated that most circuits are highly collegial, with the result that judges may be influenced by the views of their panel colleagues or may be willing to compromise with their colleagues on the final outcome. In either case, the vote of each judge is likely to be positively correlated with the political preferences of their colleagues. To capture this potential effect, the model includes the number of colleagues (ranging from zero to two) of each judge appointed by a Democratic president.

The judges we interviewed were unanimous in their assertion that one of their primary motivations is to correctly interpret and then follow existing law. Previous studies of the courts of appeals also indicate that the impact of precedent tends to be substantially greater on the courts of appeals than on the Supreme Court. While it is difficult to provide any quantitative measure that unambiguously indicates which litigants in a given case have the weight of the law on their side, the judges agreed that most of the time the trial courts "got the law right." Thus, we added a measure of the political directionality of the lower court decision (coded one for liberal and zero for conservative) as a rough surrogate indicating which side was supported by the balance of law and precedent.

Several works have found that litigant resources matter. Litigants with the greatest resources and the lowest relative stakes in litigation, especially representatives of the U.S. government, have the highest rates of success in both trial and appellate courts (Atkins 1991; Galanter 1974; McCormick 1993; Songer and Sheehan 1992; Songer, Sheehan, and Haire 2000; Wheeler et al. 1987). To control for the impact of support by the United States, two variables were added to the model, one indicating that the U.S. government supported a liberal outcome and one indicating that the government supported a conservative outcome. The excluded category is that the U.S. government did not participate and did not take a position in the case.

Finally, our judge interviews indicated that many criminal appeals raise frivolous challenges to the pro-prosecution decision of the courts below. Since most criminal defendants litigating in the federal courts are poor and thus receive free counsel through at least one appeal, there is frequently little disincentive for criminal defendants who lose at trial to appeal, even if their chances of victory on appeal are very small. Thus, we anticipate that a substantial majority of criminal defendants will lose on appeal (thus creating a decision coded as conservative) regardless of the political ideology of the panel hearing their appeal. To control for this negative impact on the likelihood of a liberal decision, we added a control variable indicating whether the appellant was a criminal defendant.

The results in table 18 provide strong support for the perspective of most of the judges we interviewed. Political preferences (as reflected by the preferences of the appointing president) continued to be associated with judge votes to a statistically significant degree in the most recent decade, confirming previous empirical studies of voting on the courts of

TABLE 18 Logistic regression model of the likelihood of a liberal vote in a random sample of published opinions in U.S. Courts of Appeals cases, 1993–2002

INDEPENDENT VARIABLE	MLE	ROBUST SE	DISCRETE CHANGES
Party of Appointing President	0.183**	0.079	0.05,0.33+
Party × Dissent	1.197***	0.193	
Female	0.108	0.103	
Black	−0.033	0.139	
Hispanic	−0.163	0.135	
Number of Democratic Colleagues	0.124***	0.036	0.026
Lower Court Directionality	0.406***	0.076	0.096
U.S. Supports Liberal Outcome	0.657***	0.083	0.163
U.S. Supports Conservative Outcome	−0.241***	0.065	−0.058
Criminal case	−0.790***	0.064	−0.176
Dissent	−0.133	0.120	
Constant	−0.799	0.073	
N	8,725		
χ^2	587.86		

Notes: Robust standard errors clustered by judge. MLE, maximum likelihood estimation.
$*P < 0.05$, $**P < 0.01$, $***P < 0.001$.
+Following Brambor, Clark, and Golder (2006), we calculated the discrete change or marginal effects of the party variable when the dissent variable was set to two values (zero, one).

appeals in the past (Goldman 1975; Richardson and Vines 1970; Songer et al. 2000; Sunstein et al. 2006). But the magnitude, or substantive significance, of these partisan attitudinal effects remains small. We estimated the size of the effects using discrete changes (discussed in chapter 2). As noted in table 18, the discrete change for political party in the unanimous decisions of the courts is only 0.05. That is, support for liberal outcomes by Democratic judges is only five percentage points higher than the support provided by Republican judges. These findings are strongly consistent with the view expressed by most judges that while there are differences among the judges in political orientation, those orientations only rarely affect the final positions supported by the judges. Thus, even in an analysis (like that in table 18) limited to the small proportion of cases that receive published opinions, the substantive effects of political preferences are modest.

However, the results also confirmed the view expressed by the judges that in the small proportion of cases in which the court is divided,[4] the division of the court often falls along the lines of political preferences reflected in the partisan nature of the appointment process. The results in table 18 indicate that in divided cases, the discrete change for the Party of Appointing President variable is 0.33. Another way of thinking about this is the following: the average judge appointed by a Democratic president would be expected to support a liberal outcome in divided cases nearly 73 percent of the time, while a similarly situated Republican appointee would be expected to support a liberal outcome in only 40 percent of the divided cases. In contrast to these effects of partisan appointment, the racial and gender characteristics of the judges were not related to their votes to a statistically significant degree.

The control variables in the model performed as expected. Most notably, the directionality of the lower court decision, reflecting in part the impact of legal influences, was statistically significant at the 0.001 level and had a discrete change that was more than double the effect of political party in unanimous cases. Support or opposition from the U.S. government also had a significant impact on the likelihood of a liberal vote, confirming past party capability studies. An examination of the discrete changes for the two variables reflecting U.S. government participation shows that with all other variables held at their mean, the expected likelihood of a liberal vote was 46 percent when the U.S. government supported such an outcome and only 26 percent when the U.S. government supported a conservative outcome.

Conclusion

The analyses presented in this chapter provide validation that attitudes matter in judicial decision making, while simultaneously showing that, at least for lower court judges, attitudinal influences are one of several important factors that influence decision making (we explore this idea further in chapter 6). More specifically, as corroborated by the judges we interviewed, political preferences exert a modest influence on the decision-making process. As Zorn and Bowie observe, "The multiplicity of goals at lower levels suggests that any single influence on lower court judges' decision making will explain relatively little, if any, of the aggregate variation in judges' decisions" (2010, 1012). In short, because of the courts of appeals' institutional position, constraints, respect for precedent, and workload, to name a few factors, ideology alone may not capture the intricacies of decision making for these middle-tier judges.

Unlike prior studies addressing the role of political ideology in the decision-making process, we included the judges' views on this theory of decision making. As noted, several of the judges were less than comfortable discussing ideology and decision making; nonetheless, many were willing to admit that at times, usually in salient cases, ideology is one of several influences on decision making. In addition to salient issues, the judges pointed out that hard cases (cases characterized by a substantial degree of legal uncertainty) often bring about ideological divisions. For example, when a dissenting vote is cast in the case, the rate of ideological disagreement increased dramatically compared to unanimously decided decisions.

Finally, we asked the judges if they noticed a discernible difference in decision-making patterns among their female and racial minority colleagues. Most of the judges noted that they had not seen any significant differences in the way their colleagues made decisions because of their sex or race status. If anything, the differences were more notable for the white male judges in that if a woman judge or one from a racial minority was participating on the panel, it would influence those judges to consider more carefully the female (or racial minority) point of view, at least in some instances (e.g., workplace discrimination cases). Our empirical model bears out our general findings from the judge interviews. Statistically, we found no significant effect of gender and racial characteristics on decision making.

In the next chapter we explore and test some of these other constraints that may affect courts of appeals judges' decision making. We explore whether the possibility of Supreme Court or circuit en banc review and reversal affects how judges reach their decisions in the cases that come before them. In particular, we test the strategic theory framework of decision making, noting that the obvious intuitional constraint judges face is review and reversal by a higher authority, whether that is the Supreme Court or the circuit sitting en banc.

SIX

Strategic Accounts of Decision Making

Strategic accounts of appellate court decision making, like attitudinal accounts, usually posit that judges have a goal of making good public policy that is consistent with their own personal political preferences (Cross and Tiller 1998; Epstein and Knight 1998, 2000; McNollgast 1995). But in contrast to attitudinal models, which hold that judges vote sincerely to support the case outcomes they most prefer, the strategic account holds that judges who vote strategically take into account the potential actions of other actors and may modify their behavior in response to the probable reactions of others (Baum 1997). The institutional setting of the intermediate federal appellate courts creates several potential opportunities for strategic behavior. For example, bargaining is likely to occur on collegial courts. The judge assigned to write the opinion of the court might bargain with the other judges over opinion content, and, as we saw in chapter 3, such bargaining is a regular feature of decision making on the courts of appeals. Additionally, panel decisions are subject to review and reversal by the circuit en banc and the Supreme Court. As such, judges might opt to author a dissenting opinion to signal the potential reviewers that they should indeed review and reverse the majority. Alternatively, the panel might select an outcome that is distant from the ideologically preferred outcomes of the panel in order to avoid reversal by the circuit en banc or the Supreme Court. Thus, because of the institutional structure of the courts of appeals, judges can act strategically in a variety of ways, including negotiating over opinion content and utilizing special opinions to signal the Supreme Court to review a case. The main strategic question facing appeals court judges, however, is usually assumed to be whether they will modify their behavior to avoid reversal by the Supreme Court (Klein and Hume 2003; McNollgast 1995; Songer, Segal, and Cameron 1994).

In this chapter we focus on whether a strategic perspective provides a useful general approach that enhances an understanding of broad patterns of decision making by judges on the U.S. courts of appeals. In particular, we examine whether it is rational in the majority of cases for appeals court judges to modify their behavior when necessary to avoid reversal by the Supreme Court or the circuit meeting en banc. We conclude that in a large majority of the cases they decide, a strategic perspective is not helpful in understanding the decision calculus of appellate court judges. That conclusion is based on a three-part argument. First, we found that circuit judges do not have a strong sense of which of their decisions are likely to be reviewed and potentially reversed by the Supreme Court or the circuit en banc.[1] Second, our analysis of actual appeals court decisions indicates that even if one made very conservative assumptions, the objective probability that all but a handful of these cases would be reviewed and reversed is so small that a rational judge would not fear reversal unless the costs of such a reversal were quite high.[2] Finally, we show that the perceived costs of reversal are much too small to motivate judges to change their behavior to attempt to avoid reversal by either the circuit en banc or the Supreme Court. Our analysis of the actual voting behavior of the judges, comparing their votes in cases with an objectively low likelihood of being reviewed by the Supreme Court and their voting in the small minority of cases most likely to be reviewed, supports this conclusion and yields little evidence of strategic voting.

Strategic Accounts of Judicial Behavior

Extant scholarship suggests that attitudes have a substantial effect on the behavior of all appellate court judges in the United States (Hettinger, Lindquist, and Martinek 2004, 123). Nevertheless, even if we restrict our focus to the policy-relevant behavior of appellate judges, there appears to be an increasing number of scholars who argue that judges do not always vote their sincere ideological attitudes but instead temper their private preferences with strategic calculations about the probable reaction of others (Epstein and Knight 1998).

An important dispute is whether appeals court judges' voting is motivated by fear of reversal by the Supreme Court. While some scholars have argued that U.S. courts of appeals judges can anticipate when the U.S. Supreme Court will review a case and will modify their decision in anticipation of the probable Supreme Court response (Cross and Tiller 1998; McNollgast 1995), others disagree and claim to find no evidence of strategic behavior (Hettinger, Lindquist, and Martinek 2004). The judges themselves also disagree with the advocates of strategic perspectives. In our interviews with more than sixty judges on the courts of appeal in the United States, we found the judges to be nearly unanimous in claiming that neither they nor their colleagues would act strategically to avoid review (although some judges hinted they believed at times their colleagues thought about possible Supreme Court reversal).[3] Furthermore, other recent interviews with judges on the U.S. Courts of Appeals came to a similar conclusion (Klein 2002). Yet advocates of strategic models continue to suggest that lower court judges fear reversal from the Supreme Court.

The underlying premise of strategic models is that judges are motivated by their policy preferences and that in order for judges to advance their policy preferences or goals, they must calculate how others will react to their decisions. Strategic models are not new phenomena. Both Schubert (1958, 1962) and Murphy (1964) methodically analyzed strategic behavior on the Supreme Court several decades ago. However, when examining scholarship on strategic judicial behavior in light of its information assumptions, it is important to distinguish between strategic interactions among judges on the same court and strategic reactions by judges to external actors. Judges can usually be assumed to have sufficient information about the preferences and probable actions of colleagues on their own court, but they may have much less information about judges on other courts or political actors outside the judicial system (see chapter 3). There is considerable evidence that Supreme Court justices make strategic calculations about the internal actions of their colleagues on the Court (Epstein and Knight 1998; Maltzman, Spriggs, and Wahlbeck 2000; Spriggs, Maltzman, and Wahlbeck 1999; Wahlbeck, Spriggs, and Maltzman 1998). Similarly, as noted in chapter 3, although the appeals court judges we interviewed were reluctant to use the word "strategic" to describe their actions, they cited many instances in which they modified portions of the opinions they wrote in anticipation of how the other judges on their panel would react, and they noted that bargaining over the content of the opinion was quite common. However, there is more controversy about whether Supreme Court justices and courts of appeals judges respond strategically to external actors (see Ferejohn and Weingast 1992; Gely and Spiller 1990; Lindquist and Yalof 2001; Marks 1989; Spiller and Gely 1992; but see Segal 1997).

Both strategic accounts of appeals court decision making and legal accounts posit that judges will depart from their private ideological preferences when deciding cases. But the accounts differ in an important way. As Cross (2007) has written, "The legal model is retrospective and calls on circuit courts to adhere to the previous rulings of the Supreme Court. The strategic model is prospective and expects that circuit courts will respond to the anticipated future holdings of the Court" (97). If lower court judges cannot predict which cases will be reviewed, then it would be impossible for them to act strategically. However, if judges can predict the likelihood of review, then it is reasonable to assume they might act differently on cases that they believe will be reviewed by the Court, especially if reversal is deemed costly.

Strategic Accounts of Decision Making on the U.S. Courts of Appeals

The evidence is relatively strong that the internal dynamics of courts of appeals decision making include extensive interaction among the judges. The nature of this internal strategic interaction came through clearly in the interviews we conducted with judges on the courts of appeals. For instance, Judge B told us that "there is a certain amount of brokering going on; I wrote a lengthy statement this morning to a colleague that said I agreed with the result but wanted to change the way the opinion was structured. In the memo I said that if the other judge was able to make those changes, I would be able to join the opinion." When asked about this comment of Judge B, his colleague Judge C went so far as to say that such accommodation "is an *integral* part of the process; it is the core of the appellate process." Similarly, Judge M was not at all reluctant to admit that bargaining went on during opinion writing, and while he did not use the word "strategic," he clearly indicated that judges frequently take into account the preferences of their colleagues. He said, "There is a lot of give-and-take at conference, but we hash out the details of the opinions as we write memos back and forth after receiving the first draft of the opinion. . . . There is a definite attempt to accommodate each other's views whenever possible."

Similar comments were made by virtually all the judges we talked to. Negotiation, compromise, and respect for the positions of colleagues are seen by appeals court judges as a normal part of crafting opinions. There is a definite attempt to accommodate each other's views "whenever possible." Bargaining is often implicit, but sometimes it is quite explicit, according to Judge D, who noted that one might say, "There are only three points in your draft that I am not comfortable with and I would be able to join if you were able to change . . . A, B, C." Judge Q used almost identical language in indicating that overt bargaining goes on among the judges. He maintained, "It is perfectly accepted that judges will sometimes write responses to an opinion draft that say something like . . . I could concur in this opinion if the following changes were made" (see chapter 3 for further elaboration on accommodation).

A common theme that came up during our discussions regarding bargaining was that such strategic interaction occurs because the judges come to know their circuit colleagues quite well, a result of the extensive interaction they have with them. In fact, Judge A said that when he starts reading the briefs for a case, the first thing that pops into his mind is how his two colleagues on the panel will react to the key issues.

Although judges may not have "perfect" information about their colleagues' preferences, they have enough information that they feel confident in their ability to predict the probable reaction of their colleagues in many situations. However, there is less agreement about whether or how frequently appeals court judges react strategically to external actors, and there is even less agreement as to whether judges have enough information to predict the probable reaction of various external actors. Appeals court judges behaving strategically would be most concerned with the potential reactions of two other institutional actors. Most immediately, judges on a three-judge panel might be concerned about the possibility of reversal by their circuit sitting en banc. Alternatively, they might consider the possibility of reversal by the Supreme Court.

In examining whether federal appeals court judges act strategically in anticipation of en banc review, researchers have focused on dissenting behavior. Van Winkle (1997), Cross and Tiller (1998), and Hettinger, Lindquist, and Martinek (2004) analyzed whether judges act strategically when deciding to dissent. Van Winkle (1997) put forth a signaling model, and analyzed search and seizure cases from 1992 through 1993. He found that appeals court judges are less likely to dissent when they are a circuit outlier on a panel of circuit mainstreamers. In addition, Van Winkle (1997) found evidence that a circuit mainstreamer judge on a panel of circuit outliers is more likely to dissent as a signal to the rest of the circuit mainstreamers. Similarly, Cross and Tiller (1998) in their examination of administrative law cases from the District of Columbia Circuit from 1991 through 1995 found evidence of strategic behavior by appeals court judges. McNollgast (1995) developed a formal model that predicts the ways in which appeals court judges might modify their opinions to avoid reversal by the Supreme Court in various scenarios. Without presenting any evidence, the McNollgast model assumes that appeals court judges are rational actors who are primarily motivated by their policy preferences, and also assumes that appeals court judges can perfectly predict the likelihood of review (1636).

In contrast, Hettinger, Lindquist, and Martinek (2004) found no evidence of strategic behavior on three-judge panels. They presented a unidimensional spatial model and found that as the ideological distance between a judge and the panel majority got larger, the likelihood of writing dissents increased (133). However, analysis of differences between the behavior of judges in different signaling regimes provides no evidence that judges make strategic calculations about the probable reactions of judges in the rest of the circuit. The authors contend this finding supports the attitudinal model rather than the strategic perspective.

Strategic accounts suggest that judges who face the possibility of review may strategically refrain from voting their personal preferences because they fear reversal. Scholars "have developed a highly credible body of evidence showing that circuit judges and other lower court judges are generally . . . responsive to the policies announced by their superiors" (Klein 2002, 7). This evidence is consistent with the theory that judges act strategically to avoid reversal, but the same evidence might also be explained by assuming that judges have been successfully socialized to believe that the job of the judge is to apply the relevant statutes and precedents regardless of their personal preferences. That is, both strategic and legal accounts of judicial behavior would lead to the same prediction regarding the responsiveness of appeals court judges to Supreme Court policy.

Perhaps the strongest evidence that appeals courts respond strategically to possible reversal by the Supreme Court comes from an analysis of changing patterns of decisions in search and seizure cases. After employing a case fact model in an attempt to control for precedent, Songer, Segal, and Cameron (1994) found that appeals court decisions were positively related both to the ideology of the appeals court judges and to changes in the current ideology of the Supreme Court. The authors concluded that these results are consistent with a principal agent perspective in which the agents (appeals court judges) attempt to advance their own policy preferences limited by their perceptions of the constraints imposed by the preferences of their principal (the Supreme Court). Partial support for this interpretation is provided by Howard (1981), who found that 57 percent of the judges who answered his mail survey rated the anticipated reaction of the Supreme Court as "important" or "very important" in their decisional calculus, but such anticipated reactions were cited as important less frequently than six other possible influences on decisions. Songer, Ginn, and Sarver (2003) took a different approach, examining cases in which there was no fear of reversal (i.e., tort diversity cases), and concluded that in such cases the judges were just as likely to follow precedent in conflict with their private preferences as they were in cases in which there was a realistic chance of review and reversal. Thus, they concluded that fear of reversal has little effect on the judges. Likewise, Klein and Hume (2003) in their analysis of search and seizure cases from 1961 to 1990 found that congruence between lower court decisions and Supreme Court decisions did not stem from a fear of reversal. A similar conclusion was reached by Klein (2002) after an extensive study of cases involving circuit conflict. He found little evidence that the judges attempted to anticipate potential Supreme Court reactions and concluded that they were no more cautious in their decision making in cases likely to be reviewed than in those that had little chance of review by the Supreme Court. Most recently, Cross (2007) reported comparable results. In his analysis of a large sample of appeals court decisions he uncovered results that were "strikingly and directly opposite of what strategic theories of compliance . . . would suggest" (104). Similarly, Benesh and Martinek (2002) in their analysis of state supreme court confessions cases found that the ideology of the Supreme Court did not enter into the judges' decision calculus.

A few of the judges who were familiar with political science research on the courts generally and with research on the courts of appeals specifically talked openly about the usefulness of strategic theory as a way to understand their decision making. Judge R did not believe the courts of appeals "work the way economics and law professors think." He explained that all the judges on his circuit "agree that their job is to follow Supreme Court precedent, and it is not their job to figure out where the Court is going." He went on to comment that even if judges tried to act "strategically" by setting the policy between their own preference and the preference of the Supreme Court to try to avoid a reversal, that would result "in a less favorable outcome—it would not be successful—the Supreme Court is too smart and would easily see through what they were trying to do." However, he (and a few other judges made a similar comment) may, as a tactic, decide a case on narrow grounds in order to avoid review by the Supreme Court. As Judge R further explained, "I might decide a case on narrow grounds to avoid a review that would result in a broad ruling that would be bad policy." He, among a few other judges, went on to say that on occasion, he has written an opinion in a manner that makes review impossible.

In a rare exchange, one judge[4] described a case in which he had written a narrow opinion in order to avoid Supreme Court review:

> The issue in the case was whether grand jury minutes could be opened up at any time in the future for use by historians. The government position was no, they could never be opened, and I thought the government's position was absurd, but there were some hints that the Supreme Court might accept this case. The specific issue related to historians' request for documents in a McCarthy era prosecution—some of the witnesses were still alive, and one could argue there were still important privacy interests to protect. The district court sided with the government in this case. I wrote an opinion that set out parameters and structure for deciding when history would trump privacy concerns and when it would be entrusted to the sound discretion of the trial court. Then I ruled that in the present case it did fit the criteria for an instance when it was at the discretion of the trial court, and the trial court had found that the minutes could not be opened, so the appeals court was bound by that exercise of valid discretion. The historians would not appeal because as a profession, they had won the larger issue, and [the] government couldn't appeal because they had won the case.

Judge V provided an insightful assessment of the strategic perspective. He suggested that at first blush, the strategic account seems to make sense, but he cautioned scholars about its practicality. As he commented, "There is some merit to strategic perspectives as long as you do not ascribe too much knowledge to the courts; there is usually too much uncertainty for the court to guess the chances of reversal."

Assessing the Application of the Strategic Account: Is It Rational?

The Supreme Court agrees to hear approximately 150 to 200 cases per term (including those that receive summary decisions from the Court). This means that the Court hears fewer than 3 percent of all petitions it receives. Moreover, many lower court decisions are never appealed. As a result, Supreme Court review of lower court decisions is a rare event (appeals courts decisions are typically reviewed in less than three-tenths of 1 percent of cases). Similarly, review of a panel decision by the circuit en banc is also a rare event. As noted in chapter 3, fewer decisions of panels of the courts of appeals are reviewed by the circuit en banc than the three-tenths of 1 percent that are reviewed by the Supreme Court. Consequently, the question of interest now is whether it is rational for appeals court judges to modify their behavior strategically to avoid reversal by the Supreme Court. Given the very low probability that a federal appeals court case will even make it to the Supreme Court, it is important to determine whether appeals court judges can reasonably predict the likelihood of Supreme Court review. Appeals court judges may not need completely perfect information, but unless appeals court judges can accurately predict the likelihood of Supreme Court review and potential reversal and its associated cost, it is impossible for them to engage in strategic behavior when deciding cases. However, if appeals court judges can predict what cases are likely to be reviewed and believe there is a substantial cost associated with reversal, then it is at least plausible that they will strategically decide those cases most likely to be reviewed.

In deciphering this puzzle, we make the following three-pronged argument. First, for U.S. courts of appeals judges to act strategically, the judges must have a strong sense of which cases will be reviewed by the Supreme Court. Second, cases for strategic action must have a high probability of review. Third, the cost of reversal must be high. Strategic action is most likely when all three conditions are present. However, the relative magnitude of the second and third conditions may affect strategic calculations.

According to most strategic perspectives, the agent is more likely to shirk if the benefits of shirking outweigh the costs. The costs are a function of the extent and likelihood of sanctions by the principal. The sanction is reversal, which has personal and policy costs. The likelihood of sanctioning by the principal is a function of the monitoring by the principal. If the principals (the circuit en banc and the SCOTUS) do not adequately monitor (review) the agent (the judge on the panel), the judge is less likely to be constrained by the principal and is therefore more likely to shirk. Presumably, monitoring is adequate only if it is relatively frequent and predictable. We find that it is infrequent and unpredictable, and therefore likely ineffective. Additionally, if the costs of shirking (sanctions from the principal, in this case reversal, resulting in policy and personal costs) are low in comparison to the benefits, the judge is more likely to shirk. The interviews with the judges suggested the costs of reversal are minimal. Therefore, given the infrequent, random monitoring combined with the minimal efficacy of the potential sanctions and the low costs of shirking, we doubt the judges factor in the preferences of the circuit en banc or the Supreme Court when deciding cases.

Can Judges Determine Which Cases Will Be Reviewed? The View of the Judges

Of the sixty judges formally interviewed, only seven expressed even a moderately high degree of confidence in their ability to predict accurately which cases would be reviewed by the Supreme Court. Only Judge R expressed unambiguous confidence, asserting, "We know what cases are likely to go to the Supreme Court." But he quickly added that what was more important was the knowledge that more than 99 percent of their decisions would not be reviewed. Judge Q seemed to agree, but was somewhat more guarded in his assessment, claiming only that "we can predict fairly well what will go to the Supreme Court—or at least which cases have a good chance of being reviewed. . . . Most of our cases clearly will not be reviewed, and we all know that." Judge WW felt confident listing several characteristics that would trigger Supreme Court review: "criminal cases, circuit conflict, intracircuit conflict, dissent, and first impression cases." Judge AA provided more specific examples: "Sometimes dissent is used to signal to the Supreme Court that the majority got the decision wrong. I have written dissents for that reason. If you favor the defendant, the Supreme Court is more likely to look at the case; in immigration cases, if you don't follow the agency ruling the SCT is more likely to look at the case; anytime we make a decision that puts limits on law enforcement, the Court will look at it." Finally, Judge UU echoed the importance of circuit conflict as triggering review, but also noted the importance of the solicitor general in positively triggering review. He stated, "For the Supreme Court if the Solicitor General gets involved and if there is circuit conflict," then review is more likely. And Judge OO, the most confident judge of the judges we interviewed, put it this way:

> I am very cognizant of the views of all the Supreme Court Justices on various issues from First Amendment, abortion, affirmative action, and rights of the accused, and I feel quite confident I know what makes a case certworthy and the types of decisions lower court judges can make that would trigger the Court to review the case. You will find lots of appeals court judges claiming they have no idea what makes the Court grant cert, but I don't believe that for a minute. We know their views and their ideologies, and we know the issues they like to take up.

Fifty-three of the sixty judges said they could not accurately predict which cases would be reviewed. At one extreme, nine of the sixty judges conveyed a sense of bewilderment at the certiorari process. Judge G volunteered, "I have been 'flabbergasted' at which cases of mine have been reviewed by the Supreme Court—so I guess I would have to say it is pretty hard to predict when the Court will grant cert." Judge A agreed, saying, "I have no idea what makes a case certworthy—it is just something I have never thought about; the chance of review of a case I'm working is simply irrelevant." Similarly, Judge O concluded, "Usually I can't predict what the Supreme Court is going to do on an issue." Judge L offered, "I'm not at all clear on what makes a case certworthy; I've never paid much attention to what the Supreme Court will do, in part because they take so few of our cases." Judge N agreed with Judge L's assessment: "I don't have a very good idea of what makes a case certworthy." Judge WW offered the following assessment: "Some [cases] go to the Supreme Court and some don't. I don't know why, and for some it is obvious but I don't predict because the case most likely will not be heard by the Supreme Court." Finally, Judge I admitted, "I have no idea what the Supreme Court will review except for a very few high-profile cases like *Padilla.*"

The remaining forty-four judges in our sample had some general ideas about either the types of cases that had moderately good chances of review or which cases certainly would not be reviewed, but professed little ability to make predictions in a large number of cases they heard. Most of the judges indicated that for at least a majority of the cases they heard, they were confident that the Court would not grant cert, but for the remainder of their docket it was difficult to predict which cases would go up and which would not. Typical of these judges was the response of Judge B: "I am not able to predict which cases the Supreme Court will review, but in 60 percent or 70 percent of the cases one can be pretty sure they are not going to review." Similarly, Judge L said, "It is easy to identify many cases that you know will not go up, but it is very hard to tell whether a specific case will be taken." Judge N presented a variation on this theme. After earlier noting that perhaps a third or so of their decisions were "slam dunks," in which all of the judges easily reached agreement, Judge N offered, "I don't have a very good idea of what makes a case certworthy. Of course, it is pretty obvious that most of the cases we think are slam dunks are not going to go up." Other judges offered more specific ideas about the types of cases that would not be reviewed. Judge P admitted that he didn't know which cases would be reviewed, but he was pretty confident about some of the types of cases that would not be reviewed. For instance, he said, "You know that criminal cases that turn on the facts won't go to the Court." Judge H pointed out that circuit splits are the most identifiable characteristic, but after that he would be unable to identify what makes a case worthy of the Supreme Court's attention. For example, he argued, "I think that circuit splits; at least if it is an issue that they care about, is that thing that is most likely to lead to cert. Other than that, I'm not sure. It is just issues that they care about, but those change, so I'm not always sure which ones those are. So even if I was worried about reversal, I couldn't predict which cases they were likely to take well enough to do anything about it."

The other common theme, mentioned spontaneously by more than half (thirty-five of sixty) of the judges, was that decisions that create circuit conflicts had an increased chance of being reviewed by the Supreme Court. The assessment of Judge C was typical of the responses: "The most obvious thing that will make it likely that the Court will grant cert is a conflict among circuits; if we get an issue that other circuits have already decided, we will take seriously what the other circuits have decided—we almost always talk about that in conference." However, he quickly added: "But even with a conflict you can't be sure at all." Similarly, Judge J suggested "It is very difficult to predict except you know that clear circuit splits are likely to lead to review," and his sentiments were echoed by Judge M, who said, "Not really sure what makes a case certworthy besides circuit conflicts." But Judge M went on to explain that they tried to avoid circuit splits when they could. "We are very careful not to produce a circuit split if we can avoid it; we talk about that a lot and are very hesitant to go the other way, especially if two or three circuits have already come out on the same side of the issue. We probably have as much concern for national uniformity as the Supreme Court does. I guess it just comes down to what they think is important."

A couple of judges modified this assessment that circuit conflicts lead to Supreme Court review, noting that "big" or "important" cases are also likely to be reviewed. Typical of these judges, Judge E suggested the following: "Circuit splits are probably the biggest factor in the Supreme Court deciding to review. Other than that it seems to be whether they think it is a big issue or an area of law that has not been addressed, but I don't think I am confident, except in a very few cases, what the Supreme Court would consider a big case. So most of the time there is no way to know if they are going to review your decision." Judge O answered, "Well, circuit conflicts—when your circuit creates a split with the decision of another circuit—you know review is likely, but other than that, I don't know what the Supreme Court is likely to do. It just never enters my mind to think about what kind of cases the Supreme Court might review. It is what *they* think is important, after all—that is pretty much all their guidelines say." Similarly, Judge K said, "It is very difficult to tell which cases are certworthy. It is very often a mystery to me. There are a few cases, like *Padilla,* where you know that cert will be granted, but a very few cases fall into a category like that. . . . Generally, whether they are going to take a case you have is a crap shoot. . . . You can be pretty sure most of the cases will not go up, but of course, circuit conflicts are more likely to be reviewed."

Overall, twenty-nine of the sixty judges formally interviewed cited national importance as a factor influencing a grant of cert, but interestingly, only a few of those twenty-nine felt confident they knew precisely what made a case "important" in the minds of the justices. In an informal conversation with six judges, all agreed that there were always a very small number of cases, perhaps a half dozen to a dozen in the country in a given year, which most judges as well as most other close observers of the legal system were pretty sure that the Supreme Court would ultimately review because of the very high political profile of the case. Cases often mentioned in this category included *Padilla, Grutter,* and recent conflicts involving phone taps by the National Security Agency and the national partial birth abortion law. But all the judges agreed that it was the nature of the issue that would prompt Supreme Court review of these high-profile cases. None of the six judges believed there was anything that the court of appeals could do in such cases to influence whether or not the Supreme Court granted cert; thus, strategic action would be impossible, they said. Moreover, several of the judges noted that even in some of those rare cases that everyone assumed would go to the Supreme Court, when the case did in fact go up, it was reversed by the Court, suggesting that either the appeals court panel decided not to worry about how the Supreme Court would react or it was unable to accurately predict the Court's response.

While the judges said that in most cases they were unable to predict the chances of review, at the extreme margins, there apparently are a very small number of cases that the judges believe they can predict quite confidently the Supreme Court will review. For example, one clerk interviewed mentioned a death penalty case in which the Supreme Court had already reversed the circuit court twice, and now the case was before the circuit court for a third time. The clerk indicated that he knew that, facing the possibility of a third reversal in the same case, the judges on the panel had informally discussed what the Supreme Court might do as they discussed how to structure their opinion. However, the clerk noted that this type of situation was very rare; his judge had indicated that he had never had a similar situation in more than thirty years on the bench. The same clerk noted that in an analogous death penalty case in the Fifth Circuit, the court of appeals was reversed the third time the case went to the Supreme Court, suggesting that those judges did not act strategically to prevent reversal even though they presumably knew that such reversal was possible.

In summary, the general view seems to be that all the judges know that review is very unlikely, and they can often be highly confident that a given case will not be reviewed. But even if a case passes some minimal hurdle of difficulty or importance, most judges claim they are almost always unable to assess what the chance is that their decision, no matter which way they decide the case, will be reviewed by the Supreme Court.

An Empirical Assessment of the Probabilities of Review

Next we determined whether cases judged by objective criteria to be the strongest candidates for review actually have a high likelihood of Supreme Court review. More specifically, we modeled the likelihood that a given case would be reviewed by the Supreme Court using only the characteristics of the case that would be known to the judges on the panel at the time of their decision. In contrast, judges on the panel do not know (though they may suspect) whether the losing party in the case will ask the Supreme Court to review, and if such an appeal is filed, they do not know what will be in the cert petition, or whether the solicitor general or other amici will file in support of or in opposition to the petition. Thus, appeals court judges cannot use such factors to decide whether or not to behave strategically.

As noted in chapter 2, a majority of the cases coming to the courts of appeals are viewed by the judges as not involving any important or contentious legal issues. Consequently, the judges have devised a number of time-saving procedures to permit expeditious handling of these cases (e.g., procedural termination on the recommendation of staff attorneys, denial of oral argument, and termination of the appeal with just a brief, nonpublished opinion). The implication of both the tiny number of appeals reviewed by the Supreme Court or the circuit en banc and the comments of the judges is that these cases are viewed by the judges as having virtually no chance of further review. So it is clear that the judges do not consider strategic behavior with regard to these cases, which make up a large majority of their cases. In the analysis below, we focus on just the small proportion of cases that present the politically and legally most important issues, those that have received oral argument and are resolved with a published opinion. As noted in chapter 3, in recent years cases that receive the "full treatment" from a panel of judges account for only about 8 percent of the total caseload coming to the courts of appeals (about five thousand cases annually) but for virtually all the cases in which review of the panel decision is possible in any practical sense.[5] So the focus of our analysis is on whether there is any evidence of strategic action in this important minority of the docket of the courts of appeals.

The interviews described above indicate that appeals court judges tend to think about cert in terms of case characteristics. When asked what makes it likely that the Court will review their decision, judges tended not to talk about the nature of their decision or opinion but instead talked about the nature of the case or issue, saying the Court might take it if it was a "big national issue" (Judge D) or if it was "an issue that they care about" (Judge H). In contrast, they suggested that review was unlikely if the precedent was so clear that it was a "slam dunk" (Judge N). Furthermore, a recent interview with a former Federal Appeals Court and Supreme Court law clerk confirmed this idea of judges viewing cases in terms of their characteristics rather than outcomes. The idea of case characteristics becomes important when assessing whether cases encompassing (or not) certain characteristics are certworthy or not. Perry (1991) has suggested that Supreme Court justices look for certain case characteristics, both positive and negative, when determining whether to grant certiorari. By positive, we mean case characteristics that will lead to cert being granted. Conversely, negative characteristics are those that will lead to denial of cert.

The next prong of our analysis was to determine whether one can accurately predict which of the cases with published opinions the Supreme Court will review, based on objective case characteristics. To do this, we analyzed the universe of appeals court published opinions that were reviewed by the Supreme Court during a three-year period and a stratified random sample of published appeals court opinions that were not reviewed by the Supreme Court. This strategy allowed us to straightforwardly evaluate the impact of characteristics of cases heard by the courts of appeals on the agenda of the Supreme Court. Only cases decided by three-judge panels were included in the analysis.

POSITIVE INDICATORS OF IMPORTANCE

Perry believes that the Supreme Court classifies importance not only in breadth but also in depth of a case (1991, 254). This suggests that if the issue is broad and far-reaching, if it has the potential to affect a large number of people, or if the outcome is vital for the polity as a whole, the Court is more likely to regard it as one that is important enough to grant cert (Giles, Walker, and Zorn 2006; Perry 1991, 253–54; Zorn 2002). Furthermore, a case may be considered important if the decision is essential to maintaining uniformity in the law, especially when there appears to be divergence over constitutional or statutory interpretation (codified as Federal Law Issue and Constitutional). This leads us to our first hypothesis regarding cases that have a broad impact:

H1: Cases that involve the interpretation of the Constitution or federal statute are likely to have broader impact than cases that simply resolve private disputes, so such cases will be more likely to be reviewed.

Several studies have found that the presence of amicus curiae briefs increases the likelihood of Court review, especially in light of the rarity of an amicus brief being filed in courts of appeals cases (Caldeira and Wright 1988). Moreover, amicus curiae briefs suggest to the Court that an issue is of great societal importance (Hansford 2004). We created a variable that indicates whether or not amici are present at the courts of appeals proceedings. This variable, designated Amicus Curiae, is coded one if one or more amici curiae briefs were filed and zero otherwise.

H2: The presence of amicus curiae briefs at the court of appeals proceedings should increase the likelihood of Supreme Court review.

Perry found through his interviews that certain types of cases, especially death penalty cases, because of the severe nature of their effects are more likely to be reviewed by Court. To test this hypothesis, we included a variable, Death Penalty, that is coded one if there was a death penalty issue and zero otherwise.

H3: The likelihood of Supreme Court review increases if there is a death penalty issue present.

Moreover, there are specific issue areas that, while they may affect only a small number of people, are viewed as so fundamental to the preservation of democracy that they also deserve special consideration from the Court. One such issue area that has been suggested to embody this special significance is First Amendment rights and guarantees. Hence we created a variable that indicates whether or not First Amendment issues are at stake; this variable, designated First Amendment Issue, is coded one if there is a First Amendment issue and zero otherwise.

H4: The likelihood of Supreme Court review increases if there exists a First Amendment issue.

Additionally, several empirical analyses of judicial voting behavior (Goldman 1969; Pritchett 1948; Schubert 1965; Tate 1981) over the past sixty years have consistently assumed that unanimously decided cases are quite often characterized as either possessing clear-cut precedent or the straightforward application of the case facts to the constitutional or statutory provision (Goldman 1969). Additionally, dissent may serve as a "whistle-blowing" mechanism (Cross and Tiller 1998; Giles, Walker, and Zorn 2006). Therefore, we conclude that it is quite reasonable to assume that cases with non-unanimous decisions are more likely to pose major jurisprudential questions than cases with unanimous decisions. As a result, we created a variable, Panel Conflict, to assess whether the presence of a dissenting opinion in the courts of appeals increases the likelihood of review by the Court.

H5: The presence of a dissent in the court of appeal's opinion increases the likelihood of review by the Supreme Court.

Finally, the most often repeated finding in previous studies of cert and in our interviews, and one of the most frequently mentioned "signals" discovered by Perry (1991), is that a conflict among the circuits on a point of federal law is likely to increase the chances that cert will be granted. Thus, the final positive indicator of the likelihood of cert is hypothesized to be Circuit Conflict:

H6: The likelihood of Supreme Court review increases if there is a conflict among the circuits on a point of federal law or national constitutional interpretation.

NEGATIVE INDICATORS OF IMPORTANCE

Perry (1991) derived from his interviews of Supreme Court justices and law clerks case characteristics that he deemed unimportant or "frivolous." Here we hypothesize that case characteristics from the appeals court decisions with negative indicators will be considered uncertworthy by the Supreme Court. We predict that these negative case characteristics will arise in a greater percentage of cases that are denied review than in those that are granted review. Perry (1991) specifically pointed to two types of cases that are considered frivolous: diversity cases and ineffective assistance of counsel. In particular, any court resolution emanating from a diversity case affects only a single state and, more important, interpretations by federal courts of the state law issues involved are not binding precedent for state supreme courts. As a result, any Supreme Court decision would have little jurisprudential significance. Therefore, we created a variable, Diversity Issue, that indicates the presence of a diversity issue in the court of appeals case. This variable was coded one if a diversity issue was present and zero otherwise.

H7: The presence of a diversity issue in the court of appeals case decreases the likelihood of review by the Supreme Court.

Cases involving questions of ineffective assistance of counsel are also considered to be in the category of frivolous cases. To test this assertion, we created a variable, Ineffective Assistance of Counsel, that indicates whether or not ineffective assistance of counsel claims were present in the appeals court case. This variable was coded one if there existed such a claim and zero otherwise.

H8: Claims involving ineffective assistance of counsel decrease the likelihood of Supreme Court review.

Perry (1991) found that law clerks and justices often mentioned that fact-specific cases are quite often denied review. Perry writes, "in most instances, the Court does not want to take a case when resolving it adds nothing to the doctrine, but turns on the facts of a particular case" (1991, 223). To test Perry's affirmations, we created a set of variables that get at this idea of fact specificity. In borrowing from Perry, we expect certain case characteristics to be negatively related to review. These include claims regarding weight of the evidence, cases involving the substantial evidence doctrine, and sufficiency of the evidence, codified as the corresponding variables Weight of Evidence, Substantial Evidence, and Sufficiency of Evidence. All of these evidentiary issues tend to be fact-specific to the case at hand and as a result would not be associated with a heightened likelihood of Court review.

H9: Cases involving issues regarding weight of evidence, substantial evidence, and sufficient evidence are negatively related to Supreme Court review.

CONTROLS

To sufficiently assess the relevance of positive and negative importance indicators, it is imperative that we control for other factors that have often been found by research to influence the Supreme Court's decision to grant cert. One of the most important factors to control for is the presence of the solicitor general representing the United States when the United States is a litigant in the case. Given the solicitor general's success in petitioning the Supreme Court for review, we believe that a government loss in the appeals court will be positively associated with review, while government success would be more apt to stand as is. These variables are designated as U.S. Government Winner and U.S. Government Loser.

Finally, congruence of the ideological direction between the lower court decisions and the Supreme Court seems to play a crucial role. That is to say, ideology matters in judicial decision making. Although we cannot test directly whether the Supreme Court grants cert as a way to correct for the ideology of the lower court decision, we indirectly tested this assertion by controlling for the ideology of the appeals court decision. During the period studied (the early Rehnquist court), the court is generally perceived to have been solidly conservative in its policy preferences. Such a conservative court would presumably have been more likely to overturn liberal than conservative decisions of the courts of appeals. By coding the direction of the appeals court decisions as either conservative or liberal (Lower Court Direction), we were clearly able to analyze, for instance, whether conservative decisions are less likely to be reviewed by a primarily conservative Supreme Court under review by this analysis.

DATA AND METHODS

The case data come from the Songer (2002) United States Courts of Appeals Database, Phase I and Phase II. Phase I involved the coding of a random sample of thirty cases with published opinions from each circuit for each year from 1960 to 1996 in addition to smaller samples for the period 1925 to 1959. In Phase II, all appeals court cases reviewed by the Supreme Court from 1953 to 1988 were coded. From each of these databases, we selected all cases from three years at the beginning of the Rehnquist Court, 1986–1988. Duplicates from the two databases were eliminated. Thus, the data for analysis include the universe of decisions reviewed by the Supreme Court and a sample of published cases not reviewed. The data in the model are weighted to reflect the sampling.

The dependent variable in our model is whether or not the Supreme Court reviewed the appeals court decision. This variable was coded one if the decision was reviewed and zero if it was not reviewed. Since our dependent variable is dichotomous, ordinary least squares regression is not suitable for this type of analysis; therefore, we instead used logistic regression.[6] Additional details of the coding and descriptive statistics for the variables in the model are provided in the technical appendix.

Results from the Case Characteristic Model

We move to the next phase of our analysis by examining whether or not the Supreme Court granted cert, given the presence of positive or negative case characteristics. The results of our logit model are presented in table 19. In general, our model performed very well. The model is significant at the 0.0001 level, and most of the independent variables have effects that are statistically significant. Overall, we found that most of our case characteristics (variables) performed as expected.

Most of the hypotheses are confirmed by the results of the logit model. Cases in which the U.S. government wins in the courts of appeals are less likely to be reviewed than cases not involving the U.S. government. Additionally, as expected, ideology matters. We found that the odds of granting cert decrease by approximately 55 percent when the lower court decision is conservative. Also as hypothesized, the chances of review are increased by the presence of our positive indicators of importance, including involvement of a federal law or constitutional issue, involvement of a First Amendment issue, the existence of circuit conflict, or the participation of amici curiae. These results in general confirm the implications of the existing literature on certiorari. Likewise, we found support for hypotheses about cases that had a negative indicator of importance; the presence of such a negative indicator dramatically decreases the likelihood of review. To highlight, when the lower court interprets the substantial evidence doctrine in agency cases, the odds of the Supreme Court reviewing the case decrease by approximately 85 percent.

Our Findings in Perspective: How Likely Is Supreme Court Review?

Although we do find support for most of our hypotheses, it is imperative to put these findings in perspective. Outwardly, our model implies that appeals court judges can accurately predict the likelihood of review. However, given the knowledge that Supreme Court review is an unlikely event, we delved further to explore how cases with several positive indicators of review stack up against the likelihood of review. While we have a high degree of confidence (for many variables, at the 0.001 level) that the presence or absence of these factors changes the probability of review to a statistically significant degree, many of the variables might still lack substantive relevance to a strategically oriented judge. To demonstrate,

TABLE 19 Model of the likelihood of U.S. Courts of Appeals cases (1986–1988) making it to the agenda of the Supreme Court

CASE CHARACTERISTIC	EXPECTATION	MLE (SE)	ODDS RATIO	PERCENTAGE CHANGE
POSITIVE INDICATORS OF IMPORTANCE				
Federal Law Issue	+	0.625** (0.199)	1.868	86
Constitutional	+	1.155*** (0.247)	3.174	217
Amicus Curiae	+	0.899*** (0.236)	2.457	146
Death Penalty	+	−0.151 (0.691)		
First Amendment Issue	+	0.724* (0.351)	2.063	106
Panel Conflict (dissent)	+	1.060*** (0.203)	2.886	189
Circuit Conflict	+	1.393*** (0.209)	4.027	303
NEGATIVE INDICATORS OF IMPORTANCE				
Diversity Issue	–	−1.273*** (0.526)	0.280	−72
Ineffective Assistance of Counsel	–	−1.247# (1.012)	0.287	−71
Weight of Evidence	–	−0.933*** (0.291)	0.393	−61
Substantial Evidence	–	−1.912* (1.009)	0.148	−85
Sufficiency of Evidence	–	−0.195 (0.533)		
OUTCOME VARIABLES—PRIOR STUDIES				
U.S. Government Loser (in appeals court)	+	0.224 (0.236)		
U.S. Government Winner (in appeals court)	–	−0.963*** (0.282)	0.381	−62
Decision Conservative (of appeals court)	–	−0.799*** (0.282)	0.450	−55
Constant		−5.203*** (0.198)		
N	1,176			
Gamma	0.704			

Notes: Degrees of freedom = 15. MLE—maximum likelihood estimation; standard errors in parentheses.

#$P < 0.10$, *$P < 0.05$, **$P < 0.01$, ***$P < 0.001$ (one-tailed).

we also calculated the probability that the Supreme Court would grant review given several selected combinations of positive case characteristics indicators.

These calculations are provided in table 20. For example, let us consider a case characterized by a combination of three characteristics, all shown by the analysis above to strongly increase the chances of review. For an appeals court case, example A, with a constitutional issue, an amicus brief filed, and panel conflict (dissent) present, the probability that the case will be reviewed by the Supreme Court is approximately 0.11. It should be stressed that it is extremely rare for such a case to be heard by the courts of appeals: only seven-tenths of 1 percent of the cases in our sample had a probability of cert that was this high. Yet even for such an out-of-the-ordinary case, one might wonder whether any rational judge would worry about reversal if the judge perceived that the chance of review was only 11 percent, even if the judge assumed that a grant of cert was tantamount to reversal, unless the potential costs of reversal were very high. Taking a hypothetical case with two other factors strongly related to the likelihood that cert would be granted, we found that the probability that an appeals court case with panel conflict (dissent) and circuit conflict, case type B, would be reviewed by the Supreme Court was only 0.06. Even in a case with five factors all of which were found to significantly increase the chance for review (a conservative decision with amicus participation, a constitutional issue, panel conflict [dissent], and circuit conflict), the probability of the Supreme Court granting cert rose only to 0.18 (case type C in table 20).

Overall, these results show that even though the probability of review is higher when combinations of positive indicators of review are present compared to negative indicators, the actual chance that a given case with multiple positive indicators will be reviewed remains small. Thus, a rational judge on a panel who understood which cases were most likely to be reviewed still would conclude that even if she had a case that was one of the types most likely to be reviewed, her particular case would most likely not be reviewed.

To gain additional perspective on the rationality of strategic action to avoid reversal, we calculated the estimated probability of review for each individual case in our sample of more than 1,100 published decisions by the courts of appeals. We found that the probability of review was less than 1 percent in 77 percent of all appeals court cases with published opinions and less than 5 percent in more than 97 percent of the cases.[7] Even if a judge assumed that reversal was likely any time a case

TABLE 20 Probability of Supreme Court granting review, given the presence of positive indicators

	VARIABLE					
POSSIBLE CASE TYPE	AMICUS CURIAE	CONSTITUTIONAL	PANEL CONFLICT (DISSENT)	DECISION CONSERVATIVE (OF APPEALS COURT)	CIRCUIT CONFLICT	PROBABILITY OF REVIEW
A	X	X	X			0.11
B			X		X	0.06
C	X	X	X	X	X	0.18

Note: X denotes an illustration of a case with the indicated case characteristics and the rest of the variables held at zero.

was reviewed (though reversal actually occurs in only two-thirds of the cases reviewed), these data suggest that judges rationally should have a very low fear of reversal for the overwhelming majority of the cases they hear.

Finally, we considered how the probability of cert might be affected by strategic decision making by the judges on the courts of appeals. The interviews with the judges revealed that the judges think it is primarily the characteristics of the cases and their issues rather than the decisions of appeals court judges that have the greatest impact on whether or not cert is granted. Our case model confirms that many of the factors that have the greatest impact on the probability of cert (e.g., whether there is a constitutional or statutory issue versus a weight of evidence or ineffective assistance of counsel issue) are beyond the control of even a judge who is inclined to act strategically. Thus, in table 21 we focus on a couple of examples of the extent to which an attempt to act strategically to avoid reversal can actually affect those odds.

First, it should be noted that in those 77 percent of cases with published opinions, in which the probability of cert is already below 1 percent, we believe it is most unlikely that any judge would act strategically in an attempt to reduce the chances of cert and possible reversal even further. So we limited our examples to cases involving some of the factors strongly and positively related in a statistical sense to the likelihood of cert being granted. Let's now consider the first example, labeled Sincere 1, a criminal case involving a constitutional issue, the participation of an amicus, and the U.S. government as a party. Our example assumes the judges all voted sincerely to support the criminal defendant (a liberal decision). The probability of cert is estimated to be 5 percent. Alternatively, the court might act strategically to change the outcome (i.e., make a conservative decision favoring the government). Such strategic action would only reduce the probability of cert from 5 percent to 2 percent (see Strategic 1a). Alternatively (see Strategic 1b), a judge wanting Supreme Court review might dissent, increasing the chances of cert from 5 percent to 13 percent.

In the second example, Sincere 2, we crafted an extreme case, once again with a constitutional issue and amicus participation, but in which the court unanimously and sincerely made a liberal decision that created a conflict with a prior decision of another circuit. The probability of cert in this case would be 14 percent (more likely than in over 99.5 percent of our actual cases). If the court in this case instead decided strategically to change the outcome to a conservative decision that was consistent with

TABLE 21 Examples of changing the probability of the Supreme Court's granting review by the strategic action of appeals court judges

	VARIABLE						
DECISION TYPE	U.S. GOVERNMENT WINNER/ LOSER (IN APPEALS COURT)	AMICUS CURIAE	CONSTITUTIONAL	PANEL CONFLICT (DISSENT)	DECISION CONSERVATIVE/ LIBERAL (OF APPEALS COURT)	CIRCUIT CONFLICT	PROBABILITY OF REVIEW
Sincere 1	Loser	Yes	Yes	No	Liberal	No	0.05
Strategic 1a	Winner	Yes	Yes	No	Conservative	No	0.02
Strategic 1b	Loser	Yes	Yes	Yes	Liberal	No	0.13
Sincere 2	—	Yes	Yes	No	Liberal	Yes	0.14
Strategic 2	—	Yes	Yes	No	Conservative	No	0.01

the policies of other circuits, the chances of cert would be reduced to just 1 percent. This last example, labeled Strategic 2, appears to represent closely the maximum marginal effect that strategic action by any appeals court panel could hope to achieve. Whether a court would act strategically even in this extreme situation might depend on the risk averseness of the judges and their perception of the likelihood that cert would lead to reversal and the cost of such reversal.[8]

Next we examined whether judges can predict the likelihood of en banc review.

En Banc Rehearings

As noted earlier, another institutional constraint courts of appeals judges face is possible en banc review by their circuit court. The courts of appeals have the discretionary option to grant an en banc rehearing, which allows all the active circuit judges to rehear a given case (with the exception of the Ninth Circuit, which, because of its size, requires only eleven judges to sit en banc rather than the full twenty-nine). There are typically two ways a case can make it to the circuit court's en banc docket. An active circuit court judge can request the circuit to rehear a case (sua sponte), or a litigant who lost can petition the circuit for an en banc rehearing. Both options require a majority of the active judges in the circuit to agree to grant the petition. Scholars have characterized the en banc rehearing process as a way for the circuit as a whole (with the exception of the Ninth Circuit) to correct panel decisions that conflict with the majority preferences of the judges in the circuit (Abramowiz 2000; Atkins 1972; Giles, Walker, and Zorn 2006; Giles et al. 2007; Van Winkle 1997). It should also be recalled that when the circuit agrees to grant a rehearing en banc, the three-judge panel ruling is vacated. Thus, when the circuit en banc "reverses" or "affirms" a ruling, it is the district court decision that is reversed or affirmed. However, in a technical sense, while the panel ruling is not reversed per se, one can still examine whether the circuit en banc agreed with the vacated panel ruling. Moreover, interviews conducted with several courts of appeals court judges revealed that judges tend to care more about being "reviewed" by their circuit en banc than by the Supreme Court.

Partly because of the rarity of en banc rehearings (Wasby 2001), scholars have been interested in understanding why circuits grant them in the first place. Prior studies examining en banc rehearings have analyzed how the circuit can control panel decisions that conflict with the majority preferences of the circuit (Banks 1999; Clark 2008; Solimine 1988;

Zarone 2000), the interactions between the circuit en banc and the Supreme Court (George and Solimine 2001), the influences of en banc review (Banks 1999; George 1999; Solimine 1988;), how circuits set their en banc agendas (Giles, Walker, and Zorn 2006; Giles et al. 2007), and how ideology influences en banc review (Banks 1999; Clark 2008; Solimine 1988; Zarone 2000). We examined whether judges have enough information to predict en banc review by combining the perspectives of the judges and empirical testing.

Determining En Banc Review: The Judges' Perspective

We asked the judges whether they could predict the factors that might persuade their circuit to grant an en banc rehearing. First, we asked the judges whether they could predict which cases would be reviewed by their circuit en banc. Second, we asked the judges to speak to the specific characteristics of a case that would make it worthy of en banc review.

In response to the first question, fifteen of the sixty judges we interviewed expressed a high degree of assurance that they could predict with accuracy the types of cases their circuit would grant en banc review. One remark made by Judge Q stood out, as it was the most confident self-estimation of a judge's ability to predict en banc review: "I am quite aware of the views of my colleagues in my circuit on various issues, from abortion, affirmative action, and rights of the accused, and I feel quite confident I know what makes a case more likely to be reviewed by my circuit en banc. We all know each other's views and know when an issue commands our attention for full court review." Judge T and Judge BB expressed similar views on their ability to predict en banc review. For example, Judge T remarked, "The two strongest indicators that our circuit will grant a rehearing is conflict within the circuit, meaning two panels decide the same type of case and come to different conclusions. We, the circuit, have to address this so as to have uniformity within the circuit. Secondly, if the case is involved in a circuit conflict we are likely to grant a rehearing, especially if it is an issue of national importance, so that we can have the full force of the circuit behind the case law."

At the other end of the spectrum, four of the sixty judges stated they were unable to predict what cases their circuit would review en banc. Judge D, for instance, claimed, "I am just not sure when the circuit wants to rehear a case. Some cases I think are clearly going to be reheard, and they are not, and then others I am certain the circuit would not rehear, and the circuit does. Unfortunately, I am not very good at predicting these sorts of things."

The remaining judges conveyed some sense of the types of case their circuit would be willing to grant a rehearing. Many judges expressed the opinion that most of the cases they routinely decided would not be reviewed by their circuit en banc, and they were more confident in identifying those sets sof cases. For example, Judge N said, "For the most part, we know a high majority of our cases will never be reheard by our circuit en banc. Look, in our circuit we may grant en banc review in eight to ten cases a year, and we decide over five thousand cases a year, so you do the math. It's not likely, and we know this."

When judges were asked whether they could identify specific case characteristics that would prompt a rehearing en banc, the overwhelming responses were intra- and intercircuit conflict. In addition to circuit conflict, several judges mentioned a filed dissent and cases dealing with issues of national importance as factors that might lead to en banc review. When pressed whether a concurring opinion would increase the likelihood of a rehearing en banc, many of the judges agreed this would be positively associated with a rehearing. The judges also noted that some case characteristics were more important than others in triggering an en banc rehearing. For example, Judge J commented, "I would say that intercircuit conflict and serious constitutional questions are the two biggest reasons our circuit would grant en banc review. And although I believe circuit conflict and issues of national importance or serious constitutional questions, like abortion, for example, are the biggest factors that get our attention, I also think dissent in a case can serve that same function, [as can] a concurring opinion, but perhaps to a lesser degree."

The judges answered questions regarding the case characteristics that would decrease the likelihood of an en banc rehearing. That is, the judges were asked whether they could identify cases that were considered frivolous or unlikely to be reheard by the circuit en banc. Most judges pointed to cases involving diversity jurisdiction issues. Furthermore, several judges noted that fact-specific cases were routine error-correcting cases their circuit would not review en banc. When pushed as to the types of cases this category included, several judges mentioned weight of evidence issues, interpretation of the substantial evidence doctrine, and questions of sufficiency of evidence.

An Empirical Analysis of the Likelihood of En Banc Review

The judges interviewed indicated that they tended to think about the potential for en banc and Supreme Court review in terms of case characteristics rather than case outcomes. Utilizing the judge interview data and findings reported in the scholarly literature, we examined whether cases deemed worthy of the full circuit court's attention have a greater chance of review than those cases deemed unworthy of the full circuit court's attention.

Scholars have noted that one of the main constraints faced by lower court judges is the possibility that their decision will be reversed (Benesh and Reddick 2002; Bowie and Songer 2009; Klein and Hume 2003). As such, judges may alter their decision-making patterns because of this potential for review and reversal. This at the very least assumes judges have enough information to make the strategic calculation to avoid review. Simply, we asked, do appeals court judges have enough information to make the necessary strategic calculations to determine the likelihood of en banc review? One way to test this informational assumption was to build a model that incorporated case characteristics that have been suggested to increase and decrease the likelihood of en banc review. Without having a reasonable assessment of the case characteristics that increase or decrease the likelihood of en banc review, appeals court judges ultimately would be unable to make accurate strategic calculations.

In addition to including the judges' views on en banc rehearings, we also examined whether cases judged by objective case characteristics to be the strongest contenders for review actually have a high probability of en banc review. Building on the framework presented above for evaluating the possibility of cert by the Supreme Court and our analysis presented earlier in this chapter, we examined only the case characteristics known to the judges on the panel at the time of their decision. For example, while judges may know whether one of their panel colleagues will write a dissenting opinion, they will not know (although they may suspect) whether the losing party in the case will ask the circuit to review. Therefore, appeals court judges cannot use factors that are not known to them at the time of the case when deciding whether to behave strategically.

In addition to what the judges believe increase (or decrease) the likelihood of en banc review, there are guidelines suggesting when circuit courts should rehear a case en banc. Rule 35 of the Federal Rules of Appellate Procedure (FRAPs) governs the use of en banc panels. According to rule 35, "*en banc* consideration is necessary to secure or maintain uniformity of the court's decision; or the proceeding involves a question of exceptional importance." Notably, two conditions warrant granting an en banc rehearing: (1) the case presents a matter of legal uncertainty, and (2) the case is deemed exceptionally important. While the first exception is straightforward, the second exception provides, at best, only a vague guideline for what constitutes "exceptional importance." Nonetheless, political scientists and the judges interviewed have proposed several distinct indicators of what makes a case worthy and unworthy of a rehearing en banc.

HYPOTHESES

Because of the similarity in the discretionary docket control mechanisms between the Supreme Court certiorari and en banc rehearing process, the guidelines regarding when circuits should rehear a case, and the rarity with which en banc rehearings occur, we proposed and tested almost identical hypotheses to those given above (see the rationales above for the analogous hypotheses).

POSITIVE INDICATORS OF IMPORTANCE

Since, like the Supreme Court, the courts of appeals care about case importance, both should be more likely to review constitutional cases (the variable is Constitution).

H1: Because cases that involve the interpretation of the Constitution are likely to have broader impact than cases that simply resolve private disputes, such cases are more likely to be reviewed by the circuit en banc.

Similarly, amicus participation (Amicus Curiae) should indicate importance to the circuit en banc, as well as to the Supreme Court.

H2: The presence of an amicus curiae brief at the federal court of appeals proceedings should increase the likelihood of en banc review.

For the same reasons that dissent on the courts of appeals is expected to serve as a cue for review by the Supreme Court, it should increase the chances of review by the circuit en banc (the variables are Dissenting Opinion—panel and Concurring Opinion—panel).

H3: The presence of a dissenting opinion in the court of appeals' panel decision increases the likelihood of review by the circuit en banc.

H4: The presence of a concurring opinion in the court of appeals' panel decision increases the likelihood of en banc review.

The most frequently mentioned indicators of en banc review are the existence of intercircuit and intracircuit conflict. Intercircuit conflict

(Intercircuit Conflict) refers to a split among the circuits on a point of federal law or constitutional interpretation. Similarly, intracircuit conflict (Intracircuit Conflict) refers to a split between two or more panels within a circuit on the interpretation of the Constitution or a federal statute. Both are likely to increase the chances that an en banc hearing will be granted. Thus, we proposed the following:

H5: The likelihood of en banc review increases if there is intercircuit conflict on a point of federal law or national constitutional interpretation.
H6: The likelihood of en banc review increases if there is intracircuit conflict on a point of federal law or national constitutional interpretation.

NEGATIVE INDICATORS OF IMPORTANCE

We expect that the circuit is not likely to review every alleged error by their panels but instead limits its review to important issues. Thus the same negative indicators of importance that reduce the likelihood of Supreme Court review may be expected to limit the likelihood of a review en banc. Specifically:

H7: The presence of a diversity issue in a case heard by the court of appeals decreases the likelihood of review by the circuit en banc.
H8: Claims involving ineffective assistance of counsel decrease the likelihood of en banc review.
H9: Fact-specific cases are negatively related to en banc review.

CONTROL MEASURES

As in our model of review by the Supreme Court, to sufficiently assess the relevance of positive and negative importance indicators, it is necessary to control for ideological factors. Presumably, a circuit en banc is more likely to overturn panel decisions that are inconsistent with the preferences of the circuit majority (Banks 1999; Clark 2008; Haire, Songer, and Lindquist 2003). Controlling for whether a decision is incompatible with the majority preferences of the whole circuit court allows one to analyze whether ideologically incongruent decisions are more likely than congruent decisions to be reviewed by a circuit en banc (the variable is Ideological Incongruence of Panel and Circuit).

Additionally, Cameron, Segal, and Songer (2000) found that the Supreme Court was less willing to grant certiorari in cases in which liberal panels rendered conservative decisions and conservative panels rendered liberal decisions. Haire, Lindquist, and Songer (2003, 152) suggest this is because the Supreme Court may "give the benefit of the doubt" to decisions that are ideologically incongruent with the panel's ideological make-up. Likewise, to control for this phenomenon, the circuit en banc may be less willing to review cases that are incongruent with a panel's preferred policy preferences (the variable is Panel Decision Incongruent with Median Panel Preferences).

Finally, political science research has often noted the high success rate of the U.S. government both before the Supreme Court (McGuire 1995) and in the courts of appeals (Songer, Sheehan, and Haire 2000). Given this influence, the circuit might be less inclined to review a case if the government wins (U.S. Government Winner) and more likely to review the panel decision if the government loses (U.S. Government Loser).

Data and Operationalization

The data for this study came from the First, Fifth, Sixth, and Ninth Circuit Court of Appeals from 1983 to 1991.[9] These circuits were selected because of their consistent record keeping on en banc rehearings.[10] A Lexis-Nexis search was conducted to identify the cases that were heard en banc.[11] The data in this study encompass all panel decisions that were reviewed by the circuits en banc and a sample of cases that were not reviewed by the circuits sitting en banc. Similar to the testing strategy we described above, to draw the sample of cases where en banc review was not petitioned or granted, the Songer (2002) United States Courts of Appeals Database was utilized (any duplicates in the Songer database and the en banc data collected were omitted). Once the cases were identified, the coding of the independent and dependent variables followed the protocol employed by the Songer (2002) United States Court of Appeals Database, with any exceptions explained below. The resulting data for this analysis include all panel decisions reviewed by the First, Fifth, Sixth, and Ninth Circuits en banc and a sample of published cases not reviewed. Because these data include all en banc rehearings and a sample of cases that were not heard en banc, the data in the model are weighted to reflect the sampling.

DEPENDENT VARIABLE

The dependent variable is whether or not the circuit granted a rehearing en banc. This variable was coded one if the three-judge panel decision was reviewed en banc and zero if it was not reviewed. Since the dependent variable is dichotomous, logistic regression is used for this analysis.[12]

INDEPENDENT VARIABLES

Beginning with the positive indicators of importance, the variable Constitution (i.e., a constitutional issue was present) was coded one if the case contained a matter of constitutional interpretation, and zero otherwise. The measure for Amicus Curiae was simply coded one if one or more amicus briefs were filed in the panel decision and zero otherwise. Dissenting Opinion (panel) was coded one if a dissent was filed in the case, and zero otherwise. Likewise, if a case included a concurring opinion (of the panel), this was coded one, and zero otherwise.

To assess whether a case possessed intercircuit and intracircuit conflict, each opinion was read and a value of one was assigned if either the majority, concurring, or dissenting opinion specifically stated that circuit conflict was present in this case, and zero otherwise. With respect to the negative indicators of importance, each variable was coded one if it involved diversity jurisdiction, ineffective assistance of counsel, or fact-specific issues, and zero if it did not

Following the coding procedure set forth in Haire, Lindquist, and Songer (2003), the variable Ideological Incongruence of Panel and Circuit was coded one if the decision was liberal and a majority of the judges on the circuit at the time of the decision were conservative, or if the decision was conservative and a majority of the judges on the circuit at the time of the decision were liberal (using the variable Party of the Appointing President as a proxy), and zero otherwise. Similarly, using the variable Party of the Appointing President as a proxy, the variable Panel Decision Incongruent with Median Panel Preferences was coded one if the decision was liberal and the median panel judge was Republican, or if the case outcome was conservative and the median panel judge was Democratic, and zero otherwise.

Finally, the Songer (2002) U.S. Courts of Appeals Database provides detailed coding of the litigants and their respective status in the case (such as appellant and apellee). Based on these litigant codes we combined any agency or official of the federal government along with information regarding the outcome of the case to create two dummy variables (the excluded category is nonparticipation of the federal government in the case) called U.S. Loser and U.S. Winner. U.S. Loser is coded one if the government lost the case at the panel decision, and zero otherwise. U.S. Winner is coded one if the government won the case, and zero otherwise.

Results from the Case Characteristic Model

The results of the model are presented in table 22.[13] Several of the hypotheses put forth are supported, and most of the variables performed as expected. In addition to the coefficient estimates, the odds ratios are reported for the variables of statistical significance.

POSITIVE INDICATORS OF IMPORTANCE

It has been hypothesized that the presence of certain characteristics in the appeals court case will increase the likelihood of review by the circuit en banc. Issues of national importance are more likely to be reviewed by the circuit en banc, and two proxies for classifying cases of national importance are amicus curiae participation and involvement of a constitutional issue. As explained earlier, amicus curiae briefs are usually submitted in a case before the Supreme Court as a way to alert the Court that there is an important issue. Likewise, the presence of an amicus curiae brief at the panel decision signals to the circuit that the case is important. The results from the case characteristic model indicate en banc review is more likely in cases where an amicus brief is filed. Specifically, when a friend of the court brief is filed in the appeals court case, the odds of circuit en banc review is approximately 3.5 times more likely than when no amicus brief is filed. Similarly, when the case involves a matter of constitutional interpretation the circuit en banc review is about 3.3 times more likely than when no constitutional issue is present. Case salience, as indicated by amicus participation and the presence of constitutional issues, certainly matters to the circuit when deciding whether or not to devote time to rehear panel decisions.

As noted previously, one of the key functions of the courts of appeals is to resolve legal uncertainty. Our results provide evidence that legal uncertainty positively influences the likelihood of en banc review. The presence of a dissenting or concurring opinion in the lower court panel decision tends to significantly increase the likelihood of review by the circuit en banc. For instance, the odds that the circuit en banc will review a case are nearly thirty-six times greater in cases with a panel split than in ones decided unanimously, and nearly eleven times greater in a case with a concurring opinion than in one without. Plainly, legal uncertainty is an important factor when the decision is made to review a case by the full complement of the circuit.

TABLE 22 Model of the likelihood of en banc review in the U.S. Courts of Appeals, First, Fifth, Sixth, and Ninth Circuits (1983–1991)

VARIABLE	EXPECTATION	MLE (SE)	ODDS RATIO
POSITIVE INDICATORS OF IMPORTANCE			
Constitutional	+	1.21* (0.56)	3.35
Amicus Curiae	+	1.26* (0.63)	3.52
Dissenting Opinion (panel)	+	3.59** (0.60)	36.23
Concurring Opinion (panel)	+	2.38** (0.45)	10.80
Intercircuit Conflict	+	3.07** (0.61)	21.54
Intracircuit Conflict	+	1.01 (0.42)	2.75
NEGATIVE INDICATORS OF IMPORTANCE			
Diversity Issue	–	−2.14** (0.70)	0.12
Ineffective Assistance of Counsel	–	−1.18* (0.65)	0.31
Fact-specific case (Weight of Evidence/ Substantial Evidence/Sufficiency of Evidence cases)	–	−1.10* (0.47)	0.33
CONTROL MEASURES			
Ideological Incongruence of Panel and Circuit	+	1.41** (0.42)	4.09
Panel Decision Incongruent with Median Panel Preferences	–	−1.33** (0.37)	0.26
U.S. Government Winner (in appeals court)	–	−2.28** (0.69)	0.10
U.S. Government Loser (in appeals court)	+	0.13 (0.61)	
Constant		−4.131*** (0.201)	
N	1,281		
Wald χ^2 (13)	136.21***		

Notes: MLE, maximum likelihood estimation; standard errors in parentheses. Percent correctly predicted: 87.

$*P < 0.05$, $**P < 0.01$, $***P < 0.001$ (one-tailed).

We hypothesized that the presence of intercircuit conflict would increase the odds that the full circuit would grant a rehearing en banc. In fact, the circuit court is twenty-one times more likely to review a panel decision if circuit conflict arises than in a case without circuit conflict. In addition, when intracircuit conflict is present the circuit en banc is nearly three times more likely to rehear the panel petition than when there is no intracircuit conflict. These findings are unsurprising insofar as one important goal of a circuit is to maintain uniformity in the case law both within the circuit and within the entire circuit courts of appeals.

NEGATIVE INDICATORS OF IMPORTANCE

Turning to those factors hypothesized to be negatively related to en banc review, we recall that two case characteristics have often been categorized as "frivolous": diversity cases and those claiming ineffective assistance of counsel. Both variables were found to substantially decrease the likelihood of review by the circuit en banc. To highlight, the presence of a diversity case decreased the odds of review by approximately 88 percent and a claim of ineffective assistance of counsel issues decreased the odds of review by roughly 69 percent.

In building on the assertion that judges do not like to grant en banc review in fact-specific cases, we hypothesized that cases concerning weight of evidence issues, interpretation of the substantial evidence doctrine, and sufficiency of evidence questions would not be worthy of review by the circuit en banc, and we found statistically significant support for this hypothesis.

CONTROL VARIABLES

Last, the ideological and litigant effects on the circuit's decision to grant en banc review were included as a way to assess the impact of the positive and negative indicators. Because of the nature of the data, we were unable to test directly whether circuit majorities use the en banc process as an error-correcting mechanism. However, this hypothesis is indirectly tested by controlling for the ideological directionality of all panel decisions examined in the model. This approach allowed us to examine whether a circuit court decides to grant review because it wishes to "correct" a lower court's decisions in direct conflict with the circuit's majority ideology. Thus, we hypothesized that panel decisions that do not conform to the circuit majority's ideology would be more likely to be reviewed by the circuit en banc. The positive statistically significant coefficient for Ideological Incongruence of Panel and Circuit provided evidence for the ideological error correction hypothesis. The likelihood of granting en banc review increases by approximately four times when the lower court decision conflicts with the circuit's prevailing ideology. For example, if a majority of the circuit's judges are Republicans, they are four times as likely to grant review to a liberal panel decision as to a conservative panel decision. Furthermore, the results illustrate that the circuit is less likely to review a case when the panel decision is incongruent with the median panel preferences, lending support to the idea that the circuit en banc does "give the benefit of the doubt" to decisions made in these situations. Finally, there is no statistically significant support that the circuit is more likely to rehear a case if the U.S. government lost. However, if the government prevails in the panel decision, the circuit is less likely to grant review.

EN BANC FINDINGS IN PERSPECTIVE

While there is support for most of the hypotheses put forth, it is important to put these findings in perspective. Even though the presence or absence of the described case characteristics changes the probability of review to a statistically significant degree, the likelihood that a case possessing these characteristics will make it to the en banc agenda is still quite small. To illustrate, the probability that the circuit en banc would grant review given several selected combinations of positive case characteristics was calculated. These calculations are provided in table 23.

For instance, consider example cases A and B. In case A the probability of review was calculated for a case that had both amicus participation and intracircuit conflict, both of which have been found to increase the likelihood of review. Case B includes the same positive indicators as case A; however, in case B the decision outcome is incongruent with the majority circuit's preferences. In case A the probability of review is approximately 0.04. In case B the probability of en banc review increases by approximately 0.06 to 0.10. Two things are of note in comparing these cases. First, even with the presence of multiple positive indicators, the likelihood of en banc review in each case is still small. Second, when the decision outcome (in these example cases) is incongruent with the preferences of the circuit majority, the likelihood of review is still only 11 percent.

Now let's consider two different cases, C and D. Case C is characterized by intercircuit conflict and dissenting opinion. The likelihood of review in this case is approximately 12 percent. To assess whether the circuit defers to panels when the decision is incongruent with panel preferences,

TABLE 23 Probability of circuit en banc granting review given the presence of positive indicators

POSSIBLE CASE TYPE	VARIABLE							PROBABILITY OF REVIEW
	AMICUS CURIAE	CONCURRING OPINION (PANEL)	DISSENTING OPINION (PANEL)	INTERCIRCUIT CONFLICT	IDEOLOGICAL INCONGRUENCE OF PANEL AND CIRCUIT	PANEL DECISION INCONGRUENT WITH MEDIAN PANEL PREFERENCES	INTRACIRCUIT CONFLICT	
A	X						X	0.04
B	X				X		X	0.10
C			X	X				0.12
D			X	X		X		0.07
E		X		X	X			0.11
F		X		X				0.09

Note: X denotes an illustration of a case with the indicated case characteristics and the rest of the variables held at zero.

we turn to case D. This case has the same characteristics as C except the decision outcome is incongruent with the median panel preferences. In case D, the probability of review decreases to 0.07. Although the circuit is less likely to rehear case D, the difference in probability between rehearing case C and rehearing case D is approximately 5 percent.

Overall, the analysis in table 23 demonstrates that even though the probability of review is higher when combinations of positive case characteristics are present than when negative case indicators are present, the probability that a given case with multiple positive case characteristics will be reviewed by the circuit en banc remains small.[14] Therefore, a strategic judge on a panel who understood which cases were most likely to be reviewed still would conclude that even if she had a case that was one of the types of cases most likely to be reviewed, the particular case would still, in most instances, not be reheard by the circuit en banc.

Next we examine the cost to a circuit judge of reversal by the Supreme Court. Since the evidence presented in the next section suggests that the cost of reversal is usually very low, we argue that a rational judge would not depart from his or her sincere preferences to avoid potential reversal.

The Costs of Reversal

Strategic theories of judicial decision making usually assume that judges are primarily policy-oriented actors who want to maximize the extent to which legal policy is shaped by their personal political preferences. In order to decide whether or not to act strategically to avoid reversal, a judge needs information to first calculate the probability of review and reversal if the policy of the appeals court panel is set at his ideal point. Next the judge needs to calculate the potential costs. Two alternative costs need to be considered: first, the cost if the Supreme Court reviews and reverses to set policy at the ideal point of the median justice on the Supreme Court, and second, the loss if the judge moves the appeals court decision away from his own ideal point and far enough toward the ideal point of the Supreme Court to avoid review. The first loss (from reversal) may have two components: the policy loss from having a decision at some distance from the preference of the judge and any additional, more personal loss that may occur from the fact of reversal. The second loss, when a judge acts strategically and avoids reversal, is only a policy loss.

On the surface, it appears that any nonpolicy costs from reversal are likely to be low. Judges on the courts of appeals have substantial independence in both law and practice. Reversals do not lead to any formal sanctions. Judges will not be removed from office or have their pay affected even by high rates of reversal, nor will any of the other material perks of their office be affected (e.g., they will not lose travel money or choice office space or assignment to panels considering interesting cases). If a reversal by the Supreme Court stigmatized appeals court judges to any substantial degree, that outcome might prove a sufficient cost to induce strategic action to avoid reversal. But one recent study concluded that there is little evidence from existing studies to support the existence of such a cost (Cross 2007). Moreover, Cross reported that there is no evidence that reversals adversely affect the chances of elevation for an appeals court judge (101). Additionally, the earliest comprehensive study of the courts of appeals concluded that the reputations of appeals court judges "appear to be independent of Supreme Court support" (Howard 1981, 139–40). Furthermore, Baum (2006) has suggested that judges want to be respected by their colleagues and gaining that respect means maintaining a reputation as a professional who adheres to the norms of the job, which include following clear law and making effective legal arguments on behalf of positions taken (54–55). But if a judge follows these professional norms and is still reversed, that reversal is not likely to negatively affect his or her professional standing. In fact, Baum cites one Ninth Circuit judge who was frequently reversed yet who received more than enough applause from his community for his principled stands to outweigh any cost from the fact of those reversals (112–13). These brief descriptions in the existing literature that suggest that the nonpolicy losses resulting from reversal are quite low are strongly supported by the evidence presented below from interviews with the judges. Before presenting that evidence in detail, we first discuss the potential policy losses.

To simplify discussion at this point, we consider potential policy losses under the assumption (which appears to be consistent with the evidence presented below) that there are no other significant losses that will accrue to judges who are reversed. To illustrate the nature of the choices facing a strategic judge, we devised the diagram in figure 14, in which COA represents the policy preference of the median judge on the appeals court panel, SCt represents the policy preference that will be adopted if the Supreme Court reviews and reverses, and SD represents the policy adopted by a strategic decision that is minimally close enough to the preferences

FIGURE 14. Strategic decision making on the U.S. Courts of Appeals

of the Supreme Court to avoid review. It is assumed that an appeals court panel need not move policy all the way to the ideal point of the Supreme Court median to avoid reversal because review always entails some cost to the Supreme Court. We assume further that the policy loss to the appeals court of having the policy moved from COA to SCt is one.

Whether or not a rational appeals court median judge will write an opinion placing the policy at SD rather than at COA will be a function of the distance between COA and SD and the estimate of the judge of the probability of reversal at COA. That is, a rational judge must be able to estimate the probability of review of a decision at his ideal point, and must also be able to estimate how much of a change of policy would be required to avoid review.

At one extreme of information, the appeals court judge will be unable to completely distinguish among cases; that is, the judge will have no idea which cases have greater chances of review than others. In such an extreme situation (no knowledge by the judge), the judge will estimate that the probability of review is 0.01 (because only one in every one hundred decisions of the courts of appeals that have published opinions are reviewed by the Supreme Court). In such a situation, a rational appeals court judge will not act strategically even if the cost of adopting SD is quite small (e.g., even if the opinion must only be moved one-tenth of the distance between COA and SCt). In such a situation, the expected loss for acting sincerely in a given case will be estimated by the judge to be 1 (the cost of reversal) × 0.01 (probability of reversal) = 0.01. In contrast, to act strategically in the case would incur a cost of 0.1, ten times as great as the expected cost of sincere action.[15]

At the other extreme, let us suppose that a judge estimates that the probability of review is 90 percent. In that case, the judge will act strategically even if the cost of the strategic decision is quite high. For instance, even if the judge must move the policy three-fourths of the way from his own ideal point toward the preference of the Supreme Court in order to avoid review, the strategic decision will be adopted. In this scenario, the expected cost of sincere action is 1 (the cost of reversal) × 0.9 (probability of reversal) = 0.9. In contrast, to act strategically in the case would incur the smaller cost of 0.75.

In summary, it appears that the policy costs of reversal are not sufficient to motivate strategic behavior except in possibly a very small number of cases. The only remaining question to be investigated is whether the judges perceive any substantial nonpolicy costs to potential reversal.

RESULTS: THE COST OF REVERSAL: THE VIEW OF THE JUDGES

Even if the likelihood of review is small, a rational, strategically oriented judge might modify her opinion to avoid review if the perceived cost of review was high enough. We argued above that the policy costs of reversal are not sufficient to motivate a rational judge to strategically modify her behavior, and that there appear to be no substantial material costs to reversal. The only remaining possible cost is whether the reputation of judges is harmed by reversal. To assess this possibility, we asked the judges about the "cost" of being reversed. The consensus among most of the judges was that the cost was insignificant. In two different informal dinner conversations, all ten of the judges agreed with the sentiment expressed by some that the founding fathers had done a pretty good job of insulating them from political reprisals for their actions. Thus, they all agreed that even a string of reversals would not result in impeachment proceedings being brought against them, or in having their pay reduced, or in any kind of disciplinary action from the chief judge. Moreover, none of them could think of any appeals court judge whose chances of being "promoted" to the Supreme Court had been hurt by having been reversed a number of times. In fact, a couple pointed out that being reversed for an opinion that supported the political preferences of a future president might actually improve a judge's chances for elevation. Additionally, a few judges noted the unlikelihood of promotion to the Supreme Court in the first place. Judge N explained, "Younger judges probably think about it on occasion, but you soon learn that there isn't much you can do about it. It takes lightning to strike to move up in the federal judiciary." Or as Judge P described, "I think that it is absolutely unimaginable that your possible elevation to the Supreme Court would affect anything that is done on this court. You know that elevation is a fantasy, so it isn't an influence."

When asked about informal sanctions that might result from being reversed, not a single judge voiced any concern about the effect of a given reversal or a string of reversals. There appeared to be a consensus that one would be viewed negatively by one's colleagues if one ignored the law or precedents or accepted canons of legal reasoning, but any fear of such approbation was independent of any concern about reversal. Several judges argued that such a concern was just as great on cases like diversity cases, in which there was no chance of review, as on high-profile cases likely to be granted cert. In other words, many of the judges explained their motivation was more about "getting the law right" and less about avoiding reversal. Judge WW explained, "What bothers you is you want to make the right decision and want to get the right precedent. We are motivated by what is correct law. The Supreme Court is unpredictable, and let the chips fall where they may. If they want to overturn me that is fine."

The judges expressed these views in a variety of ways. For example, Judge C said, "If they do review and they see it differently, so be it—it is their job, after all, to make law. Why would I care? I can't be fired, and it wouldn't even be embarrassing. The only thing that would embarrass me to my colleagues is if I hadn't done a good job—if my analysis were sloppy, or if I had missed an important case—but if the Supreme Court simply wants to define the law in a different way, no one will blame me." Similarly, Judge YY said, "I don't care about Supreme Court reversal. The thing that does bother me or concerns me vis-à-vis the Supreme Court is if they had the view we were defying the Supreme Court. The Supreme Court has reversed me before and it did not bother me—it's their job, I don't get bothered. Once they decide the issue, you apply it." The same point was made by Judge G: "If I am satisfied that I am doing my job, why should I be concerned if the Supreme Court reverses me? Of course, I will follow precedent, but that has nothing to do with being reversed." Similarly, Judge H opined, "Why should I worry if I get reversed? It is not very likely, but if it happens, so what? As long as I'm convinced that I have the law right, reversal doesn't matter." Judge K noted, "The Supreme Court reviews such a small percentage of your cases that there is no point in worrying about them. In that sense our position is very different from that of district judges, for whom review is an everyday fact of life." Judge UU explained that the workload demands are too high for judges to worry. He stated, "Too many cases to deal with to be worrying about being overruled." Along these same lines, Judge UU went on to state that because of time constraints, he does not have time to predict review. "I don't try to predict because I don't have time." And Judge O succinctly summed up the view he believed most of his colleagues shared, saying, "I don't worry about reversal—everyone gets reversed."

Judge D specifically addressed the question of how his colleagues would respond, saying, "Review is so rare that most of us don't worry about it; I don't think anyone is embarrassed by Supreme Court reversal." Judge J agreed, saying, "So if I'm reversed, I feel bad for about an hour, and then turn to my next project and don't worry anymore." One of the more academically inclined judges, Judge R, said that he was familiar with the strategic literature and had actually given the matter a good bit of thought. He said that he had concluded that if one thought a case was likely to go to the Supreme Court,

> our job—as an intermediate court—is to present the Supreme Court with a menu of options and point out the consequences of taking one option rather than another. That is, our job is to make it easier for the Court to frame issues and focus on the important issues. Of course, we also tell the Court what we think the resolution should be—but that is not our main role because it is the Supreme Court that is ultimately going to make the policy, so in these cases there is no reason to "fear" reversal—the Court is going to make the policy regardless of what we do and regardless of what our preferences are. It is a fact of life, so no one worries about it. So our job is to do our best to ensure that the Supreme Court's consideration of the alternatives is as rational as possible.

These views were presented during a lunch conversation at the Second Circuit retreat, and although a couple of the judges indicated that they didn't worry as much about laying out all the options as Judge R had suggested, they all agreed with the sentiments expressed about why no one worried about reversal. Finally, Judge S said, "I don't think at all about what will happen if my case goes to the Supreme Court."

From our interviews, the judges accept the conventional wisdom that no overt sanctions from the external world will be imposed on a judge who is reversed, even if those reversals are frequent. Additionally, none of the judges interviewed worried that informal sanctions from their colleagues might be a cost of reversal. As Judge S succinctly stated, "Getting reversed doesn't cost you a dime!"

Further Tests of the Strategic Perspective

In chapter 5 we provided several empirical tests of the attitudinal model, that is, we examined the voting behavior of appeals courts judges in a variety of situations to determine the extent to which the political or ideological preferences of the judges were correlated with their support of liberal versus conservative outcomes. In a nutshell, we found that the statistical analyses were generally consistent with what we learned from the interviews with the judges, namely, there is a statistically significant relationship between the political preferences of the judges and their votes, especially in cases in which the court is split, but the strength of that relationship is modest. Political attitudes are only a relatively small part of the explanation of why judges vote the way they do. In this final section, we extend those analyses to explore the extent to which the impact of the political preferences of the judges is modified or constrained by a strategic concern with the possibility of review by the Supreme Court.

The logic of the strategic perspective is that judges should be constrained from voting their sincere political preferences when they are concerned that the Supreme Court may review and reverse their decision. From this perspective, one would anticipate that the relationship between the political preferences of the judges and their voting choices will be strongest when there is little or no chance of Supreme Court review and that the impact of those political preferences will decrease as the chance of review by the Supreme Court increases. Moreover, most of this decreased influence of political preferences would be expected to occur for judges whose private preferences are most out of line with the preferences of the majority of the Supreme Court.

To test these propositions, we used the results of table 19 to identify those cases that had the greatest chance of Supreme Court review and compared the impact of judge preferences in those cases with those in two other categories of cases: all cases with published opinions in a given time period and those cases that were the least likely to be reviewed. Specifically, we first examined all the cases in the ten most recent years (1993–2002) of the United States Courts of Appeals Database (Songer 2002) in which it was possible to unambiguously categorize the outcome as liberal or conservative.[16] We chose these years because during that period, the Rehnquist court was consistently conservative with stable membership. We next examined cases from the same period that had at least two of the four case characteristics that substantially increase the odds of Supreme Court review (i.e., the presence of a constitutional issue, a statutory construction issue, the participation by one or more amici in the case, or the presence of a dissent by one of the judges on the panel) and had none of the case characteristics that decrease the likelihood of review. This sample of the decisions most likely to be reviewed by the Supreme Court comprised 912 cases, roughly 15 percent of the total sample of cases with published opinions in which the decision could be unambiguously classified as liberal or conservative. Finally, we examined the 165 cases (3 percent of the total sample) that had the lowest probability of review by the Supreme Court (those cases that did not have any of the four factors that increase the chances of review but had at last one of the factors identified in table 19 as decreasing the likelihood of review).

With each of these three samples, we ran a multivariate model to assess the impact of judicial preferences on the judges' support for liberal versus conservative outcomes. Since our dependent variable—whether the judge vote was liberal or conservative—was dichotomous, we used logistic regression to model the relationship. The main variable of interest was an indicator of the ideology of the judge based on the party of the appointing president (Democratic president, coded one, or Republican president, coded zero).[17] The prediction derived from a strategic perspective was that the relationship between this measure of judicial preferences and judges' votes on outcomes should be strongest in the sample of cases least likely to be reviewed by the Supreme Court and be weakest in the sample most likely to be reviewed. Moreover, since the Supreme Court was quite conservative during this period, the votes of conservative (Republican) judges should be least affected by the changing likelihood of reversal, while Democratic judges should feel constrained from voting their sincere liberal preferences in the sample of cases most likely to be reviewed.

Three control variables were added to the model to capture some of the other factors that past studies have found to influence votes on the courts of appeals. First, we added a control for the ideological direction of the lower court decision to reflect possible legal constraints on the decision. Next, we added a control for the ideology of the two colleagues of each judge on the panel to reflect the pressures related to collegiality noted in our judge interviews. Finally, in light of the numerous studies on party capability (Atkins 1991; Galanter 1974; McCormick 1993; Sheehan, Mishler, and Songer 1992; Songer and Sheehan 1992) that have noted the high rate of success of the U.S. government, we added two dummy variables to reflect whether the United States was a party to the case. The variable U.S. Liberal was coded one if the U.S. government was a party and favored a liberal outcome, and otherwise it was coded zero. Analogously, the variable U.S. Conservative was coded one if the U.S. government favored a conservative outcome, and otherwise it too was coded zero. The excluded category was nonparticipation of the United States in the case.

The results of these analyses, displayed in table 24, provide little support for the predictions of the strategic perspective. In table 24 we note that in the sample of all cases with published opinions, the impact of judicial preferences on their vote is similar to what was found in analogous analyses reported in chapter 5. Judges appointed by Democratic presidents are more likely than those appointed by Republican presidents to support liberal outcomes to a statistically significant degree. But the magnitude of the effect of judicial preferences is quite modest; the

TABLE 24 The likelihood of a liberal vote in published opinions of the U.S. Courts of Appeals versus cases most likely to be reviewed by the Supreme Court, 1993–2002

	RANDOM SAMPLE OF PUBLISHED U.S. COURTS OF APPEALS CASES		MOST LIKELY TO BE REVIEWED BY THE SUPREME COURT	
INDEPENDENT VARIABLES	MLE (SE)	MARGINAL EFFECTS	MLE (SE)	MARGINAL EFFECTS
Lower Court Direction (liberal or conservative)	0.981*** (0.089)	0.219	0.838*** (0.187)	0.192
Party of Appointing President	0.248*** (0.084)	0.052	0.816*** (0.189)	0.184
U.S. Liberal (U.S. supports liberal outcome)	0.773*** (0.097)	0.177	1.126*** (0.229)	0.268
U.S. Conservative (U.S. supports conservative outcome)	−0.570*** (0.069)	−0.117	−0.358* (0.175)	−0.077
Number of Democratic Colleagues	0.106** (0.045)	0.022	−0.128 (0.124)	−0.028
Constant	−1.177 (0.085)		−1.146 (0.206)	
N	5,990		912	
χ^2	587.55***		99.15***	

Note: MLE, maximum likelihood estimation; robust standard errors clustered on individual judge. $*P < 0.05$, $**P < 0.01$, $***P < 0.001$.

marginal effect on the likelihood of a liberal vote if one switches from a judge appointed by a Republican to one appointed by a Democrat while all other variables are held constant is only slightly more than five percentage points. In contrast, the impact of judicial preferences on votes on outcomes is much stronger in the small sample of cases in which review by the Supreme Court is more likely. The results show that the relationship between the party of the appointing president and the judicial vote on outcomes is positive and significant at the 0.001 level. Moreover, the marginal effect of switching from a Republican to a Democratic judge is more than eighteen percentage points. That is, in the cases in which Supreme Court review is most likely, the impact of judicial political preferences on the likelihood of a liberal vote is more than three times as great as it is in the larger sample of all published opinions in which the average likelihood of Supreme Court review is much lower (we recall from the analyses above that the likelihood of review for the average published opinion is less than 1 percent).

When we examined the small sample of cases in which review by the Supreme Court was least likely, the relationship between judicial preferences and votes on outcomes was near zero and not statistically significant (results not displayed). These results are also inconsistent with the predictions based on a strategic perspective.

When we examined the raw proportion of times that Democratic and Republican judges supported a liberal outcome in the three samples, we discovered that the votes of Republican judges are nearly identical in the three samples (varying from 30 percent liberal to 32 percent liberal). That is, in the absence of controls, the tendency of Republican judges to vote in support of their sincere preferences appears to be unaffected by the likelihood of review. In contrast, Democratic judges were most likely to vote in support of their sincere preferences when the likelihood of review was greatest by a Supreme Court with opposing political preferences. That is, the results were directly opposite to expectations based on a strategic perspective. Strategic judges appointed by Democratic presidents would presumably have the most to lose from review by a Supreme Court with a Republican majority that was widely viewed as solidly conservative in its political preferences. Nevertheless, Democratic judges supported a liberal outcome in 43 percent of cases having the greatest chance of review but in only 36 percent of cases that had the lowest chances of review.[18]

In summary, not only does the empirical analysis of judicial votes in cases with the greatest chance of review compared to votes in cases with the least chance of review fail to provide support for the strategic perspective, the results are actually sharply opposite to what would be expected from a strategic perspective. When we looked at the judges who should be most concerned about review by the Supreme Court and concentrated just on the small percentage of cases most likely to be reviewed, the analysis demonstrated that they were more likely to vote their sincere preferences than they were in cases with a lower chance of review. It is useful to remember that because this entire analysis was conducted on cases with published decisions, which already amounted to just 8 percent of all cases decided by the courts of appeals, the sample analyzed above designated as the cases most likely to be reviewed out of all published decisions represents just 1 percent of all cases decided by the courts of appeals. Consequently, while there may be a handful of cases per year in which the courts of appeal react strategically to the possibility of reversal by the Supreme Court, the failure to find any evidence of strategic behavior in even the 1 percent of cases most likely to be reviewed makes it clear that appeals court judges rarely (if ever) change their votes on outcomes because of fear of reversal by the Supreme Court.

Conclusion

In this chapter, we examined several types of strategic behavior. We first noted that the judges themselves universally agree (see chapter 3) that they bargain over opinion content, and that this bargaining can lead to accommodations.

Strategic models that point to fear of reversal as a motivating force in courts of appeals decision making rely on several key assumptions. First, they assume that judges have a good idea of what the Supreme Court will review. Next, strategic models presume that cases that are the strongest candidates for review have a high probability of review. Last, advocates of strategic models assume that appeals court judges view reversal as costly. That is, for circuit courts of appeals judges to act consistently strategically, not only must they be able to accurately predict which cases will be reviewed and overturned by the Court, they must also believe that reversal would impose unacceptably high costs on them.

We also examined whether the fear of reversal by the circuit en banc or the Supreme Court influences the judges. Our findings do not suggest that these conditions for strategic action exist. The interviews suggest that the judges do not believe that they can predict accurately which cases will be reviewed except perhaps in a very small number of extraordinary cases. And although in our statistical analysis of cert decisions we found support for almost all our hypotheses relating to the case characteristics that substantially affect the chances that a case will be reviewed, it is important to restate that our data show that the likelihood of review in the most positive cases is still marginal at best.[19] Moreover, the chances of reversal are actually lower than the chances of cert displayed in our tables because only about two out of every three decisions accepted for review are actually reversed. We do not know what the perception of judges is about the conditional probability of reversal given the assumption that a particular decision of theirs is reviewed. But even if they made the conservative assumption that every one of their decisions reviewed would be reversed, the probability of review would still be so low that a rational judge would perceive the probability of reversal as extremely low in almost all cases. Finally, objective factors, previous findings reported in the judicial literature, and the judges themselves all agree that the costs of reversal are quite low. Consequently, strategic theories that argue that rational appeals court judges can be expected to substantially modify their behavior to avoid reversal in any substantial number of cases have little support in the evidence. It might be possible to find anecdotal accounts that suggest a particular panel acted strategically in a given case, but the evidence presented above suggests that such strategic behavior would be relatively rare.

The results from the empirical analysis of case outcomes dovetail very nicely with the results of the interviews of appeals court judges. Our case characteristics model indicated that it was possible to identify types of cases that had virtually no chance of review, and our judges indicated that they were confident that they could also identify such cases. Moreover, the judges suggested that a substantial portion of all the cases they decide fell into this category of cases with no realistic chance of review. The judges generally indicated that they had some rough idea about broad categories of cases in which review was possible, and when they offered specific case characteristics those characteristics were similar to those that had positive effects in our statistical model. However, almost all the judges interviewed indicated that they had little confidence in their ability to predict which of the cases in which review was possible would actually be reviewed. This seems consistent with the findings of our model that cases exhibiting multiple indicators that enhance the probability of review still often have very low chances of review. Finally, the judges themselves agreed with the conclusion of this analysis that strategic models are not very useful for understanding their behavior.

SEVEN

The Congruence of Social Science and the Perceptions of the Judges

We began this research with the idea of providing a comprehensive overview of the way in which the modern courts of appeals go about their business. In particular, we focused on the extent to which the perspectives of the judges are congruent with the picture painted in mainstream analyses of the courts by empirical social scientists. But before venturing too far into a description of how the courts operate, we sought to craft a description of the main actors who are the central focus throughout this book, the judges. Although courts of appeals judges are among the most powerful political actors in the country, they are virtually unknown to the vast majority of Americans. Of particular interest to social scientists, and arguably of importance to all who are interested in the evolving nature of American democracy, is the increasing diversity of the backgrounds of the judges. Because of the constitutional guarantee of lifetime tenure, no single president has been able to fill the court with his own partisans: the current courts of appeals have a substantial number of judges appointed by each of the past six presidents, with no presidential appointment cohort reaching even 30 percent of the judiciary. Also of interest, the past three to four decades have witnessed an increasing diversification of the courts in terms of gender, race, and ethnicity. The most obvious explanation for the tendency toward appointing more women and ethnic minorities is the increasing proportion of these groups in the pipeline (i.e., the proportion graduating from law school a quarter of a century before the date of appointment). However, the analysis reported in chapter 1 shows that this does not appear to be the sole factor behind the increased numbers of women and minority judges appointed to the courts of appeals. In fact, diversification of the federal bench has been occurring more rapidly than would be expected from the increasing diversity of U.S. law schools and thus appears to also reflect an increasing commitment by both political parties to advancing affirmative action and diversification goals (though Democratic presidents have been much more supportive of this movement toward diversity). The culmination of this trend was President Obama's drawing substantially less than half his appointments from the ranks of white men—the first president to do so.

Chapter 1 also detailed the tremendous explosion in the workload of the courts that has occurred since the 1960s. Because the number of new judges appointed has not kept up with the increasing number of cases appealed, the courts have been forced to adopt innovations that provide more efficient means of resolving the disputes appealed to them. The detailed presentation of the perspectives of the judges and the new supplementary analyses presented in the first two chapters fill a major shortcoming in the extant literature on the courts of appeals by detailing the internal processes by which the courts handle their exploding dockets through extensive screening of the cases, followed by detailed examination of the substance of the claims of the competing parties, an examination that entails extensive interaction between the judges and their clerks. The first ever published statistical analysis of the likelihood of an appeal receiving an oral argument provides strong support for the view of the judges that increasing caseloads are a major reason for the declining use of oral arguments, and that circuit rules are also important. In fact, the analysis reinforces the views of the judges that one of the shortcomings of previous research has been the tendency to treat all the circuits as if the courts of appeals were a single institution instead of twelve different courts with substantial differences in basic practices. For instance, the frequency of use of oral argument and the implementation of different rules across the circuits have produced meaningful differences among the circuits in their actual practices. Thus, the first chapter ended with an empirical analysis not previously undertaken by political scientists, an investigation prompted by what we learned from the judicial interviews, and the subsequent statistical analysis provided empirical confirmation of the qualitative conclusions based on those judge interviews.

We began the second chapter by analyzing the agenda of the courts, which again showed substantial variance across circuits, reinforcing the conclusion of the first chapter that much is missed when the courts of appeals are treated as a single institution rather than as a set of a dozen somewhat related institutions (i.e., the circuits). Moving on to the selection and composition of the three-judge panels that decide most appeals, our interviews noted that in all circuits, the use of designated judges is seen as one of the devices that the circuits have used to handle increasing caseload pressures. Designated judges are assigned at the discretion of the chief judge of the circuit, but their appointment appears to be noncontroversial. All the judges we interviewed appeared to be comfortable with the idea of using designated judges to reduce workload pressures, and no one complained about the criteria used by his or her respective chief judge to select these additions to the panels. Most previous treatments of the courts of appeals gave scant attention to the practice of using district judges and judges on senior status as designated judges, relegating the practice to footnote status, but the judges interviewed for this project were unanimous in seeing it as an important part of the strategy for dealing with the caseload explosion. Thus, in this instance, our interviews did not so much provide new information about the operation of the courts of appeals that was absent from previous empirical analyses as it offered a useful corrective view on the importance of a practice that had been somewhat ignored in the past. The interviews also highlighted the importance of the increasing number of judges who are continuing to serve on the courts after reaching "normal" retirement age by taking senior status, a strategy that permits the appointment of an additional regular appeals court judge while the judge on senior status continues to hear a reduced caseload, and thus contributes to the ability of the circuit to keep up with its expanding docket.

No empirical studies exist that directly assess the effectiveness of oral argument at the court of appeals, but our interviews provided the most extensive look ever published at the way the custom works in practice. While all judges viewed oral arguments as providing useful perspectives for the judges, they disagreed among themselves on the extent to which any minds were changed on the ultimate question of who would win the appeal. Similarly, there are no previous empirical analyses of what happens during the judges' conference following oral argument, and so our interviews provided essentially a first look at this important process. While it is widely known that one of the key decisions during conference is who will write the opinion of the court, no previous statistical analyses attempted to model that critical decision. The second chapter first explored the views of the judges as to the factors that influenced the assignment of opinion writing and then used those insights to provide the first detailed analysis of the factors that influence the assignment of the opinion of the court. We found strong support for the theory that judges consider efficiency when making assignments, even though there was only ambivalent support for this theory among the judges we interviewed. This finding reaffirms the perspective that although the courts of appeals are clearly important political decision makers, they remain at heart legal institutions in which legal expertise and competence matter. To highlight one of several findings, and in what may come as a surprise to the advocates of affirmative action, judge gender has no apparent effect on assignment of the majority opinion. There is virtually no difference in the likelihood that male rather than female judges will receive the majority opinion assignment. Finally, consistent with the views expressed by the judges, but very different from an expectation that might be generated by the results of studies of opinion assignment on the Supreme Court, strategic considerations appear to have little relevance on the courts of appeals.

Chapter 3 offered the most detailed look ever published at the politics of opinion writing and the extensive negotiation and bargaining that occur on the courts. Data necessary to conduct a statistical analysis of the frequency of bargaining or the nature of bargaining during opinion writing simply do not exist. Thus, there are no existing empirical studies of opinion writing that can be compared to the view of the process provided in this chapter; the descriptions, while qualitative, are the only evidence that exists. Virtually all the appeals court judges we interviewed understood the process of opinion writing to involve extensive feedback for the opinion author from the other judges on the panel after the author circulated a first draft of the opinion. Most of the judges indicated there is considerable give-and-take among the judges, with the final opinion often reflecting bargaining and compromise among the judges on the panel. Moreover, the judges indicated that consensus often is reached after much give-and-take, not as the result of compromise but rather as the end result of a serious, candid evaluation of legal arguments that results in all the judges coming to a sincere agreement about the best way to resolve the conflict before them. That is, persuasion on the legal merits of the controversy often (though not always) brings together judges whose different political preferences might have initially led them to take opposing positions, and from our findings it seems that only in a few salient cases and issues do the judges believe it is worth their time to dissent.

There has been considerable debate among scholars who study the U.S. Supreme Court about whose preferences should be assumed to control the policy created by opinions of that Court; some argue that opinions most nearly reflect the preferences of the opinion writer, others contend it is the preferences of the median justice on the Court that are most influential, and still others argue that it is the median justice in the opinion coalition whose preferences dominate. While it cannot be automatically assumed that findings for the courts of appeals are also applicable to the Supreme Court, it was clear from the interviews with appeals court judges that opinions on their courts are not simply an expression of the preferences or approach of the opinion author but reflect input from everyone on the panel. This discussion of the judges' perceptions about the opinion-writing process was supplemented by our statistical analysis of the factors influencing the time the opinion-writing process takes and the eventual length of the majority opinion. These analyses largely reinforced the importance attributed by the judges to the complexity and salience of the issues and the extent of the differences in political preferences on the panel. But the analyses also highlighted that the experience and legal qualifications of the opinion writer are also important.

As both the interviews with the judges and previous statistical analyses of judicial behavior have indicated, consensus is achieved in a large majority of the cases decided by the courts of appeals. The focus of chapter 4 shifted to those relatively few cases in which the judges end up disagreeing either on the outcome or on the reasoning in the opinion. The analyses in chapter 4 of the causes of dissent largely support the views expressed by the judges of the importance of legal factors, including case complexity and legal ambiguity, and the lack of importance of strategic considerations in producing divided decisions. But the statistical analyses suggested that both attitudinal differences among the judges on the panel and variations in the legal qualifications of the opinion writer may be more important than the judges admit. Thus, the statistical analyses present a partially different picture of the causes of dissent than one would get from talking to the judges, perhaps reflecting the reluctance of the judges to admit the influence of "political" factors on their work.

Chapters 5 and 6 took up the topics that have been most frequently explored in previous empirical analyses of appellate courts: attitudinal and strategic explanations of judicial behavior. At first glance, the new statistical analyses presented in chapter 5 appear to reinforce the conventional wisdom among social scientists that the political preferences of the judges exert a major impact on their voting choices. In partial contrast, the judges acknowledged that political preferences on occasion influence the positions taken by judges on their court, but insisted that the influence of such preferences occurs only in a very small minority of cases.[1] Further examination of the statistical evidence presented throughout the book results in a picture that is substantially closer to the general perspective of the judges. The chapter shows that although partisan and ideological differences are critical in the cases in which the court is publicly divided, the overwhelming levels of unanimity present when all cases are considered (including those disposed of without full merits treatment or a published opinion) are consistent with the views expressed by the judges of the relative infrequency of ideological influence on final outcomes.

While previously published work on the courts of appeals contains an increasing number of studies that argue that judicial decision making is best understood within a strategic framework, both the judge interviews and the statistical analyses presented in chapter 6 refute such conventional wisdom. The judges were in near total agreement that strategic models of judicial decision making are seriously flawed, with the exception of the bargaining and compromise that take place during the opinion-writing phase of their decision making. Given this consensus among the judges, we reexamined the previous evidence cited in support of strategic approaches and designed some new statistical models to more adequately test the differences between the judges' views and the conventional social science perspective. The results of these new statistical analyses were found to be more supportive of the judges' position than of previous studies cited in support of a strategic perspective. The statistical analyses presented in the chapter suggest that the judges will rarely have the information necessary for rational strategic action, and further demonstrate that several critical predictions of strategic accounts are not confirmed by the actual pattern of judicial decision making.

Conclusion

In the introduction, we presented two themes for this book. We wanted to leverage a mixed methods approach to both compare (and contrast) the views from the bench and chambers with available quantitative evidence, and we wanted to test our integrated theory of judicial decision making across the full spectrum of appellate processes and choices. With respect to the latter, we took a minority position, at least among published works. Unlike most judicial scholars, we do not advocate a particular explanation for the behavior of judges. Indeed, as our combination of qualitative and quantitative analyses suggests, a complex variety of factors influence judges. Of course, our multifaceted approach could be a function of the broad scope of our analyses. Instead of focusing on one aspect of judicial behavior (e.g., whether a judge casts a liberal or a conservative vote), we examined a variety of processes and outcomes. Depending on the context, the behavior of U.S. Courts of Appeals judges can be explained by attitudinal, legal, strategic, or institutional models, alone or in combination.

We first provided evidence of the integrated model in chapter 2. The decision to hear oral arguments is a function of a variety of institutional factors, including local rules. But within these institutional constraints the judges are goal-oriented. For example, panelists appear to consider minimizing workloads when determining whether to hear oral arguments, or utilize other summary decision-making tools, such as the nonpublication of opinions.

Similarly, throughout the book, we found and noted evidence that courts of appeals judges are influenced by institutional norms. In particular, most of the judges we interviewed identified powerful consensual norms on their circuits. This was reflected in a variety of contexts. The overall dissent rates across circuits are low—typically below 10 percent. While some of this can be explained by the nature of the circuits' dockets, which include a variety of legally simplistic, nonsalient discretionary cases, the effects of consensual norms permeated our discussion throughout the book. For example, the judges are willing to negotiate, bargain, and compromise. Sometimes this happens during the conference, but it also occurs most frequently between the conference and the public release of the panel's decision. As noted in chapter 3, in five circuits drafts of the panel's opinion are circulated to the whole circuit before their formal release, and judges outside the panel are invited to comment on any problems in the draft opinion. Our interviews indicated that most of the time, the panel takes these comments very seriously and will often make changes to the opinion, either to reduce the chance of en banc review or more generally out of respect for the views of their colleagues. While the judges interviewed thought this practice of prepublication circulation of opinions reduced the likelihood of en banc review, our analysis of the actual occurrence of en banc review found no evidence to support the views of the judges. Of course, consistent with our integrated model, it is the presence of consensual norms that appears to encourage strategic behavior during this stage.

In other contexts, we found little evidence of strategic behavior, including the decisions to cast dissenting votes and to assign the opinion of the court. In chapter 6, we noted that randomness of en banc and Supreme Court review diminishes the likelihood that courts of appeals judges will strategically factor in the preferences of the circuit as a whole or of the High Court. In these contexts, the judges suggested that the law is the most important factor, and attitudes are a distant second. Our quantitative evidence certainly does not contradict this belief.

One thing is apparent: context matters when determining which factors dominate the behavior of the judges. More procedural decisions such as case management are influenced by institutions and nonattitudinal goals, while those decisions that affect outcomes are more likely to be affected by law, ideology, and perhaps strategic calculations. Also, even within a particular type of process (e.g., the decision to assign the opinion of the court or the case outcome), context matters. For example, salience is a major contextual factor. Presiding judges are significantly more likely to self-assign in salient cases, and judges are more ideological in cases that include a dissenting vote.

With respect to our other, perhaps more important theme, we are convinced that the initial decision to present an analysis that combined and critically compared the insights of the judges themselves with the picture of the courts gained from both past empirical research and our own new statistical models of judicial behavior produced the richest perspective. The high degree of congruence between the perspectives gained from the judge interviews and the picture of the courts that emerged from the statistical analyses probably will come as a surprise to many social scientists. The judges appeared to be both thoughtful and attentive observers of the processes they were immersed in and, once guaranteed anonymity, and guaranteed that they would not be asked to reveal confidential information about any specific cases, they appeared willing to speak openly and honestly with us. Moreover, because they had "insider information," they were able to provide details about the process of decision making, such as how they prepare for oral argument and how they bargain over opinion content—details that are simply not available to researchers limited to what is available in the public record. On the other hand, the addition of sophisticated statistical analyses to the interview results enabled us to detect trends and patterns that were not always apparent to the judges, immersed as they are in the day-to-day operations of their courts. We hope that the rich picture that has emerged from the combination of these approaches will encourage other scholars to more systematically attempt to incorporate interviews with judges, and perhaps with other participants in the U.S. legal system, to supplement the growing use of increasingly sophisticated quantitative techniques that characterize much of the best recent scholarship on the courts.

TECHNICAL APPENDIX: DATA AND METHODS

Overall Methods Issues

ESTIMATES OF SUBSTANTIVE SIGNIFICANCE

DISCRETE CHANGES. In most chapters, for binary regression models we estimated the substantive significance using what Long and Freese (2006) call "discrete changes": the differences in the predicted probability that the dependent variable equals one when the independent variable of interest is set to two distinct values while all other covariates are held to their appropriate measure of central tendency (e.g., continuous variables are set to the mean, dummy variables are set to the mode). Dummy independent variables of interest are set to their two possible values, 1 and 0. Following one of the typical conventions, unless otherwise noted, we set continuous independent variables of interest to one standard deviation above and below the mean.

As an example, we presented the logistic regression model of the decision to hear oral arguments in table 4. In that model, the Constitutional variable (coded one if the case included an issue of U.S. constitutional law, zero if it did not) had a discrete change value of 0.04. We could interpret this in the following manner: the probability of the court hearing an oral argument is 0.04 higher in cases that raise constitutional issues, when the other independent variables are held constant at their appropriate measures of central tendency. Similarly, in the same model, the continuous variable Number of Issues has a discrete change of 0.08. One could interpret this as the difference in the probability the court will hear an oral argument when the Number of Issues variable is one standard deviation above and below the mean. While this latter interpretation is not particularly elegant, it does allow us to roughly compare substantive effects across continuous variables.

PERCENT CHANGES. Additionally, in some instances (e.g., the model of dissent in chapter 4), we also estimated what we call "percent changes." Unfortunately, because of the nature of logistic regression models, predicted probabilities are significantly constrained when the dependent variable is skewed. Percent changes arguably account for this and provide a more accurate reflection of the effects of the independent variables when the binary dependent variable is skewed. The percent changes are equal to the discrete change divided by the probability that the dependent variable is equal to one when the independent variable of interest is set to the lower of the two variables (e.g., zero for a dummy variable), multiplied by 100. Substantively, this tells us the percentage increase in the probability that the dependent variable is equal to one when we increase the independent variable of interest from the lower to the higher value while holding the other covariates constant at the appropriate measures of central tendency.

CHANGES IN EXPECTED COUNTS. Two of the models presented in chapter 3 (Days to Decision, table 8; Opinion Length, table 9) estimate substantive significance using an analogous procedure that we call changes in expected counts. Unlike discrete changes, these are calculated using estimates of the expected counts of the dependent variable. However, like the discrete changes and percent changes, the changes in expected counts are differences generated following the same conventions for setting the independent variables (described above). For example, the first change in expected counts presented in the text estimates the effects of Complexity on disposition times. The estimate of the change in the expected count is just over 23. In other words, on average, a case that is one standard deviation above the mean with respect to complexity would, on average, take an additional twenty-three days to decide, compared to an otherwise similar case with a Complexity value that is one standard deviation below the mean.

JUDGE-LEVEL MEASURES. As we discuss in the text, both active circuit court judges and designated judges (including retired U.S. Supreme Court justices and retired appellate judges from the circuit, as well as active district court judges and active appellate judges from other circuits) sit on courts of appeals panels. All of our judge-level variables are measures for both active judges from that circuit and the designated judges. Of course, sometimes the measure will vary systematically by status. For example, a district court judge sitting by designation will by definition have a 0 value for our judge tenure variable, which measures the length of service as a U.S. courts of appeals judge.

Chapter 2 Methods

VARIABLES IN TABLE 4: ORAL ARGUMENTS

Orally Argued Case: This variable is dichotomous, coded one if the case was orally argued and zero if it was not orally argued. The variable was constructed using the Federal Judicial Center's (FJC's) Federal Court Cases: Integrated Database (2005), which includes a variable noting whether the case was orally argued.

Circuit Docket Size: The measure is the total number of terminations by the circuit divided by the total number of three-judge panels (which is the number of active judges divided by three). While it might be more intuitive to utilize the total number of cases per active judge, the Administrative Office of the United States Courts (AOC) suggests that the per-panel caseload measure is more appropriate for the U.S. courts of appeals (see http://www.uscourts.gov/fcmstat/intro97/pgv.pdf, last accessed November 5, 2009). For example, the per-judge method would assume that a single judge in a circuit of twelve with a docket of 120 cases would hear ten cases. However, since the circuit meets in three-judge panels, the judge would actually participate in thirty cases, or 120/(12/3). Of course, beyond measurement validity concerns, panel-level data were available for the entire time period, while judge-level data were not available for four of the years we examined. Finally, we note that both measures are correlated above 0.80.

Circuit Judge Vacancies: Using data compiled from the AOC Reports, we measured vacancies by the number of months a judgeship was left open during the year the case was decided. For example, if a circuit had three positions open for the entire year and one position open for four months, the variable value for that circuit year would be 40.

Panel Opinion Caseload: Ideally, the panel caseload variable would measure the number of outstanding majority opinions assigned to the judge at the time the court decided whether to hear oral arguments. Unfortunately, we do not have access to the processing dates, and the data collection would be impracticable.[1] Given these limitations, we generated a proxy variable. First, we summed the total number of opinions authored by the judge in the two months prior to the decision date. Then, to account for the sample, we adjusted that number by the per-panel/per-month caseload for the circuit during that year. Next, we generated the difference of the judge and circuit mean (for that year) weighted number of opinion assignments in the previous two months. Finally, to account for diminishing marginal utilities, we added a constant to adjust the difference so that the minimum value was 1, and then took the natural log. We then took the mean opinion caseload for each of the three panelists. Higher values indicate that the panelists had, on average, relatively more assignments than their brethren.

Circuit Rules: We also hypothesized that circuits with rules that discouraged oral arguments were less likely to hear oral arguments. While no obvious construct exists, we created one based on a content analysis of the relevant local rules and internal operating procedures (IOPs). For each circuit rule or IOP that discouraged oral arguments, the variable value increased by one point. For example, the Second and Sixth Circuit rules creating a waiver presumption when parties do not file a request for oral argument by a certain time are worth a point. If the circuit rules or IOPs expressly stated that the circuit utilized a prescreening method by a staffer, the value increased by one. Additionally, the variable increased by one if circuit rules prohibited oral arguments in a subset of cases. If any provision explicitly stated a preference against a party requesting oral argument or the reconsideration of the circuit decision not to hear oral arguments, the variable increased by one. Finally, if the circuit rules or IOPs encouraged oral arguments, such as the Seventh Circuit rule requiring oral arguments in direct death penalty appeals, the variable decreased by one. The variable is a dummy variable coded one if the circuit had rules discouraging oral argument and zero if it did not.[2] As such, we expect to find a positive coefficient.

Amicus Curiae: This variable is measured as the natural log of the number of amicus briefs filed in the case.[3]

Panel Ideological Range: The variable is the absolute value of the difference between the highest and lowest ideology values for the three judges sitting on the panel that decided the case on the merits. The judges' ideologies were measured using a proxy measure of the mean ideologies of the primary actors in the selection of U.S. courts of appeals judges: the president and the senators from the president's party in the nominee's home state. Early measures relied solely on the ideology (Kuersten and Songer 2003; Randazzo 2004; Songer, Ginn, and Sarver 2003) or party (Goldman 1975; Howard 1981; Songer, Sheehan, and Haire 2000) of the appointing president. Giles, Hettinger, and Peppers (2001, hereinafter GHP) modified these measures by utilizing the average scores of the home state senators from the president's party (when they existed). However, both approaches miss a key aspect of the process. The initial measures ignored the influence of the norm of senatorial courtesy, while the GHP measure ignores the possibility that the president still plays a major role when senatorial courtesy applies. Specifically, available evidence suggests that home state senators from the president's party rarely dictate to the president who the nominee should be. Instead, the process usually involves a degree of negotiation between the president and the home state senators (Goldman 1997; Howard 1981; Kuersten and Songer 2003). Given this more nuanced understanding of the selection process, we utilized the following method for estimating the ideologies of the judges. If the judge's home state did not have a senator from the president's party, the ideology score for that judge was set equal to the Poole and Rosenthal common-space NOMINATE scores of the appointing president.[4] Unlike the GHP scores, however, when the home state senators were from the president's party, the ideology score for the judge was set equal to the mean of the NOMINATE scores of the president and the home state senators from his party.[5]

Panel Law School Prestige: To determine elite status, we borrowed the measure developed by Slotnick (1983)[6] and employed by Sarver, Kaheny, and Szmer (2008) and Szmer, Kaheny, and Sarver (2010).

MULTICOLLINEARITY DIAGNOSTICS FOR TABLE 4: ORAL ARGUMENTS

Because we included a variety of measures that are potentially correlated with one another, particularly the circuit-level measures, high multicollinearity could create problems with our hypothesis tests. Following Gujarati and Porter (2009), we estimated the variance inflation factors for each variable to estimate the amount of multicollinearity. They suggest that values above 10 indicate high multicollinearity (Gujarati and Porter 2009, 340). We did have two measures that approached this level: Circuit Rules (7.94) and Circuit Active Judges (6.81). Of course, neither is problematic. First, the Circuit Rules measure tests one of our hypotheses, and the coefficient is statistically significant. Since the one concern with high multicollinearity is that it inflates standard error estimates, making it difficult to find statistically significant relationships, clearly this is not a concern. With respect to the Circuit Active Judges measure, because it is a control variable, we are not concerned with tests of statistical inference for it.

VARIABLES AND METHODS FOR TABLE 7: OPINION ASSIGNMENT. ESTIMATION METHOD

Because our dependent variable is dichotomous, we needed to employ a variant of either logistic or probit regression. However, because we had clusters of votes within a case (either two or three in each case), the within-case error terms are likely correlated. As Maltzman and Wahlbeck (2004) note, there are several alternative estimation techniques that can correct for this, including fixed and random effects models. As Maltzman and Wahlbeck suggest, however, conditional (fixed effects) logit has certain limitations that make it unattractive in this context. As they note, fixed effects models are problematic for models estimating interactions with a variable that does not vary across the cluster (in the case).[7] Since we wanted to test several of these interactions, we followed the lead of Maltzman and Wahlbeck and estimated the coefficients using random effects probit.[8] Additionally, we included dummy variables for circuit and year to account for additional sources of correlated errors.

Equity: Ideally, an equity variable would measure the number of outstanding majority opinions assigned to the judge at the time of the conference. Unfortunately, we only had access to a sample of cases, without information regarding the panel conferences. Given these limitations, we generated a proxy variable. First, we summed the total number of opinions authored by the judge in the previous two months. Then, to account for the sample, we adjusted that number by the per-panel/per-month caseload for the circuit during that year. Next, we generated the difference of the judge and circuit mean (for that year) weighted number of opinion assignments in the previous two months. Finally, to account for diminishing marginal utilities, we added a constant to adjust the difference so that the minimum value was 1, and then took the natural log.

Law School Prestige: To determine elite status, we borrowed the measure developed by Slotnick (1983) and employed by Sarver, Kaheny, and Szmer (2008) and Szmer, Kaheny, and Sarver (2010).

Salience: The Salience (or importance) variable reflects the scores from principal components factor analysis of three separate proxy indicators derived from the literature: amicus curiae participation (Hettinger, Lindquist, and Martinek 2004, 2006; Lindquist 2007; Maltzman, Spriggs, and Wahlbeck 2000; Maltzman and Wahlbeck 2004; Wahlbeck, Spriggs, and Maltzman 1999),[9] the presence of a civil liberties or rights issue (Hettinger, Lindquist, and Martinek 2004, 2006; Lindquist 2007), and the exercise of judicial review by the court (Hettinger, Lindquist, and Martinek 2004; Maltzman, Spriggs, and Wahlbeck 2000; Maltzman and Wahlbeck 2004; Wahlbeck, Spriggs, and Maltzman 1999).[10] The constitutive variables are the natural logs of the number of amicus curiae,[11] a dummy variable coded one if the case involved a civil rights or liberties claim, and a dummy variable coded one if the case involved a constitutional question.[12] The factor analysis resulted in one factor with an eigenvalue greater than 1. Higher values indicate increased salience. We separately multiplied Salience times Ideological Distance and Opinion Assigner, generating two different multiplicative terms (not shown).

Chapter 3 Methods

STATISTICAL METHOD USED IN TABLE 8: A MODEL OF DISPOSITION TIME

Since the dependent variable is both a duration and count measure, we could have estimated the models using either a duration model or an appropriate count-based technique. We did not choose the former, which is more appropriate when the duration is right-censored or the covariates of interest are time-varying during the duration—neither of which applied in this case (Box-Steffensmeier and Jones 2004). Instead, we treated the dependent variable as a count. Since there was evidence of high overdispersion, we estimated the model parameters using negative binomial regression (Long and Freese 2006). Additionally, we calculated the White-Huber robust standard errors clustered by year.[13]

VARIABLES IN TABLE 8: A MODEL OF DISPOSITION TIME

Disposition Time: The day when the court received the appellant's brief can be found in the FJC's Federal Court Cases: Integrated Database (2005). The decision date is found in the both the FJC and USCA databases. Alternatively, we could have used the docket assignment date or the oral argument date. We chose the brief submission date because the time from the docket date is in part a function of the behavior of court processing staff and, more important, of external actors (the litigants and litigators). Moreover, the date of the last brief filing reflects a point in time at which the judges have received important information from both parties, such that they (or, more likely, their clerks) can initiate the decision-making process. Alternatively, we could have utilized the oral argument date. While this date arguably might more accurately reflect the initial point at which the judges begin to decide the case, it would have forced us to exclude a significant number of cases—those that were not orally argued. Insofar as just over 16 percent of the cases in the USCA data set during this time period were not orally argued, we chose not to report the results of the models utilizing the oral argument date. However, the results were close to those we present here. Only two of the thirteen statistically significant coefficients (in the hypothesized direction) were not statistically significant in the model using the oral argument date (the amount of judicial vacancies on the circuit and the ideological range of the panel), while one variable that was not statistically significant in the hypothesized direction in the presented results (Salience) was statistically significant in the unreported model.

Salience: The discussion of Salience under chapter 2 methods above is referenced here.

Complexity: Previous studies utilized a variety of case complexity measures. Some, such as the number of legal provisions relevant to the case (Benesh and Reddick 2002; Maltzman, Spriggs, and Wahlbeck 2000, 46), are not included in the Songer (2002) United States Courts of Appeals Database. Also, since the length of the opinion of the court (Hettinger, Lindquist, and Martinek 2006; Lindquist 2007) could reflect both salience and complexity (see the Black and Spriggs 2008 study of opinion length, as well as our subsequent analysis), it was not included in the measure.[14] That left three appropriate proxy measures employed in prior studies as proxy measures of complexity: the presence of a cross appeal (Hettinger, Lindquist, and Martinek 2004, 2006; Lindquist 2007), the number of parties participating in the litigation (Hettinger, Lindquist, and Martinek 2004), and the number of substantive issues (Benesh and Reddick 2002; Hansford 2004; Hettinger, Lindquist, and Martinek 2004, 2006; Lindquist 2007; Maltzman, Spriggs, and Wahlbeck 2000; Wahlbeck, Spriggs, and Maltzman 1999). Additionally, we identified a fourth proxy measure that we calculated but that is not part of the Songer (2002) database (and therefore has not been employed in prior studies): whether the case was orally argued. Indeed, two of the three Federal Rules of Appellate Procedure 34(a)(2) standards for determining whether to allow oral arguments reflect complexity (whether the case is frivolous; whether the legal issues "have been authoritatively decided" in prior cases). In the end, we generated an index using the factor scores of a principal components factor analysis of three of the constructs: the number of issues, the presence of a cross appeal, and whether the case was orally argued.[15] We chose to exclude the number of parties based on the results of the factor analysis, which indicated that it was not a reliable indicator of the same underlying dimension as the other three components.[16] The factor analysis generated one factor with an eigenvalue above 1. Higher values of the scale indicate more complexity.

MOW Senior Judge/Visiting Active Appeals Judge/District Court Judge: Judges vary in terms of their employment status. They typically fall into one of four categories: active judges on the circuit, senior appeals court judges from the circuit, visiting active judges from other circuits, and district court judges sitting by designation. As this is a nominal variable, we included three dummy variables: MOW Senior Judge, MOW Visiting Active Appeals Judge, and MOW District Court Judge. We posited a negative coefficient for the senior judge variable. The reference category is active judges on the circuit.

Circuit Docket Size: The measure is the total number of terminations by the circuit divided by the total number of three-judge panels (which is the number of active judges divided by three). While it might be more intuitive to utilize the total number of cases per active judge, the AOC suggests that the per-panel caseload measure is more appropriate for the courts of appeals (see http://www.uscourts.gov/fcmstat/intro97/pgv.pdf, last accessed November 5, 2009). For example, the per-judge method would assume that a single judge in a circuit of twelve with a docket of 120 would hear ten cases, However, since the circuit meets in three-judge panels, the judge would actually participate in thirty cases, or 120/(12/3). Of course, beyond measurement validity concerns, the panel-level data were available for the entire time period, while the judge-level data were not available for four of the years we examined. Finally, we note that both measures are correlated above 0.80.

MOW Opinion Caseload: This measure used the same proxy to estimate the opinion caseload discussed above for the Panel Opinion Caseload variable included in chapter 2. However, instead of taking the mean value for the three panelists, this variable is the opinion caseload for the author of the opinion of the court.

Chapter 4 Methods

GENERAL ISSUES FOR MODELING DISSENT

Since Dissent is a binary variable, we estimated the model coefficients using logistic regression. Additionally, to account for possible autocorrelation resulting from correlated errors within cases, we estimated robust standard errors clustered by the case.[17] Owing to the scarcity of Latino and Asian American judges, we focused only on white and African American judges. As such, we excluded votes cast by other minority judges. However, the results do not change when we include dummy variables for other racial or ethnic minorities.

Unlike some prior studies of dissent (e.g., Hettinger, Lindquist, and Martinek 2006), we did not exclude the majority opinion writer. While the decision to dissent can be affected by the identity of the majority opinion assigner, initial dissenting votes are typically cast at the conference before the opinion has been assigned to a member of the majority coalition. Given this temporal issue, we preferred to include the decisions of all the judges in the analysis. However, as a robust check, we did analyze the model using only those judges who did not author the opinion of the court. Only two of the hypotheses tests resulted in different outcomes. One variable coefficient was statistically significant only in the model without the majority opinion assigner; another coefficient that was significant in the full model was statistically significant only at the 0.0725 level in the model without the majority opinion assigner.

Of course, logistic regression models of rare events can lead to biased coefficient estimates (King and Zeng 2001). To account for this, we also estimated the model using rare events logit, part of the ReLogit software package developed by Tomz, King, and Zeng (2003). The results are generally consistent with those reported, with one exception: the Judge Gender × Panel Gender multiplicative term coefficient was only borderline statistically significant (the observed probability level was 0.0685).

Because of the nature of logistic regression models, the discrete changes presented in table 15 are very conservative measures of predicted probabilities (see King and Zeng 2001).[18] The sigmoid shape of the logit curve is such that independent variables have muted effects on the probability that the dependent variable is equal to one when that probability is close to zero or one, while it will have much higher effects when that probability is closest to 0.5 (Long 1997). Thus, table 15 also presents the percent changes in predicted probabilities resulting from the discrete changes.

VARIABLES IN TABLE 15: A MODEL OF JUDGE DISSENTING VOTES

Signal En Banc Review: The measure was constructed to denote the degree to which a judge would prefer to have the panel's decision overturned by the circuit sitting en banc. To construct the measure, we had first to estimate the preferences of the judge, the panel, and the circuit. We employed the adjusted GHP ideology measure (discussed in chapter 1) to estimate the preferences of the individual judge. Also, following convention, the circuit preference is the median ideology score for all the active judges sitting on the circuit during that year. Similarly, panel preferences are measured using the ideology of the median judge sitting on the panel.[19] To best reflect the underlying concept, the actual Signal En Banc Review variable is the absolute value of the difference between the judge and circuit preferences minus the absolute value of the difference between the judge and the panel preferences. Positive values indicate the judge is closer to the circuit median and therefore more likely to dissent.

Signal SCOTUS Review: The measure was created using the same formula as for the en banc variable except that we substituted the SCOTUS preference for the circuit preference. Like the circuit measure, the SCOTUS preference is the ideology of the median justice for the year the case was decided. We used the Judicial Common Space score (Epstein et al. 2007), which is set to the same continuum as our GHP-based measure, to estimate the ideal point for the median justice. Again, positive values suggest the panelist's preference is more proximate to the SCOTUS median than to the panel median.

NOTES

Introduction

1. U.S. Constitution, Article 3, Section 1.
2. The major exception is that, because of the constitutional prohibition against double jeopardy, the government may not appeal a criminal decision that resulted in a "not guilty" verdict for the defendant.
3. On average, another one hundred cert petitions are disposed of by a summary decision of the Supreme Court.
4. The United States Courts of Appeals Database, 1925–1996 (Songer 2002), is a multi-user database created by a grant from the National Science Foundation (SES 8912678) under the direction of Donald R. Songer, Principal Investigator. The database includes a stratified random sample of fifteen published cases per circuit for each year from 1925 to 1960 and thirty published cases per circuit for each year from 1961 to 1996. The Update to the United States Courts of Appeals Database (Ashlyn Kuersten and Susan Haire, co-Principal Investigators) extended this coding through 2002. The database, its update, and its documentation may be obtained from several websites, including http://www.artsandsciences.sc.edu/poli/juri. Additionally, we incorporated judge background data from the Attributes of U.S. Federal Judges Database (Gryski and Zuk 2004). This multi-user database was created under the auspices of National Science Foundation grant no. SBR-93-11999 (Gerard S. Gryski and Gary Zuk, Principal Investigators). It is also available at http://www.artsandsciences.sc.edu/poli/juri.

ONE The Judges and Cases

1. For studies examining retirement decisions of court judges on the courts of appeals, see Barrow and Zuk (1990), Nixon and Haskin (2000), Spriggs and Wahlbeck (1995), Vining (2009a), and Yoon (2005). The Constitution provides that judges on the U.S. courts of appeals, like other federal judges, may be impeached by a majority vote in the U.S. House of Representatives and removed from office by a two-thirds vote in the Senate. However, only one judge has actually been removed

from office by the impeachment process. Robert Archibald of the Third Circuit was removed in 1913 (Vining 2009b).

2. However, as Steigerwalt (2010) notes, over time, the home state senators who are not from the president's party have also gained power. For example, some recent Senate Judiciary Committee chairs have blocked nominations when home state senators from the party opposite the president cast blue slips. Additionally, in some instances, when the senatorial delegation is split along party lines, the senator from the party of the president has shared the power with the colleague from the opposing party (Steigerwalt 2010).
3. When a judge takes senior status, a vacancy is created that can be filled by the appointment of a new "regular" appeals court judge.
4. Based on our interviews and the internal operating procedures of the circuits, in the Sixth, Tenth, and District of Columbia Circuits a judge on senior status may elect to sit with the court en banc when the court is reviewing a decision made by a panel on which the senior judge sat. But other circuits do not follow this rule. Additionally, judges on senior status may not vote on whether to grant an en banc rehearing.
5. The judge data described in figures 2 through 4 and discussed in this section are derived from the authors' calculations based on the Attributes of U.S. Federal Judges Database (Gryski and Zuk 2004). The database and its documentation can be downloaded from the JuRi website at the University of South Carolina: http://www.artsandsciences.sc.edu/poli/juri.
6. When the data displayed in figures 2 through 4 were collected.
7. For example, appeals from the Federal Communications Commission, the Securities and Exchange Commission, the National Labor Relations Board, the Interstate Commerce Commission, and the Immigration and Naturalization Service.
8. While the overwhelming majority of cases decided by the courts of appeals are mandatory appeals (or "appeals as of right"), the courts also have a limited discretionary docket ("appeal by permission" cases). For example, litigants do not have a statutory right to an appeal of an interlocutory decision (in other words, a decision made at some intermediate stage during the course of the litigation, such as a ruling on a motion that does not lead to dismissal) of the lower court. The United States Code Title 28, Section 1292, sets out the limited circumstances in which the adversely affected litigant may appeal an interlocutory decision, but the court of appeals may choose whether to grant the petition (thereby agreeing to hear the appeal).
9. Article III, Section 2, of the U.S. Constitution defines a narrow set of circumstances in which U.S. courts may hear cases where only state law questions are at issues. These diversity of citizenship cases include civil disputes between citizens of different states, as well as disputes between U.S. citizens and a foreign country or citizens/subjects of a foreign country. Additionally, under United States Code Title 28, Section 1332, the federal district courts may entertain such diversity suits only when the amount in contention is at least $75,000.
10. This is not surprising, in that the court was formed in 1982 when Congress merged two relatively diverse courts, the appellate division of the U.S. Court of Claims and the U.S. Court of Customs and Patent Appeals.
11. The most recent Federal Rules of Appellate Procedure can be found here: http://www.uscourts.gov/RulesAndPolicies/FederalRulemaking/Overview.aspx.

12. As noted above, in most instances the party that is subjected to the adverse decision by the district court has an appeal of right. In those cases, that party initiating the appeal (by filing the notice of appeal) is designated the "appellant," and the opposing party is the "appellee." However, when the appeal is initiated or requested by a petition, the party filing the petition is typically called the "petitioner," while the party responding is labeled "respondent." For example, in the limited circumstances in which the courts of appeals have discretionary jurisdiction over district court decisions, the party requesting an appeal must file a petition for permission to appeal to the court (FRAP 5). Additionally, there are certain instances in which the court of appeals must hear the appeal but the initiating party still must file a petition (as opposed to the notice of appeal). For example, appeals of administrative orders are initiated when the challenging party files a petition for review (FRAP 15). Finally, parties that are unhappy with prior appeals court decisions may petition for rehearing by the three-judge panel or the entire court (en banc).
13. As with most circuit court procedures, there are always exceptions to the general rule. For example, the Seventh Circuit judges report that they typically meet as a panel for a single day.
14. There are, of course, some variations in the process. For example, according to the Eighth Circuit's internal operating procedures and Local Rule 34A, the circuit's chief judge assigns either the clerk, the senior staff attorney, or one or more panels of judges to prescreen cases to determine whether the court will hear oral arguments. If oral argument is not recommended, the parties have the opportunity to request a reclassification of the case to the oral argument docket. At that point the case is randomly assigned to one of at least three different three-judge panels that are specifically constituted to decide cases without oral argument. That panel may, either on its own or following a party's motion for reclassification, decide to transfer the case to the oral argument calendar. Following FRAP 34, only one judge need vote in favor of reclassification.
15. The circuit publication rules are such that the nature of the issue agenda in unreported cases is certainly different than those that are reported. Moreover, since reporting rules vary across circuits, further distortion exists. Issue creation (i.e., judges addressing issues not raised by the parties) is an additional source of bias. As such, our observations about the issue agenda are direct reflections of the reported opinions; they are biased reflections of the underlying docket.
16. In recent years about 5 percent of the cases resulting in published opinions were reviews by the courts of appeals of the decisions of U.S. district courts on petitions to the federal courts made by prisoners who contested the constitutionality of their conviction by state courts and their confinement in state prisons. Such habeas corpus petitions provide an indirect way for federal courts to review the legality of state court criminal decisions.

TWO The Preliminaries

1. Not only does FRAP 34 not specify that the three-judge panel determining whether to hear argument must be the same three-judge panel that decides the case, in some circuits, local rules or operating procedures allow the creation of one or more separate panels to prescreen for oral arguments before a case is assigned to a separate panel for a decision on the merits.

2. We depart from our usual convention of attributing comments to judges identified by a letter to preserve anonymity because this comment by its nature already identifies the judge as being from the Seventh Circuit.
3. This "duty panel" is appointed by the chief judge of the circuit and rotates membership, typically once a year.
4. Our focus on the characteristics of the panelists here, and with respect to some of the control variables discussed in the subsequent research design, is not ideal. In a minority of the circuits, a separate screening panel typically determines whether the case will be argued—though the merits panel typically can override this decision.
5. Like any cue, this is an imperfect one, as illustrated by historic landmark pro se cases (e.g., *Gideon v. Wainwright* 372 U.S. 335).
6. The initial year, 1971, is the first full year in which we could find variables for some of the main independent variables using the Federal Judicial Center data, such as Circuit Docket Size and Circuit Judicial Vacancies. The end year, 2002, was the last year of USCA publicly available data when we started the analysis.
7. We recognize this measure has temporal problems, as the final decision regarding the number of substantive issues addressed in the opinion of the court is made after the decision to hear oral arguments. However, we believe the problem is minimal, as the number of issues addressed in the opinions should be highly correlated with the number of issues addressed in the briefs, which are submitted prior to the decision regarding oral hearings.
8. We recognize that prior publication could also reflect complexity. However, including this as a control, as opposed to a measure of complexity, only made our tests of the complexity hypothesis more conservative.
9. Of course, the ABA no longer uses the extremely well qualified rating. As such, we also estimated the model using a dummy variable that combined nominees that received either a well qualified or an extremely well qualified rating. The results of the model were consistent with the one we reported.
10. This case was 347 U.S. 483 (1954).
11. One judge noted that during the controversy over school desegregation, judges on the Fourth Circuit were concerned about the charges being raised about panel stacking in the nearby Fifth Circuit and vowed they would not have a similar controversy on their own circuit. Consequently, for a period of several years, whenever an appeal raising a desegregation order reached the Fourth Circuit, the chief judge would bypass the normal procedure of selecting a three-judge panel to hear the appeal and instead schedule the appeal to be initially heard by the full circuit sitting en banc.
12. According to Title 28, Sections 291–94, of the U.S. Code, the chief judge of the circuit may "designate and assign temporarily" a district court or senior (retired) judge from that circuit to sit as an appellate judge on the circuit. Similarly, the chief justice of the United States has the power to designate a variety of judges to sit on a court of appeal. He may designate and assign active or retired district court or appellate judges from one circuit to temporarily sit on another circuit. Additionally, the chief justice may assign retired Supreme Court justices to sit by designation on a circuit.
13. While we never performed any statistical tests of possible differences between active judges and those on senior status, we divided our interviews into two stacks by judge

status, active and senior, and comparatively read through the interviews in each stack topic by topic. We did not discern any differences between the groups.

14. Interview by Tim Russert of Justice O'Connor on CNN, April 2005.
15. And on the Fourth Circuit, a panel will sometimes sit for a single day once a year, hearing three or four cases, at some of the law schools in the circuit to enable law students to satisfy their bar requirements to observe a given number of trials before admission to the bar.
16. In sharp contrast, judges on the Court of Appeal for England and Wales interviewed for a different project were scandalized by the practices in the American courts of appeals. The English judges were unanimous in their belief that it was not possible to thoroughly understand the issues in a case without extensive oral argument (and hearings in England often lasted a day and a half to two days per case).
17. This conclusion of our judges is confirmed by other accounts of the courts of appeals (see Cohen 2002, 72; Howard 1981, 234). Howard's conclusion about the rules for opinion assignment was based on his interviews with appeals court judges in the 1960s. Cohen's interviews were conducted in the early 2000s. Interviews we have conducted in the past six years confirm that the same rules have continued to the present, as does our reading of the internal circuit rules.
18. Curiously, in coding the United States Courts of Appeals Database, 1925–1996 (Songer 2002), which involved coding a random sample of about 20,000 cases decided between 1925 and 2002, coders discovered three cases (0.015 percent of all cases) in which the dissenting judge also wrote the majority opinion. We asked a few of our judges about this anomaly, but no one had any explanation.
19. Based on our calculation of the dissent rate using the United States Courts of Appeals Database (Songer 2002) for the period 1960–2007, the court was unanimous in 90.5 percent of all cases with published opinions.
20. This multi-user database was created by National Science Foundation grant no. SBR-93-11999 (Gerard S. Gryski and Gary Zuk, Principal Investigators). It is available for download from the JuRi website at the University of South Carolina (http://www.artsandsciences.sc.edu/poli/juri).
21. As a result of the idiosyncratic case assignment procedures in the Ninth Circuit, we also estimated the models presented in table 6, excluding Ninth Circuit cases. The results of the significance tests were virtually identical.
22. That said, if we remove the self-assignment variables, judges are significantly less likely to assign to ideologically distant judges, as posited (though the relationship is not moderated by case salience). In this case, ideological distance is likely a proxy for self-assignment, particularly in light of the relatively moderate level of multicollinearity when self-assignment is included in the model.
23. In a subsequent model, not included in this chapter, we discovered that the gender of the presiding judge was also unrelated to the likelihood that a male rather than a female judge would receive the majority opinion assignment.
24. In analyses not presented, it was determined that there was no difference in the probability that the opinion assignment would go to an African American rather than a Latino. Therefore, for the sake of parsimony, these two categories were combined into a single category of minority racial status.
25. Given the increasing electronic availability of many decisions, the courts increasingly

refer to opinions not available in the *Federal Reporter* as "not for citation" rather than "unpublished." The term "publication" is actually somewhat anachronistic at this point. Initially, panels either published the decision in the *Federal Reporter* (published by West) or the decision (often just a memorandum announcing the holding of the court without any exposition of the rationale behind the decision) was not released for publication. Of course, the published and unpublished decisions were always available for inspection by the public at the office of the clerk of the circuit, or in any of the official circuit libraries (and often, slip opinions were made available at federal repository libraries located within the circuit). The line between published and unpublished opinions has blurred over the last twenty years, however. First, many of the circuits began releasing unpublished opinions to the two major electronic legal services, Lexis and Westlaw, in the early 1990s. The publication nomenclature actually became a misnomer in 2001, when West started the *Federal Appendix,* which "publishes" the cases not included in the *Federal Reporter.* At one point, the term "not for citation" appeared to replace "published" as the more accurate description of the cases not included in the *Federal Reporter,* as a majority of circuits prohibited citation to these opinions in litigant briefs and oral arguments. However, when FRAP 32.1 was promulgated in 2006 to prohibit circuits from preventing parties from citing "unpublished" opinions, this "not for citation" term also became an anachronism.

THREE Decision Making and Writing the Opinion of the Court

1. Most decisions of the courts of appeals are now available to the public online at no cost, but even old opinions are by law matters of public record and are available either in published form in a series of journals called the *Federal Reporter,* available in any law library, or may be obtained by any person from the clerk's office of the circuit.
2. The time period is limited by the availability of the dates used to construct the processing time variables. As noted in the text, some of the information used to construct the data set was found in the Federal Judicial Center's Federal Court Cases: Integrated Database. Unfortunately, though the database accurately coded the information necessary to generate the dependent variable (including the year, month, and day) through 1996 (and for some of the 1997 cases, as the FJC database uses the fiscal year), more recent years did not include the day for the initial stages of the litigation (brief filing, docket assignment, and oral argument).
3. See the discussion of published decisions in chapter 2, note 24.
4. For example, see the Second Circuit's Internal Operating Procedure (IOP) 32.1.1 and the Third Circuit's IOP Chapter 5.
5. The only reference to publication is FRAP 32.1, which took effect in 2007 and prohibits circuits from circumscribing litigant citations of unpublished opinions.
6. With the exception that if the government loses a criminal case in the district court, the constitutional prohibition against double jeopardy prevents the government from appealing.
7. There are two variations on this procedure. In the Ninth Circuit, en banc review is heard by a panel consisting of the chief judge of the circuit and ten other non-senior appeals court judges chosen randomly. In the Sixth, Tenth, and District of Colum-

bia Circuits, if a senior appeals court judge from the circuit sat on the panel whose decision is subjected to en banc review, that judge may participate in the en banc decision. Other judges sitting by designation (e.g., district judges or appeals court judges from other circuits) are not extended this right.

8. *Shepard's* does not reliably report all the instances in which a petition for rehearing is filed by either the litigants or the judges. Thus, we have no information on how frequently the circuit is asked to review a decision of one of its panels.

FOUR Separate Opinion Writing on the Courts of Appeals

1. One could argue this does not necessarily reflect strategic considerations. Indeed, the observed pattern—judges who agreed with each other in the past continue to agree with one another—could result from a variety of factors not accounted for in the model. For example, while the study by Wahlbeck, Spriggs, and Maltzman (1999) controlled for ideological attachments, it did not directly measure nonideological shared attitudes or nonattitudinal attachments like friendships.
2. The extent of consensus on the courts of appeals is even more striking when one remembers that the 91 percent rate of unanimity reported is based only on those cases decided on the merits that resulted in reported opinions, and that such reported opinions represent only 8 percent of all cases decided by the courts of appeals. Using the data analyzed in the publication model in chapter 3, we found that judges dissent in less than one-half of 1 percent of all unreported decisions. So the overall rate at which the judges publicly express disagreement over the outcome is actually only 9 percent of 8 percent, or seven-tenths of 1 percent of the total workload of the courts of appeal.
3. An alternative perspective is that leisure preference plays a greater role in judicial behavior than in most other forms of employment, and because "a dissent is always added work," judges will often refrain from dissenting even when they disagree with the majority's opinion (Epstein, Landes, and Posner 2013, 36–37). However, none of the judges we interviewed articulated this perspective.
4. This is not surprising, in light of the overall low rate of dissents. Dissents occurred in just over 9.6 percent of the cases in our estimation sample. Since two of the three judges in a case with a dissent vote with the majority, the rate of dissents among individual judge votes is closer to 3 percent.

FIVE Explaining Attitudinal and Legal Influences on Decisions

1. The judge commenting on this case did not participate in the case; he was providing an example of how men and women would see a particular issue.
2. If one combines the finding from chapter 1 that only about one-half of the cases coming to the courts of appeals are decided in merits terminations with the data in table 10 that shows that in recent years fewer than one-fourth of all merits terminations result in published opinions, the conclusion is that the Songer (2002) United States Courts of Appeals Database contains a sample of only 10 percent to 15 percent of all appeals court cases.
3. Indeed, one recent study of forestry cases concluded court of appeals judges behave ideologically in published cases, but not in those that are not reported (Keele et al. 2009).

4. As indicated in figure 13, divided cases represent roughly 9 percent of the cases with published opinions, and since in recent years only 10 percent to 15 percent of the cases have been decided with a published opinion, cases in which the court was divided represent less than 2 percent of all appeals court terminations.

SIX Strategic Accounts of Decision Making

1. This finding is in contrast to the assumption made by a number of proponents of strategic approaches, including McNollgast (1995).
2. This finding is also contrary to assumptions made by many strategic accounts, including that of McNollgast (1995).
3. Similar interview results were also found in interviews with thirty-five courts of appeals judges from Canada and England.
4. To protect the anonymity of the judge, we do not refer to him or her by letter because other comments made by the judge are utilized throughout this book.
5. There are, of course, rare exceptions, such as the Second Circuit's New Haven firefighters affirmative action case, *Ricci v. DeStefano,* which was reversed by the Supreme Court (557 U.S. 557 [2009]). The case was originally unreported by the three-judge panel. Even then, after the Second Circuit announced it would vote to rehear the appeal en banc, the panel withdrew the unpublished opinion and replaced it with a published summary per curiam opinion.
6. Since certiorari is arguably a rare event, as a check on robustness we also estimated the model in table 18 using a rare event specification (see King and Zeng 2001). The results of that estimation are identical to those presented here.
7. The probability of cert reached 10 percent in only six-tenths of 1 percent of all cases.
8. Of course, to avoid review, a judge might strategically decide to make some alteration in the wording of the opinion that would fall short of changing the outcome. Since such a minor change might be perceived as less costly to the judge, it might be undertaken even when the probability of review was low. While this result is theoretically possible, no evidence that such action was ever taken could be uncovered in our interviews with the judges.
9. The Fifth Circuit en banc data were provided by Michael Giles and Thomas Walker, and part of the First and Ninth Circuit en banc data was provided by Stephen Wasby.
10. Additionally, during this period the ideological use of en bancs became more prevalent (Giles, Walker, and Zorn 2006; Schwartz 1988).
11. To identify the en banc cases, we employed the technique pioneered by Giles, Walker, and Zorn (2006). Specifically, "A Lexis-Nexis query consisting of the names of four circuit judges was employed to generate a list of cases. Each of these cases was then examined to see if it was decided *en banc.* The query was run again with a different combination of judges' names and the resulting list of cases checked for nonduplicative *en banc* cases. This procedure was repeated with different combinations of judges until no new *en banc* cases were generated" (Giles, Walker, and Zorn 2006, 858).
12. Since en banc review is a rare event, as a check on robustness, a model using a rare-event specification (see King and Zeng 2001) was estimated, and those results were found to be substantively identical to the results presented here.

13. Overall, the model performed as anticipated. The model correctly predicted 85 percent of the observations and the reduction in predictive error was approximately 28 percent. Due to possible heteroskedastic error variance we used robust standard errors. The technical appendix provides the descriptive statistics about the unweighted values of each of the variables included in the model.
14. In addition, we calculated the probability of review for cases that had more than one negative indicator of review, and in all of the calculations the likelihood of en banc review was approximately 0.0002 to 0.0004.
15. It is theoretically possible that the policy cost for an appeals court judge might be somewhat higher than these figures indicate because a judge might consider that a reversal implied that the disfavored policy was now a national policy. However, none of the judges interviewed gave any indication that they thought in those terms.
16. For example, we excluded from the analysis cases whose outcome had no meaning on a liberal to conservative scale, such as contract disputes between two corporations, as well as cases with mixed outcomes that were liberal in part and conservative in part.
17. In an alternative model, not displayed, we used the more nuanced measure of ideology based on the Nominate scores for the appointing president and the home state senator(s) of the judge at the time of appointment, which are described in chapter 2. The results were essentially identical for these alternative measures of judge ideology.
18. For all cases, Democratic judges supported liberal outcomes with 38 percent of their votes—a level of support that was lower than their support for liberal outcomes in the cases most likely to be reviewed to a statistically significant degree.
19. One might even suggest that if Supreme Court outcomes could be easily predicted, very few cases would actually get to the Supreme Court. If prediction were easy, litigants would rarely bring cases they knew they would lose in the Supreme Court, and appeals court judges would not make decisions that they knew would be reversed.

SEVEN The Congruence of Social Science and the Perceptions of the Judges

1. This view is consistent with the observations of one former clerk on the courts of appeals, who identified himself as politically to the left of President Obama but who noted that he had clerked for a judge appointed by Reagan. The former clerk noted that while there were occasional issues, such as abortion, on which he and his judge disagreed as to the proper outcome of the case, in the overwhelming majority of cases, including almost all criminal appeals, he and the judge reached the same conclusions after they had both carefully read the briefs and discussed with each other the opposing arguments raised by each side.

Technical Appendix

1. While the processing dates are available for a portion of the most recent cases (mid- to late 1990s onward) on PACER, the temporal and financial costs of collecting the data are prohibitive. Moreover, our experience with PACER suggests that the extent of the information available varies dramatically across circuits. Finally, the information pre-PACER is likely only maintained at official circuit offices, which would require extensive travel, and is likely not available across all circuits for the period of interest.

2. Of course, the variable is subject to a variety of criticisms. Among them are that we coded the most recent rules, which may have changed over time, and we weight each type of rule equally.
3. We used the natural log to account for the diminishing marginal returns of amicus briefs as a signal (or reflection) of case salience. Also, since the log of zero is undefined, the measure is the natural log of the number of amicus briefs plus one.
4. These can be found at www.voteview.org.
5. We also ran the models estimating ideological distance using the GHP scores (which are also known as the court of appeals Judicial Common Space scores; see Epstein et al. 2007), which are correlated with our measure at just below the 0.94 level. The results were consistent with our findings; if anything, they were slightly more robust.
6. According to Slotnick (1983), the following fifteen schools are prestigious: Harvard, Yale, Chicago, Stanford, Columbia, Michigan, Berkeley, Pennsylvania, New York University, Duke, Virginia, Texas, Cornell, Northwestern, and UCLA. It should be noted that this measure is highly correlated with several independent measures, indicating substantial criterion and construct validity (see Adcock and Collier 2001, 537). For example, with respect to criterion validity, fourteen of the fifteen elite schools are ranked in the top fifteen of the 2008 *U.S. News and World Report* rankings. With respect to construct validity, the Slotnick measure is highly correlated with several concepts that should be interrelated with law school quality. For example, from 1950 to 2001, thirteen of Slotnicks's schools were among the fifteen largest producers of U.S. Supreme Court clerks; fourteen were in the top sixteen, and all fifteen were in the top twenty-one (Szmer 2005). Similarly, using data from the Multi-User Database on the Attributes of United States Appeals Court Judges, 1801–2004 (Zuk and Gryski 2004), of the top producers of U.S. courts of appeals judges, the first nine schools are elites, according to Slotnick (1983), as are eleven of the top sixteen.
7. We also estimated the models using probit regression with clustered standard errors. The results did not change.
8. We used the xtprobit command in Stata 11 to generate the random effects estimates.
9. Amici curiae, particularly membership-based groups (Hansford 2004) and the Office of the Solicitor General (Nicholson and Collins 2008), are more likely to participate in salient cases. Similarly, Hettinger, Lindquist, and Martinek (2006) suggest that judges are more likely to pay attention to civil rights and civil liberties cases. Moreover, Epstein and Segal (2000) note that both measures are highly correlated with other measures of Supreme Court salience (the *Congressional Quarterly* list of important cases and their own measure using *New York Times* front-page coverage). Finally, the decision to exercise judicial review as a challenge to traditional policymakers should be of special interests to followers of politics, and as such should be an indicator of political salience (Hettinger, Lindquist, and Martinek 2004). Additionally, because these cases are more likely to be cited (at least at the Supreme Court level; see Maltzman, Spriggs, and Wahlbeck 2000), it is also an indicator of legal salience.
10. Lindquist, Martinek, and Hettinger (2007) utilized prior publication status as a measure of importance. The publication standards for the district courts encompass both saliency and complexity (Swenson 2004). Indeed, when we included prior

publication status in the factor analyses for both complexity and saliency, the factor loadings were fairly high and fairly consistent (between 0.5 and 0.6). As such, we excluded it from both indices. However, we note that when it was included in the salience measure but not complexity—and vice versa—the results did not significantly change.

11. This was transformed to account for diminishing marginal utility. Again, the actual value is the log of one plus the number of amicus briefs, since the log of zero is undefined.
12. Hettinger, Lindquist, and Martinek (2004) note that civil rights and liberties cases are highly salient to most judges, and probably the general public. Moreover, with respect to criterion (and, arguably, construct) validity, Epstein and Segal (2000) found that 75 percent of the U.S. Supreme Court cases covered on the front page of the *New York Times* were civil rights or liberties cases, as were 90 percent of the cases deemed important by *Congressional Quarterly.*
13. Of course, unobserved circuit-level factors could lead to correlated errors within circuits. While using robust standard errors is one alternative method for correcting for this, other solutions include using circuit-level fixed effects, using robust standard errors clustered by circuit, or including relevant circuit-level covariates. We chose the last method, including five circuit-level independent variables in the model. We did, however, estimate unreported models using the two other methods. The fixed effects method proved problematic, generating outrageously high multicollinearity (in one case, above 1,000). Moreover, the signs switched for several of the variables, an expected side effect of the multicollinearity. Still, nine of the thirteen significant coefficients in the reported model were still statistically in the posited direction. Of course, the multicollinearity indirectly suggests that we included the relevant circuit-level variables, reducing the likelihood that the error terms are correlated within circuits. However, we also estimated the models using clustered standard errors. The results are fairly similarly to the reported model; ten of thirteen coefficients significant in that model are significant at the 0.1 level or better in the model with the clustered standard errors. Only Panel Ideological Range, Docket Size, and Judge Law School Prestige of the majority opinion assigner are not robust to this specification.
14. However, we note that the results did not change substantively when we used a complexity index that included Opinion Length.
15. We identified whether the case was orally argued using data from the FJC's Federal Court Cases: Integrated Database (2005).
16. Specifically, the uniqueness for the number of parties component was less than 0.015, and the variable had a factor loading of 0.03 on one dimension (the next lowest was 0.57) and 0.99 on the second dimension (the loadings for the other three components were all under 0.09 for that dimension).
17. We recognize that there could be autocorrelation within circuits resulting from unaccounted-for intracircuit factors as well. To account for this, we borrowed the strategy employed by Hettinger, Lindquist, and Martinek (2006): we included a Circuit Opinion Rate variable (discussed below). However, if we do include circuit-level fixed effects along with the Circuit Opinion Rate variable and the case clustered standard errors, the results of the hypotheses tests are identical to the results that we present.

18. Discrete changes in predicted probabilities reflect the difference in probability that the judge will cast a dissenting vote in the case when the independent variable is set to two interesting values, while holding all other covariates at the appropriate level of central tendency. For dichotomous variables, the two interesting values are 1 and 0; for continuous variables, they are one standard deviation above and below the mean.

    Percent changes are the percentage increase (or decrease) in the probability of dissent from the lower to the higher important value of the independent variable used to generate the discrete changes. This is calculated by the following formula: {[Pr(Y = Dissent | X = higher value) – Pr(Y = Dissent | X = lower value)]/[Pr(Y = Dissent | X = lower value)] × 100}.

19. Here we again differ from Hettinger, Lindquist, and Martinek (2006) and other studies that estimated panel preferences using the ideology of the majority opinion author. As before, we chose not to focus on the majority opinion assigner because of our belief that most dissenting votes are cast during the conference, prior to the assignment to draft the opinion of the court. Of course, when we estimated the models using the preferences of the majority opinion assigner, the results did not change.

BIBLIOGRAPHY

Abramowicz, Michael. 2000. "*En Banc* Revisited." *Columbia Law Review* 100: 1600–41.

Adcock, Robert, and David Collier. 2001. "Measurement Validity: A Shared Standard for Qualitative and Quantitative Research." *American Political Science Review* 95: 529–46.

Agarwal, S., S. Chomsisengphet, R. McMenamin, and P. M. Skiba. 2010. "Race, Gender and Political Ideology in Personal Bankruptcy Outcomes." *SSRN eLibrary.*

Alexander, Deborah, and Kristi Andersen. 1993. "Gender as a Factor in the Attribution of Leadership Traits." *Political Research Quarterly* 46: 527–45.

Atkins, Burton. 1972. "Decision-making Rules and Judicial Strategy on the United States Courts of Appeals." *Western Political Quarterly* 25: 626–42.

Atkins, Burton M. 1973. "Judicial Behavior and Tendencies Towards Conformity in a Three Member Small Group: A Case Study of Dissent Behavior in the US Courts of Appeals." *Social Science Quarterly* 54: 41.

———. 1974. "Opinion Assignments on the United States Courts of Appeals: The Question of Issue Specialization." *Western Political Quarterly* 27: 409–28.

———. 1991. "Party Capability Theory as an Explanation for Intervention: Behavior in the English Court of Appeal." *American Journal of Political Science* 35: 881–903.

Atkins, B. M., and W. Zavoina. 1974. "Judicial Leadership on Court of Appeals: Probability Analysis of Panel Assignment in Race Relations Cases on Fifth Circuit." *American Political Science Review* 18: 701–11.

Atkins, Burton M., and Henry R. Glick. 1976. "Environmental and Structural Variables as Determinants of Issues in State Courts of Last Resort." *American Journal of Political Science* 20: 97–114.

Atkins, Burton M., and Justin J. Green. 1976. "Consensus on the United States

Courts of Appeals: Illusion or Reality?" *American Journal of Political Science* 20: 735–48.

Bailey, Michael A., and Forrest Maltzman. 2011. *The Constrained Court: Law, Politics, and the Decisions Justices Make.* Princeton, NJ: Princeton University Press.

Banks, Christopher P. 1999. *Judicial Politics in the D.C. Circuit.* Baltimore, MD: Johns Hopkins University Press.

Barrow, Debora J., and Gary Zuk. 1990. "An Institutional Analysis of Turnover in the Lower Federal Courts, 1900–1987." *Journal of Politics* 52: 457–76.

Bast, Carol M., and Susan W. Harrell. 2004. "Ethical Obligations: Performing Adequate Legal Research and Legal Writing." *Nova Law Review* 29: 49–73.

Baum, Lawrence. 1977. "Judicial Specialization, Litigant Influence, and Substantive Policy: The Court of Customs and Patent Appeals." *Law & Society Review* 11: 823–50.

———. 1980. "Responses of Federal District Judges to Court of Appeals Policies: An Exploration." *Western Political Quarterly* 33: 217–24.

———. 1994. "Specialization and Authority Acceptance: The Supreme Court and Lower Federal Courts." *Political Research Quarterly* 47: 693–703.

———. 1997. *The Puzzle of Judicial Behavior.* Ann Arbor: University of Michigan Press.

———. 2006. *Judges and Their Audience: A Perspective on Judicial Behavior.* Princeton, NJ: Princeton University Press.

Beiser, Edward N. 1974. "The Rhode Island Supreme Court: A Well Integrated political System." *Law & Society Review* 8: 167–86.

Benesh, Sara C., and Wendy L. Martinek. 2002. "State Supreme Court Decision Making in Confessions Cases." *Justice System Journal* 23: 109–33.

Benesh, Sara C., and Malia Reddick. 2002. "Overruled: An Event History Analysis of Lower Court Reaction to Supreme Court Alteration of Precedent." *Journal of Politics* 64: 534–50.

Biernat, Monica, and Diane Kobrynowicz. 1997. "Gender- and Race-Based Standards of Competence: Lower Minimum Standards but Higher Ability Standards for Devalued Groups." *Journal of Personality and Social Psychology* 72: 544–57.

Binder, Sarah A., and Forrest Maltzman. 2009. *Advice & Dissent: The Struggle to Shape the Federal Judiciary.* Washington, DC: Brookings Institution Press.

Black, Ryan C., and James F. Spriggs II. 2008. "An Empirical Analysis of the Length of U.S. Supreme Court Opinions." *Houston Law Review* 45: 621–83.

Block, Frederic. 2007. "Senior Status: An 'Active' Senior Judge Corrects Some Common Misunderstandings." *Cornell Law Review* 92: 533–47.

Bowie, Jennifer Barnes, and Donald R. Songer. 2009. "Assessing the Applicability of Strategic Theory to Explain Decision Making on the Courts of Appeals." *Political Research Quarterly* 62: 393–407.

Box-Steffensmeier, Janet M., and Bradford Jones. 2004. *Event History Modeling: A Guide for Social Scientists.* Cambridge: Cambridge University Press.

Boyd, Christina L., Lee Epstein, and Andrew D. Martin. 2010. "Untangling the Causal Effects of Sex on Judging." *American Journal of Political Science* 54: 389–411.

Brace, Paul, and Melinda Gann Hall. 1990. "Neo-Institutionalism and Dissent in State Supreme Courts." *Journal of Politics* 52: 54–70.

———. 1993. "Integrated Models of Judicial Dissent." *Journal of Politics* 55: 914–35.

Brambor, Thomas, Roberts Clark, and Matt Golder. 2006. "Understanding Interaction Models: Improving Empirical Analysis." *Political Analysis* 14: 63–82.

Brenner, Saul. 1982. "Strategic Choice and Opinion Assignment on the U.S. Supreme Court: A Reexamination." *Western Political Quarterly* 35: 204–11.

———. 1984. "Issue Specialization as a Variable in Opinion Assignment on the U.S. Supreme Court." *Journal of Politics* 46: 1217–25.

———. 1993. "The Chief Justices' Self Assignment of Majority Opinions in Salient Cases." *Social Science Journal* 30: 143–50.

Brenner, Saul, and Timothy M. Hagle. 1996. "Opinion Writing and Acclimation Effect." *Political Behavior* 18: 235–61.

Brenner, Saul, and Jan Palmer. 1988. "The Time Taken to Write Opinions as a Determinant of Opinion Assignment." *Judicature* 72: 179–84.

Brenner, Saul, and Harold J. Spaeth. 1986. "Issue Specialization in Majority Opinion Assignment on the Burger Court." *Western Political Quarterly* 39: 520–27.

———. 1988. "Majority Opinion Assignments and the Maintenance of the Original Coalition on the Warren Court." *American Journal of Political Science* 32: 72–81.

Brenner, Saul, and Joseph M. Whitmeyer. 2009. *Strategy on the United States Supreme Court.* New York: Cambridge University Press.

Brudley, James J., and Corey Distlear. 2001. "Designated Diffidence: District Court Judges on the Courts of Appeals." *Law & Society Review* 35: 565–606.

Caldeira, Gregory, and John R. Wright. 1988. "Organized Interests and Agenda Setting in the U.S. Supreme Court." *American Political Science Review* 82: 1109–27.

Cameron, Charles M., and Craig Cummings. 2003. "Diversity and Judicial Decision Making: Evidence from Affirmative Action Cases in the Federal Courts of Appeal, 1971–1999." Paper presented at the Annual Meeting of the Midwest Political Science Association, Chicago, April 3–6.

Cameron, Charles M., Jeffrey A. Segal, and Donald R. Songer. 2000. "Strategic Auditing in a Political Hierarchy: An Informational Model of the Supreme Court's Certiorari Decisions." *American Political Science Review* 94: 101–16.

Canon, Bradley C., and Dean Jaros. 1970. "External Variables, Institutional Structure, and Dissent on State Supreme Courts." *Polity* 4: 185–200.

Carp, Robert A., and C. K. Rowland. 1983. *Policymaking and Politics in the Federal District Courts.* Knoxville: University of Tennessee Press.

Carp, Robert A., and Ronald Stidham. 1991. *The Federal Courts,* 2nd ed. Washington, DC: Congressional Quarterly Press.

Carter, Lief H., and Thomas F. Burke. 2010. *Reason in Law,* 8th ed. New York: Longman.

Cauthen, James N. G., and Barry Latzer. 2008. "Why So Long? Explaining Processing Time in Capital Appeals." *Justice System Journal* 29: 298–312.

Cheng, Edward K. 2008. "Opinion Specialization." *Judicature* 92: 103–5.

Christensen, Robert K., and John Szmer. 2012. "Examining the Efficiency of the U.S. Courts of Appeals: Pathologies and Prescriptions." *International Review of Law and Economics* 32: 30–37.

Clark, Tom S. 2008. "A Principal-Agent Theory of En Banc Review." *Journal of Law, Economics, & Organization* 25: 55–79.

Coffin, Frank M. 1994. *On Appeal: Courts, Lawyering and Judging.* New York: W. W. Norton.

Cohen, Jonathan Matthew. 2002. *Inside Appellate Courts: The Impact of Court Organization on Judicial Decision Making in the United States Courts of Appeals.* Ann Arbor: University of Michigan Press.

Collins, Paul T., and Wendy L. Martinek. 2011. "The Small Group Context: Designated District Court Judges in the U.S. Courts of Appeals." *Journal of Empirical Legal Studies* 8: 177–205.

Collins, Todd, and Laura Moyer. 2008. "Gender, Race, and Intersectionality on the Federal Appellate Bench." *Political Research Quarterly* 61: 219–27.

Cross, Frank B. 2007. *Decision Making in the U.S. Courts of Appeals.* Stanford, CA: Stanford University Press.

Cross, Frank B., and Emerson H. Tiller. 1998. "Judicial Partisanship and Obedience to Legal Doctrine: Whistleblowing on the Federal Courts of Appeals." *Yale Law Journal* 107: 2155–76.

Epstein, Lee, and Jack Knight. 1998. *The Choices Justices Make.* Washington, DC: Congressional Quarterly Press.

———. 2000. "Toward a Strategic Revolution in Judicial Politics: A Look Back, a Look Ahead." *Political Research Quarterly* 53: 625–61.

Epstein, Lee, William M. Landes, and Richard A. Posner. 2013. *The Behavior of Federal Judges: A Theoretical and Empirical Study of Rational Choice.* Cambridge, MA: Harvard University Press.

Epstein, Lee, Andrew D. Martin, Jeffrey A. Segal, and Chad Westerland. 2007. "The Judicial Common Space." *Journal of Law, Economics, & Organization* 23: 303–25.

Epstein, Lee, and Jeffrey A. Segal 2000. "Measuring Issue Salience." *American Journal of Political Science* 44: 66–83.

———. 2005. *Advice and Consent: The Politics of Judicial Appointments.* New York: Oxford University Press.

Farhang, Sean, and Gregory Wawro. 2004. "Institutional Dynamics on the U.S. Court of Appeals: Minority Representation under Panel Decision Making." *Journal of Law, Economics, & Organization* 20: 299–330.

Federal Judicial Center. 2005. Federal Court Cases: Integrated Database, 1970–2000 (Computer file). Conducted by the Federal Judicial Center (Study no.

8429). ICPSR Version. Ann Arbor, MI: Inter-university Consortium for Political and Social Research (producer and distributor).

Ferejohn, John, and Barry Weingast. 1992. "A Positive Theory of Statutory Interpretation." *International Review of Law and Economics* 12: 263–79.

Galanter, Marc. 1974. "Why the 'Haves' Come Out Ahead: Speculations on the Limits of Social Change." *Law & Society Review* 9: 95–160.

Gely, Rafael, and Pablo T. Spiller. 1990. "A Rational Choice Theory of Supreme Court Statutory Decisions: With Applications to the 'State Farm' and 'Grove City' Cases." *Journal of Law, Economics, & Organization* 6: 263–300.

George, Tracy. 1999. "The Dynamics and Determinants of the Decision to Grant En Banc Review." *Washington Law Review* 74: 213–74.

George, Tracey E., and Lee Epstein. 1992. "On the Nature of Supreme Court Decision Making." *American Political Science Review* 86: 323–37.

George, Tracey E., and Michael E. Solimine. 2001. "Supreme Court Monitoring of the United States Courts of Appeals En Banc." *Supreme Court Economic Review* 9: 171–204.

Gerber, Scott D., and Keeol Park. 1997. "The Quixotic Search for Consensus on the U.S. Supreme Court: A Cross-Judicial Empirical Analysis of the Rehnquist Court Justices." *American Political Science Review* 91: 390–408.

Giles, Michael W., Virginia A. Hettinger, and Todd Peppers. 2001. "Picking Federal Judges: A Note on Policy and Partisan Selection Agendas." *Political Research Quarterly* 54: 623–41.

Giles, Michael W., Virginia Hettinger, Christopher Zorn, and Todd Peppers. 2007. "The Etiology of En Banc in the U.S. Courts of Appeals." *American Journal of Political Science* 51: 449–63.

Giles, Michael W., Thomas G. Walker, and Christopher Zorn. 2006. "Setting a Judicial Agenda: The Decision to Grant En Banc Review in the U.S. Courts of Appeals." *Journal of Politics* 68: 852–66.

Gillman, Howard, and Cornell W. Clayton. 1999. "Beyond Judicial Attitudes: Institutional Approaches to Supreme Court Decision-Making." In *Supreme Court Decision-Making: New Institutionalist Approaches,* edited by Cornell W. Clayton and Howard Gillman. Chicago: University of Chicago Press.

Ginsburg, Ruth Bader, and Laura W. Brill. 1995. "Women in the Federal Judiciary: Three Way Pavers and the Exhilarating Change President Carter Wrought." *Fordham Law Review* 64: 281–90.

Glick, Henry Robert, and Kenneth N. Vines. 1973. *State Court Systems.* Englewood Cliffs, NJ: Prentice Hall.

Glick, Henry Robert, and George W. Pruet, Jr. 1986. "Dissent in State Supreme Courts: Patterns and Correlates of Conflict." In *Judicial Conflict & Consensus: Behavioral Studies of American Appellate Courts,* edited by Sheldon Goldman and Charles M. Lamb. Lexington: University of Kentucky Press.

Goff, Brian. 2006. "Supreme Court Consensus and Dissent: Estimating the Role of the Selection Screen." *Public Choice* 127: 375–91.

Goldman, Sheldon. 1966. "Voting Behavior on the United States Courts of Appeals, 1961–1964. *American Political Science Review* 60: 374–83.

———. 1969."Backgrounds, Attitudes, and the Voting behavior of Judges: A Comment on Joel Grossman's Social Backgrounds and Judicial Decisions." *Journal of Politics* 31: 214–22.

———. 1975. "Voting Behavior on the United States Courts of Appeals Revisited." *American Political Science Review* 69: 491–506.

———. 1997. *Picking Federal Judges: Lower Court Selection from Roosevelt through Reagan.* New Haven, CT: Yale University Press.

Goldman, Sheldon, and Charles M. Lamb, eds. 1986. *Judicial Conflict & Consensus: Behavioral Studies of American Appellate Courts.* Lexington: University of Kentucky Press.

Gryski, Gerard, and Gary Zuk. 2004. *Attributes of U.S. Federal Judges Database.* Available at http://www.artsandsciences.sc.edu/poli/juri.

Gujarti, Damodar N., and Dawn C. Porter. 2009. *Basic Econometrics.* New York: McGraw-Hill Education.

Haire, Susan B., and Ashlyn K. Kuersten. 2007. United States Courts of Appeals Database, 1997–2002. Available at http://www.artsandsciences.sc.edu/poli/juri/appealscourt.html.

Haire, Susan B., Stefanie A. Lindquist, and Donald R. Songer. 2003. "Appellate Court Supervision in the Federal Judiciary: A Hierarchical Perspective." *Law & Society Review* 37: 143–68.

Halpern, Stephen C., and Kenneth N. Vines. 1977. "Institutional Disunity, the Judges Bill and the Role of the US Supreme Court." *Western Political Quarterly* 30: 471–83.

Hand, Learned. 1958. *The Bill of Rights.* Cambridge, MA: Harvard University Press.

Handberg, Roger. 1978. "Leadership in State Courts of Last Resort: The Interaction of Environment and Procedure." *Jurimetrics* 19: 178–85.

Hansford, Thomas G. 2004. "Lobbying Strategies, Venue Selection, and Organized Interest Involvement at the U.S. Supreme Court." *American Politics Research* 32: 170–97.

Hausegger, Lori, and Stacia Haynie. 2003. "Judicial Decisionmaking and the Use of Panels in the Canadian Supreme Court and the South African Appellate Division." *Law & Society Review* 37: 635–57.

Hawkesworth, Mary. 2003. "Congressional Enactments of Race-Gender: Toward a Theory of Raced-Gendered Institutions." *American Political Science Review* 97: 529–50.

Hettinger, Virginia A., Stefanie A. Lindquist, and Wendy L. Martinek. 2003. "The Role and Impact of Chief Judges on the United States Courts of Appeals." *Justice System Journal* 24: 91–117.

———. 2004. "Comparing Attitudinal and Strategic Accounts of Dissenting Behavior on the U.S. Courts of Appeals." *American Journal of Political Science* 48: 123–37.

———. 2006. *Judging on a Collegial Court: Influences on Federal Appellate Decision Making.* Charlottesville: University of Virginia Press.

Hoffman, Daniel N. 1981. "Nonpublication of Federal Appellate Court Opinions." *Justice System Journal* 6: 405–34.

Howard, J. Woodford. 1981. *Courts of Appeals in the Federal Judicial System: A Study of the Second, Fifth, and District of Columbia Circuits.* Princeton, NJ: Princeton University Press.

Humphries, Martha Anne, and Donald R. Songer. 1999. "Law and Politics in Judicial Oversight of Federal Administrative Agencies." *Journal of Politics* 61: 207–20.

Hurwitz, Mark S., and Drew Noble Lanier. 2008. "Diversity in State and Federal Appellate Courts: Change and Continuity Across 20 Years." *Justice System Journal* 29: 47.

Johnson, Timothy R. 2004. *Oral Arguments and Decision Making on the United States Supreme Court.* Albany: SUNY Press.

Johnson, Timothy R., Paul J. Wahlbeck, and James F. Spriggs II. 2006. "The Influence of Oral Arguments on the U.S. Supreme Court." *American Political Science Review* 100: 99–113.

Kagan, Robert A., Bliss Cartwright, Lawrence M. Friedman, and Stanton Wheeler. 1978. "The Evolution of State Supreme Courts." *Michigan Law Review* 76: 966–98.

Kastellac, Jonathan P. 2010. "The Statistical Analysis of Judicial Decisions and Legal Rules with Classification Trees." *Journal of Empirical Legal Studies* 7: 202–30.

———. 2011. "Panel Composition and Voting on the U.S. Courts of Appeals over Time." *Political Research Quarterly* 64: 377–91.

Keele, Denise M., Robert W. Malmsheimer, Donald W. Floyd, and Lianjun Zhang. 2009. "An Analysis of Ideological Effects in Published versus Unpublished Judicial Opinions." *Journal of Empirical Legal Studies* 6: 213–39.

Kim, Pauline T. 2009. "Deliberation and Strategy on the United States Courts of Appeals: An Empirical Exploration of Panel Effects." *University of Pennsylvania Law Review* 157: 1319–81.

King, Gary, and Langche Zeng. 2001. "Logistic Regression in Rare Events Data." *Political Analysis* 9: 137–63.

Klein, David E. 2002. *Making Law in the United States Courts of Appeals.* Cambridge: Cambridge University Press.

Klein, David E., and Robert J. Hume. 2003. "Fear of Reversal as an Explanation of Lower Court Compliance." *Law & Society Review* 37: 579.

Koch, Jeffrey W. 2000. "Do Citizens Apply Gender Stereotypes to Infer Candidates' Ideological Orientations?" *Journal of Politics* 62: 414–29.

Kuersten, Ashlyn, and Donald R. Songer. 2003. "Presidential Success through Appointments to the United States Courts of Appeals." *American Politics Research* 31: 107–37

Lamb, Charles M. 1986. "A Microlevel Analysis of Appeals Court Conflict: Warren Burger and His Colleagues on the DC Circuit." In *Judicial Conflict & Consensus: Behavioral Studies of American Appellate Courts,* edited by Sheldon Goldman and Charles M. Lamb. Lexington: University of Kentucky Press.

Landes, William M., Lawrence Lessig, and Michael E. Solimine. 1998. "Judicial Influence: A Citation Analysis of Federal Courts of Appeals Judges." *Journal of Legal Studies* 27: 271.

Lax, Jeffrey R., and Kelly T. Rader. 2010. "Legal Constraints on Supreme Court Decision Making: Do Jurisprudential Regimes Exist?" *Journal of Politics* 72: 273–84.

Lindquist, Stefanie A. 2007. "Bureaucratization and Balkanization: The Origins and Effects of Decision-Making Norms in the Federal Appellate Courts." *University of Richmond Law Review* 41: 659–706.

Lindquist, Stefanie A., Susan B. Haire, and Donald R. Songer. 2007. "Supreme Court Auditing of the U.S. courts of Appeals: An Organizational Perspective." *Journal of Public Administration Research and Theory* 17: 607–624.

Lindquist, Stefanie A., and Wendy L. Martinek. 2009. "Response: Psychology, Strategy, and Behavioral Equivalence." *University of Pennsylvania Law Review, PENNumbra* 158: 75–81.

Lindquist, Stefanie A., Wendy L. Martinek, and Virginia A. Hettinger. 2007. "Splitting the Difference: Modeling Appellate Court Decisions with Mixed Outcomes." *Law & Society Review* 41: 429–56.

Lindquist, Stefanie A., and David A. Yalof. 2001. "Congressional Responses to Federal Circuit Court Decisions." *Judicature* 85: 60–68.

Long, J. Scott. 1997. *Regression Models for Categorical and Limited Dependent Variables.* Thousand Oaks, CA: Sage.

Long, J. Scott, and Jeremy Freese. 2006. *Regression Models for Categorical Dependent Variables Using Stata.* College Station, TX: Stata Press.

Maltzman, Forrest, James F. Spriggs II, and Paul J. Wahlbeck. 2000. *Crafting Law on the Supreme Court: The Collegial Game.* New York: Cambridge University Press.

Maltzman, Forrest, and Paul J. Wahlbeck. 1996. "May It Please the Chief? Opinion Assignment in the Rehnquist Court." *American Journal of Political Science* 40: 421–43.

———. 2004. "A Conditional Model of Opinion Assignment on the Supreme Court." *Political Research Quarterly* 57: 551–63.

Marks, Brian A. 1989. "A Model of Judicial Influence on Congressional Policymaking: *Grove City College v. Bell.*" PhD diss., Washington University.

McCormick, Peter. 1993. "Party Capability Theory and Appellate Success in the Supreme Court of Canada, 1949–1992." *Canadian Journal of Political Science* 3: 535–540.

———. 2003. "With Respect: Levels of Disagreement on the Lamer Court, 1990–2000." *McGill Law Journal* 48: 89–116.

McGuire, Kevin T. 1995. "Repeat Players in the Supreme Court: The Role of Experienced Lawyers in Litigation Success." *Journal of Politics* 57: 187–96.

McNollgast. 1995. "Politics and the Courts: A Positive Theory of Judicial Doctrine and the Rule of Law." *Southern California Law Review* 68: 1631–83.

Merritt, Debora Jones, and James J. Brudney. 2001. "Stalking Secret Law: What

Predicts Publications in the United States Courts of Appeals." *Vanderbilt Law Review* 54: 71–121.

Murphy, Walter F. 1964. *Elements of Judicial Strategy.* Chicago: University of Chicago Press.

Newman, Jon O. 1992. "A Study of Appellate Reversals." *Brooklyn Law Review* 58: 629–40.

Nicholson, Chris, and Paul M. Collins, Jr. 2008. "The Solicitor General's Amicus Curiae Strategies in the Supreme Court." *American Politics Research* 36: 382–415.

Nixon, David C., and J. David Haskin. 2000. "Judicial Retirement Strategies: The Judge's Role in Influencing Party Control of the Appellate Courts." *American Politics Research* 28: 458–89.

Norrander, Barbara. 1999. "The Evolution of the Gender Gap." *Public Opinion Quarterly* 63: 566–76.

Ostberg, C. L., and Matthew E. Wetstein. 2007. *Attitudinal Decision Making in the Supreme Court of Canada.* Vancouver: University of British Columbia Press.

Ostberg, C. L., Matthew Wetstein, Donald R. Songer, and Susan W. Johnson. 2009. "Ideological Consistency and Attitudinal Conflict: A Comparative Analysis of the U.S. and Canadian Supreme Courts." *Comparative Political Studies* 42: 763–92.

Peck, Sidney. 1969. "A Scalogram Analysis of the Supreme Court of Canada, 1958–1967." In *Comparative Judicial Behavior: Cross-Cultural Studies of Political Decision-Making in the East and West,* edited by Glendon Schubert and David J. Danelski. New York: Oxford University Press.

Pelled, Lisa Hope. 1996. "Demographic Diversity, Conflict, and Work Group Outcome: An Intervening Process Theory." *Organizational Science* 7: 615–31.

Peresie, Jennifer L. 2005. "Female Judges Matter: Gender and Collegial Decisionmaking in the Federal Appellate Courts." *Yale Law Journal* 114: 1759–90.

Perry, H. W., Jr. 1991. *Deciding to Decide: Agenda Setting in the United States Supreme Court.* Cambridge, MA: Harvard University Press.

Peterson, Steven A. 1981. "Dissent in American Courts." *Journal of Politics* 43: 412–34.

Pinello, Daniel R. 1999. "Linking Party to Judicial Ideology in American Courts: A Meta-Analysis." *Justice System Journal* 20: 219–54.

Posner, Richard A. 1983. "Will the Federal Courts of Appeals Survive until 1984? An Essay on Delegation and Specialization of the Judicial Function." *Southern California Law Review* 56: 761–91.

———. 1996. *The Federal Courts: Challenge and Reform.* Cambridge, MA: Harvard University Press.

Pritchett, C. Herman. 1948. *The Roosevelt Court.* New York: Macmillan.

Randazzo, Kirk A. 2004. "Foreign Affairs Litigation in the U.S. Courts of Appeals: A Preliminary Analysis." *Justice System Journal* 25: 227–38.

Randazzo, Kirk A., Richard W. Waterman, and Jeffrey A. Fine. 2006. "Checking the Federal Courts: The Impact of Congressional Statutes on Judicial Behavior." *Journal of Politics* 68: 1006–17.

Revesz, Richard L. 1997. "Environmental Regulation, Ideology and the D.C. Circuit." *Virginia Law Review* 83: 1717–72.

Richards, Mark J., and Herbert M. Kritzer. 2002. "Jurisprudential Regimes in Supreme Court Decision Making," *American Political Science Review* 96: 305–20.

Richardson, Richard J., and Kenneth N. Vines. 1970. *The Politics of Federal Courts: Lower Courts in the United States.* Boston: Little, Brown.

Richman, William M., and William L. Reynolds. 1988. "Appellate Justice Bureaucracy and Scholarship." *University of Michigan Journal of Law Reform* 21: 623–46.

Robertson, David. 1998. *Judicial Discretion in the House of Lords.* New York: Oxford University Press.

Rohde, David W. 1972. "Policy Goals, Strategic, Choice and Majority Opinion Assignments in the U. S. Supreme Court." *Midwest Journal of Political Science* 16: 652–82.

Rohde, David W., and Harold J. Spaeth. 1976. *Supreme Court Decision Making.* San Francisco: W. H. Freeman.

Sarver, Tammy A., Erin B. Kaheny, and John Szmer. 2008. "No Room for Women at the Top: The Attorney Gender Gap in the U.S. Supreme Court." *Judicature* 91: 238–50.

Scalia, Antonin. 1994. "The Dissenting Opinion." *Journal of Supreme Court History* 19: 33–44.

Schubert, Glendon 1958. "The Study of Judicial Decision-Making as an Aspect of Political Behavior." *American Political Science Review* 52: 1007–25.

———. 1962. "Policy without Law: An Extension of the Certiorari Game." *Stanford Law Review* 14: 284–327.

———. 1965. *The Judicial Mind: The Attitudes and Ideologies of Supreme Court Justices, 1946–1963.* Evanston, IL: Northwestern University Press.

Schwartz, Herman. 1988. *Packing the Courts: The Conservative Campaign to Rewrite the Constitution.* New York: Scribner.

———. 1997. "Separation-of-Powers Games in Positive Theory of Congress and Courts." *American Political Science Review* 91: 28–44.

Segal, Jeffrey A., and Albert D. Cover. 1989. "Ideological Values and the Votes of U.S. Supreme Court Justices." *American Political Science Review* 83: 557–65.

Segal, Jeffrey A., and Harold J. Spaeth. 1993. *The Supreme Court and the Attitudinal Model.* New York: Cambridge University Press.

———. 2002. *The Supreme Court and the Attitudinal Model Revisited.* New York: Cambridge University Press.

Sheehan, Reginald S., William Mishler, and Donald R. Songer. 1992. "Ideology, Status, and the Differential Success of Direct Parties before the Supreme Court." *American Political Science Review* 86: 464–71.

Slotnick, Elliot E. 1979a. "The Equality Principle & Majority Opinion Assignment on the United States Supreme Court." *Polity* 12:318–32.

———. 1979b. "Judicial Career Patterns and Majority Opinion Assignment on the Supreme Court." *Journal of Politics* 41:640–48.

———. 1983. "Federal Trial and Appellate Judges: How Do They Differ?" *Western Political Quarterly* 36: 570–78.

———. 1984. "Gender, Affirmative Action, and Recruitment to the Federal Bench." *Golden Gate University Law Review* 14: 519–71.

Smith, Rogers M. 1988. "Political Jurisprudence, the 'New Institutionalism,' and the Future of Public Law." *American Political Science Review* 82: 89–108.

Smyth, Russell. 2005. "The Role of Attitudinal, Institutional, and Environmental Factors in Explaining Variations in the Dissent Rate on the High Court of Australia." *Australian Journal of Political Science* 40: 519–40.

Sniderman, Paul M., Thomas Piazza, Philip E. Tetlock, and Ann Kendrick. 1991. "The New Racism." *American Journal of Political Science* 35: 423–47.

Solimine, Michael. 1988. "Ideology and En Banc Review." *North Carolina Law Review* 67: 29–76.

Songer, Donald R. 1982. "Consensual and Nonconsensual Decisions in Unanimous Opinions of the United States Courts of Appeals." *American Journal of Political Science* 26: 225–39.

———. 1986. "Factors Affecting Variations in Rates of Dissent in the U.S. Courts of Appeals." In *Judicial Conflict & Consensus: Behavioral Studies of American Appellate Courts,* edited by Sheldon Goldman and Charles M. Lamb. Lexington: University of Kentucky Press.

———. 1987. "The Impact of the Supreme Court on Trends in Economic Policy Making in the United States Courts of Appeals." *Journal of Politics* 49: 830–841.

———. 2002. United States Courts of Appeals Database, 1925–1996. Available at http://www.artsandsciences.sc.edu/poli/juri/appealscourt.html.

———. 2008. *The Transformation of the Supreme Court of Canada: An Empirical Examination.* Toronto: University of Toronto Press.

Songer, Donald R., Sue Davis, and Susan Haire. 1994. A Reappraisal of Diversification in the Federal Courts: Gender Effects in the Courts of Appeals. *Journal of Politics* 56: 425–39.

Songer, Donald R., Martha Humphries Ginn, and Tammy A. Sarver. 2003. "Do Judges Follow the Law When There Is No Fear of Reversal?" *Justice System Journal* 24: 137–62.

Songer, Donald R., and Susan B. Haire. 1992. "Integrating Alternative Approaches to the Study of Judicial Voting: Obscenity Cases in the U.S. Courts of Appeals." *American Journal of Political Science* 36: 963–82.

Songer, Donald R., Susan B. Haire, and Stefanie A. Lindquist. 2000. "Supreme Court Monitoring of the Federal Circuit Courts: An Institutional Perspective." Presented at the 2000 meeting of the American Political Science Association, Washington, DC.

Songer, Donald R., and Stefanie A. Lindquist. 1996. "Not the Whole Story: The Impact of the Justices' Values on Supreme Court Decision Making." *American Journal of Political Science* 40: 1049–63.

Songer, Donald R., Jeffrey A. Segal, and Charles M. Cameron. 1994. "The Hierarchy of Justice: Testing a Principal-Agent Model of Supreme Court–Circuit Court Interactions." *American Journal of Political Science* 38: 673–96.

Songer, Donald R., and Reginald S. Sheehan. 1992. "Who Wins on Appeal? Upperdogs and Underdogs on the United States Courts of Appeals." *American Journal of Political Science* 36: 235–58.

Songer, Donald R., Reginald S. Sheehan, and Susan B. Haire. 2000. *Continuity and Change on the United States Courts of Appeals.* Ann Arbor: University of Michigan Press.

Spiller, Pablo T., and Rafael Gely. 1992. "Congressional Control or Judicial Independence: The Determinants of U.S. Supreme Court Labor-Relations Decision, 1949–1988." *RAND Journal of Economics* 23: 463–92.

Spriggs, James F., II, Forrest Maltzman, and Paul J. Wahlbeck. 1999. "Bargaining on the U.S. Supreme Court: Justices' Responses to Majority Opinion Drafts." *Journal of Politics* 61: 485–506.

Spriggs, James F., II, and Paul J. Wahlbeck. 1995. "Calling it Quits: Strategic Retirement on the Federal Courts of Appeals, 1893–1991." *Political Research Quarterly* 48: 573–97.

Steigerwalt, Amy. 2010. *Battle over the Bench: Senators, Interest Groups, and Lower Court Confirmations.* Charlottesville: University of Virginia Press.

Stidman, Ronald, and Robert A. Carp. 1982. "Trial Courts' Responses to Supreme Court Policy Changes." *Law and Policy Quarterly* 4: 215–31.

Sunstein, Cass R., David Schkade, Lisa M. Ellman, and Andres Sawicki. 2006. *Are Judges Political? An Empirical Analysis of the Federal Judiciary.* Washington, DC: Brookings Institution Press.

Swenson, Karen J. 2004. "Understanding the Publication Process for District Court Opinions." *Justice System Journal* 25: 121–42.

Szmer, John J. 2005. "Unequal Justice under Law? The Effects of Party and Attorney Capability on United States Supreme Court Decision Making." PhD diss., University of South Carolina.

Szmer, John, Robert K. Christensen, and Ashlyn Kuersten. 2012. "The Efficiency of Federal Appellate Decisions: An Examination of Published and Unpublished Opinions." *Justice System Journal* 33: 318–38.

Szmer, John, and Martha Humphries Ginn. Forthcoming. "Examining the Effects of Information, Attorney Capability, and Amicus Participation on U.S. Supreme Court Decision Making." *American Politics Research.* 1532673X13502219. First published on September 19, 2013, as doi:10.1177/1532673X13502219.

Szmer, John, Erin B. Kaheny, and Tammy A. Sarver. 2010. "Have We Come a Long Way, Baby? The Influence of Attorney Gender on Supreme Court Decision Making." *Politics and Gender* 6: 1–36.

Szmer, John, Erin B. Kaheny, Tammy A. Sarver, and Mason DeCammillis. 2013.

"The Impact of Attorney Gender on Decision Making in the United States Courts of Appeals." *Journal of Women, Politics, and Policy* 34: 72–100.

Tate, C. Neal. 1981. "Personal Attribute Models of the Voting Behavior of U.S. Supreme Court Justices: Liberalism in Civil Liberties and Economic Decisions, 1946–1978." *American Political Science Review* 75: 355–67.

Tate, C. Neal, and Panu Sittiwong. 1989. "Decision Making in the Canadian Supreme Court: Extending the Personal Attributes Model Across Nations." *Journal of Politics* 51: 900–916.

Tobias, Carl. 2010. "Diversity and the Federal Bench." *Washington University Law Review* 87: 1197.

Tomz, Michael, Gary King, and Langche Zeng. 2003. "ReLogit: Rare Events Logistic Regression." *Journal of Statistical Software* 8.

Ulmer, S. Sidney. 1970. The Use of Power in the Supreme Court: The Opinion Assignments of Earl Warren, 1953–1960." *Journal of Public Law* 19: 49–67.

———. 1973. "Social Background as an Indicator to the Votes of Supreme Court Justices in Criminal Cases: 1947–1956 Terms." *American Journal of Political Science* 17: 622–30.

Van Winkle, Steven. 1997. "Dissenting as a Signal: Evidence from the U.S. Courts of Appeals." Paper presented at the Annual Meeting of the American Political Science Association, Washington, DC, September.

Vining, Richard L., Jr. 2009a. "Politics, Pragmatism, and Departures from the U.S. Courts of Appeals, 1954–2004." *Social Science Quarterly* 90: 834–53.

———. 2009b. "Judicial Departures and the Introduction of Qualified Retirement, 1892–1953." *Justice System Journal* 30: 139–57.

Wahlbeck, Paul J., James F. Spriggs II, and Forrest Maltzman. 1998. "Marshalling the Court: Bargaining and Accommodation on the United States Supreme Court." *American Journal of Political Science* 42: 294–315.

———. 1999. "The Politics of Dissents and Concurrences on the U.S. Supreme Court." *American Politics Quarterly* 27: 488–514.

Walker, Thomas G., and Deborah J. Barrow. 1985. "The Diversification of the Federal Bench: Policy and Process Ramifications." *Journal of Politics* 47: 596–617.

Wasby, Stephen L. 2001. "The Supreme Court and the Courts of Appeals En Bancs." *McGeorge Law Review* 33: 17–73.

———. 2004. "Unpublished Court of Appeals Decisions: A Hard Look at the Process." *Southern California Interdisciplinary Law Journal* 14: 67–124.

Wheeler, Stanton, Bliss Cartwright, Robert Kagan, and Lawrence Friedman. 1987. "Do the 'Haves' Come Out Ahead? Winning and Losing in State Supreme Courts, 1870–1970." *Law & Society Review* 21: 403–45.

Wilson, Bertha. 1990. "Will Women Judges Really Make a Difference?" *Osgood Hall Law Journal* 28: 507–522.

Wold, John T., and Greg A. Caldeira. 1980. "Perceptions of Routine Decision Making in Five California Courts of Appeals." *Polity* 13: 334–47.

Yoon, Albert. 2005. "As You Like It: Senior Federal Judges and the Political Economy of Judicial Tenure." *Journal of Empirical Legal Studies* 2: 495–49.

Zarone, Phil. 2000. "Agenda Setting in the Courts of Appeals: The Effect of Ideology on En Banc Re-hearings." *Journal of Appellate Practice and Process* 2: 157–89.

Zorn, Christopher. 2002. "U.S. Government Litigation Strategies in the Federal Appellate Courts." *Political Research Quarterly* 55: 145–66.

Zorn, Christopher, and Jennifer Barnes Bowie. 2010. "An Empirical Analysis of Hierarchy Effects in Judicial Decision Making." *Journal of Politics* 72: 1212–21.

Zuk, Gary, Deborah J. Barrow, and Gerard Gryski. 2004. Multi-User Database on the Attributes of United States Appeals Court Judges, 1801–2004. Available at http://www.cas.sc.edu/poli/juri/databases.htm.

INDEX